A School of Praise

MW01223356

"This is really a highly scientific and informative work . . . truly romantic and fascinating."
—Herbert Palmer, *The Spectator*

"The clarity of the Gallic mind . . . is well shown in this chastely popularized book by Professor Roule of the National Museum of Natural History in Paris. One does not need the suggestion on the jacket to compare him with Izaak Walton. . . . For modern readers, he will probably serve better than Walton."
—R. L. Duffus, *The New York Times*

"The general reader will, we believe, obtain much pleasure and profit from its perusal. It is full of the outdoors, the mystery of the waters, of beauty, and never strays far from the practical human aspect of life. The great amount of information it contains is made unobtrusive. It unfolds the philosophy of a Frenchman and a scholar."
—J. T. Nichols, *Saturday Review of Literature*

"The subject is to Mr. Roule one of dramatic interest and he endeavors to keep it on that plane. The book will please the nature student, the Izaak Walton enthusiast, or the reader who delights in believe-it-or-nots."
—*Springfield Republican*

"Professor Roule is a learned zoologist, but [he] is also an artist in description. [His book] is full of information, exact and curious."
—*Times Literary Supplement*

FISHES
Their Journeys and Migrations

FISHES
THEIR JOURNEYS AND
MIGRATIONS

BY LOUIS ROULE

PROFESSOR OF THE NATIONAL MUSEUM OF
NATURAL HISTORY IN PARIS

WITH AN INTRODUCTION BY
WILLIAM BEEBE

AND A NEW INTRODUCTION BY
GEORGE REIGER

TRANSLATED FROM THE FRENCH BY
CONRAD ELPHINSTONE

KODANSHA INTERNATIONAL
New York • Tokyo • London

Kodansha America, Inc.
114 Fifth Avenue, New York, New York 10011, U.S.A.

Kodansha International Ltd.
17-14 Otowa 1-chome, Bunkyo-ku, Tokyo 112, Japan

Published in 1996 by Kodansha America, Inc.
by arrangement with W. W. Norton & Company.

First published in 1933 by W. W. Norton & Company, Inc.

This is a Kodansha Globe book.

Library of Congress Cataloging-in-Publication Data

Roule, Louis, b. 1861.
    Fishes : their journeys and migrations / by Louis Roule ; with an
introduction by William Beebe and a new introduction by George
Reiger ; translated from the French by Conrad Elphinstone.
        p.   cm. — (Kodansha globe)
    Originally published: New York : W. W. Norton & Co., c1933.
    ISBN 1-56836-103-3 (pbk.)
    1. Fishes—Migration. I. Beebe, William, 1877–1962. II. Reiger,
George, 1939–   . III. Title. IV. Series.
QL639.5.R68   1996
597'.0525—dc20
                                                    96-35722

Printed in the United States of America

96 97 98 99 00 Q/FF 10 9 8 7 6 5 4 3 2 1

CONTENTS

CONTENTS

FIGURES IN THE TEXT

FIGURES IN THE TEXT

INTRODUCTION TO THE 1996 EDITION

BECAUSE Louis Roule's *Fishes, Their Journeys and Migrations* was written at a time when fishing was largely a local activity, and when a naturalist was often a poet as well as a scientist, this book is rich in history and philosophy. Today, these elements are more critical to the restoration and sustenance of migratory fishes than most of the statistical surveys and computerized models currently in vogue. Yet history and philosophy are rarely mentioned in regional and international conferences on how to revitalize the earth's depleted marine fishes.

History is essential, for without memory, we have little idea of original conditions and, hence, few reference points for recovering what we've lost. How can we truly restore Atlantic salmon, cod, mackerel, tuna, sturgeon, even eels, if we have no higher standards of abundance than the already overexploited conditions we've tolerated during the past twenty-five years?

When I wrote "Farewell to the Bluefin" for the July, 1974, issue of *Audubon*, stocks of bluefin tuna were already fleeting remnants of once mighty schools that roamed the world's temperate and subtropical oceans during the first half of this century, comparable to the herds of bison that thundered across the North American prairies in the first half of the nineteenth century.

Migration made such superabundance possible. By satisfying their compulsion to wander, vast schools of fishes, sun-darkening flocks of birds, and huge herds of mammals were able continuously to discover and rediscover fresh feeding grounds. Disease and predation had little long-term effect— until that superpredator, the human entrepreneur, got involved.

Today, governmental biologists hope to restore the bluefin tuna only to 1970s' population levels. The biocrats are unable to conceive of anything more than a token recovery for this or any other depleted species, because they lack memory. And because they have never read Louis Roule, they cannot imagine the abundance and diversity of sea life that Roule and his contemporaries took for granted.

Philosophy is a function of leisure, and leisure is only possible in a world where a balance—Roule preferred the word *harmony*—exists between our own species and those that sustain us. Roule distinguished human intelligence from the "irrational instinct" that characterizes, for example, the drive of salmon and eels to reach their respective spawning grounds. Then he asked, "But is there so great a difference as there seems to be between instinct and intelligence? Is not everything, in the last resort, instinctive? Intelligence seems to be rather a choice of instincts than an entirely new quality."

If intelligence—and its most sophisticated manifestation, philosophy—are based on a broad range of intuitive options, the question now seems to be: will our own species' ever-expanding population eventually eliminate all choices but the one between extinction and mere survival?

Roule alludes to records reaching back before the birth of Christ showing that bluefin tuna once provided an annual bounty to shore-based fishermen in Sardinia, Sicily, and Tunisia. Why did these and other tunas—after more than two thousand years of sustained abundance—begin to decline everywhere in the world in the 1950s? Roule provides the answer when he presciently observes that "even the strongest [tuna] net can only be used for a short season which lasts five or six weeks. . . . Afterwards it is taken up again, and not put back until the same time next year."

When the world's fisheries were industrialized following World War II, nets far larger than anything imagined by Roule were taken to sea aboard ships larger than prewar freighters, so that all pelagic species could be followed and caught wherever they roamed. Cod, pollack, haddock, and mackerel were no longer taken only on hook and line; salmon, shad, herring, and tuna were no longer fished only when they came near shore. The word *harvest* was used to disguise the reality of huge trawl nets vacuuming the bottom, while drifting gillnets and longlines combed the surface waters. Sea resources were no longer treated as renewable. They were strip-mined, pure and simple, and it's a wonder the prime plundering lasted as long as it did.

As fish populations declined, and as our own species doubled and then tripled in number, fish prices quintupled. In some cases, the rise was astronomical. Giant bluefin tuna that sold for a penny a pound in the 1950s now fetch more than $30 a pound dockside. One particularly choice bluefin sold for nearly $70,000 in Tokyo. Live baby eels, for which there was no market thirty years ago, now sell for $570 a pound, even before they reach the rearing ponds and gourmet restaurants of Asia.

Louis Roule never anticipated such staggering change. Yet his philosophy did anticipate the consequences, for he observed that "nature has a soul, compact of all the energies which traverse it, made up of all the movements which give life to it, even in the depths of the sea." That's why he felt we must follow nature's rules and not those we design from our arrogant illusion that we're unique and, hence, superior to nature.

Roule concludes *Fishes, Their Journeys and Migrations* with what amounts to a warning: "We utilize for our own purposes the resources which Nature has so lavishly distributed and, by our industry and our science, we often put our own power in its place. We shelter our human achievements behind the achievement which it called into being. We must, therefore, follow its rules and try to understand them. We must strive to know Nature, to know how to use Nature, and, bringing ourselves into harmony with Nature, to profit by the understanding which it has brought into being."

Louis Roule was born in France in 1861. In addition to dozens of scientific monographs on a spectrum of aquatic creatures, he wrote profiles of such famous French naturalists as Buffon, Daubenton, Cuvier, Lamarck, Benardin de Saint-Pierre, and Lacepede. We know relatively little of his private life. Roule catalogued the fresh and saltwater fishes of Corsica, the invertebrates of the Bay of Biscay, the aquatic fauna of the Pyrenees, and was particularly interested in salmon, sturgeon, eels, and creatures of the abyss. He may have accompanied the Prince of Monaco on some of his trips to collect oceanic fauna in the North Atlantic (1886–1902), and he probably participated in the second French expedition aboard the *Pourquoi-Pas* to Antarctica (1908–1910). He classified and catalogued much of the material collected during these expeditions, which was housed, respectively, at Monaco's Oceanographic Institute and the National Museum of Natural History in Paris. Roule was ranked "Professor" at the Paris Museum when the French edition of *Fishes, Their Journeys and Migrations* was first published in 1925.

The English translation (1933) which follows is generally excellent, but it has some idiosyncracies. For example, male fish have *testes*, not "testicles"; the sexual organs of fishes produce *milt* and *eggs*, not "germs"; and we don't usually think of fish as going through "puberty."

Roule himself made some errors. He believed, for example, that Atlantic salmon are drawn upstream by increasingly higher levels of oxygen in river systems. Thanks to research involving Pacific salmon, but completed decades after Roule's death, we now believe that taste and smell are more likely to bring salmon back to their natal streams than a craving for oxygen. Roule also identified the twaite shad as the "Rhone shad," and we're still perplexed by what he called "the golden perch."

Yet these are trivial flaws in an otherwise monumental achievement. It was Roule who deduced the deep-ocean origins of the eel due to its "dread" of light; and Roule who first demonstrated the importance of water temperature in the migration of shad and herring. George Washington complained these anadromous fishes favored the Maryland side of the Potomac rather than migrate upstream along the Virginia shore (and into his nets at Mount Vernon). Had he known rivers are frequently warmer along one bank than the other, he would have appreciated it was nothing personal among the shad, herring, and himself; it's just that these fishes prefer the warmer current near the Maryland shore.

Then there is Roule's poetry. He looked on sardines as "Nature's jewels," whose colors combine "the vast spaces of the sea: the blue of the depths and the white of the foam that tips the waves." He writes, too, of the "clever fisherman" who continues to set his net

until he thinks he has caught enough for the day. Then
he hauls up his sail again, and goes back to harbour.
Since most of his companions do as he does, at the same
hour on their own boats, almost all come back together,
forming a returning caravan, which gradually draws close
together as it nears the harbour. This return to port as
the sun is setting, with the sea sparkling with purple
light, is one of the most delightful sights the ocean has
to offer us.

Roule valued what ordinary fishermen could teach him
about the sea. "I have gone with Breton, Spanish, Provencal
fishermen in their boats," Roule writes. "I have gathered a
scientific harvest beside theirs. I have learned by their experience and by my own."

As it turned out, German oceanographers also learned from
Spanish fishermen, or from Roule himself, something which
U-boat commanders used to their advantage during World
War II. This is how Roule described the phenomenon:

The Mediterranean Sea, enclosed between lands which
are temperate and warm, is continually evaporating. It
loses more water than its rivers bring down to it, in spite
of the considerable volume of some of them. This deficit
is made up by the Atlantic Ocean, which sends into it,
through the Straits of Gibraltar, a current which moves
along the surface, passing along the coast of Algeria and
gradually mixing with the rest of the water. But the
ocean, when it gives its satellite sea the water it needs
to maintain its level, supplies more than is necessary.
Consequently, so as to keep the balance, the Mediterranean returns to the ocean the equivalent of this excess.
Under the surface current of the Straits of Gibraltar there
is a deeper current, going in the reverse direction and
carrying off the superfluous water.

In order to avoid detection by British hydrophones at Gibraltar, U-boat skippers would rise or fall to the appropriate
depth, cut all power, and drift silently with the current, in
or out of the Mediterranean. The war was more than half

over before Allied intelligence learned what the German sub-mariners were doing.

Insatiable curiosity is a hallmark of all great naturalists. Roule's was linked to his love of history. "I am very fond," he wrote, "of rummaging through old archives, ancient documents and family papers. And, I think, rightly so. In the faded pages of such relics we have the direct traces, the immediate imprint, as it were, of what life used to be."

This extended memory enabled Roule to create maps, not only illustrating the surviving salmon rivers of Western Europe in his time, but as they were when Norse raiders caught salmon in all the navigable streams of the North and Baltic seas, and when Roman legionnaires in Gaul and Spain depended on salmon for their summer rations. "Still further in the past," Roule wrote, "our prehistoric ancestors carved on the walls of their caves the outlines of this fish, which they used to catch in the river that flowed past their rough houses."

An irony of Roule's research is that anglers today would be thrilled to have Atlantic salmon restored just to those rivers that were still viable seventy-five years ago. A further sorrow is that the point Roule makes about the decline of salmon is now applicable to every migratory species in the world:

> From the economic point of view, these losses must be considered very serious. Except for those who are immediately concerned, fishermen, amateur and professional, the general public knows very little about them. These migratory fishes were a source of food; they are replaced by other food products, and the demand of the consumers takes another direction. But this substitution does not make up for the loss, which can never be repaired.

In his heart, however, Roule was not a pessimist. His effort to popularize marine science through *Fishes, Their Journeys and Migrations* (1933) and its sequel, *Fishes and Their Ways of Life* (1935), indicates a faith in education and a hope that we may yet use what we know to recover what we've lost. And by restoring what Roule calls "the greatness of the migrating fishes," we may yet restore reality and harmony in our own lives.

GEORGE REIGER
May 1996

INTRODUCTION

THIS volume is concerned with the Travels and Migrations of Fish, and the very able author, Dr. Louis Roule, has condensed into the space of nineteen chapters the sum of present day knowledge of these subjects. But best of all, he has put this into understandable language and has brought out all the mystery, the drama, the amazing actions, many of them still unexplained, which accompany this phase of the lives of fish. What is known of this fascinating aspect of life in the waters of the earth has hitherto been locked up in technical books. So here we find a double translation—first from the dry recitation of facts into a moving, living account, and secondly from the original French into most excellent English.

The translator has wisely kept as much as possible to the clear style and the pleasant individuality of writing of the author, and has made use of an amazingly extensive English vocabulary to cope adequately with the delicate shades of meaning for which the French language is deservedly famed.

This is one of a series of popular volumes which the author has published for the French reading public, and their welcome has been most cordial. Dr. Roule is a well-known scientific student of fish, with many authoritative researches to his credit, so he brings to this popular work a sound background of knowledge, leavened with an emotional appreciation of its wide appeal.

The subject of the Migration of Fish is here given the play of imagination in the recording of actual facts which it deserves, and the layman will find an astonishing field of interest in an aspect of life which is as dramatic and absorbing as it is new to the scope of popular literature.

WILLIAM BEEBE

FOREWORD

THERE is something delightful about travel. To travel is to live more intensely; it is to conquer. Every part of us is concerned in it. We acquire a more vivid knowledge, more extensive resources. We learn to profit more from ourselves and from others. Distant lands are brought closer to us; their mysteries become clearer; dream becomes reality. The most thrilling stories of adventure, the greatest epics, are travellers' tales.

But our own strength is not sufficient for such exploits. We need help, we have to make use of apparatus which, by multiplying our capacity, compensates for our deficiencies. So, adventitious, artificial organs, invented and constructed by us, supplement those which our body possesses of itself. With their help we discover and make use of Nature beyond the limits of our own possibilities. Yet there is a limit, and sometimes Nature, offended, resists our intrusions. The myth of Icarus only too often becomes a reality.

Our attention is easily awakened when we come to consider creatures which, provided like ourselves with the means of locomotion, are able to make use of them without any assistance from outside. The migratory bird flies from one hemisphere to the other, with only its wings to carry it. The migratory fish comes up from the depths of the sea to the running water of the river, under its own power. Their journeys are greater than ours, if not in extent, at any rate as regards the ease with which they are accomplished. The natural machine is sufficient. In them the power to utilize things reaches a greater perfection. Thanks to this capacity, not only do these creatures provide us in profusion with a source of nourishment, but they teach us a lesson we shall do well to heed. They are careful to follow Nature's lead, and through them, the greatness, the splendour, the might of Nature are revealed even in the depths of the sea.

FOREWORD

The world of the fishes is a new world to us.   No novel
has so much interest, no fairy tale such charm, no work of
imagination so strange a diversity as the simple story of
their journeys.   In seeking to discover all that is to be
known about them scientific observation is employed to the
fullest degree.   In this volume I have brought together the
results of long years of research, observation, and reflection.
No study has ever brought me more delight.

Louis Roule

FISHES
Their Journeys and Migrations

.H.D.Tee Van.

CHAPTER I

I. At definite periods, the sea provides places of rendezvous to certain species of fishes. In proportion to its immensity, such rendezvous cover an area of many square miles ; they go down sometimes hundreds of fathoms, and to them hasten thousands, millions, and thousands of millions of fishes, all those, in fact, whose business in life takes them there. These rendezvous move and alter like the sea itself; the water which forms them is like any other water; but none the less, they have special characteristics and a place of their own. The only attraction they have to offer is that of the water which composes them, yet, at the proper time, they are always ready, always welcoming, always full. In them and near them there are neither guides, nor landmarks; there is only water, favourable water. That is enough.

So, each year, at certain times, and in certain places, there is an unaccustomed activity of fishermen with their boats and their nets. The times are always the same, the places are always the same; they are the times and the places where shoals of fish appear for a while. And the fishes too always belong to the same species, appearing at the same time, at the same place. When that time has come, the fish arrive in hosts, and the fishermen hasten after them. For days, weeks, and even months, the boats take up their position, nets are spread, lines put out, and the harvest is gathered from the water in which it was sown. Previously, there were no fishermen there; afterwards, they are there no longer. And the fish, which a little while ago were so abundant, have themselves almost disappeared.

I

So, for the fishermen, the year is broken up into periods, each devoted to a particular one of these rendezvous. Boats and tackle are prepared beforehand; a beginning is made at the exact moment; and, when the work is done, the fishermen return. On the coasts of the English Channel, winter is the season of the herring fisheries, summer that of mackerel. In the Gulf of Gascony, the sardine and tunny are caught during the summer. In the spring the cod fishers embark for the shoals of Newfoundland, where they stay until the beginning of autumn. The great barrier-nets are set across the streams in April before the shad come up, and taken down in July when their passage is over. The regular rhythm of the appearances and disappearances of these fish extends to the catching of them, and makes it appear seasonal.

This regularity is striking. Like the labours of the farmer which, succeeding one another at definite intervals, take place with perfect regularity, those of the fisherman usually follow a similar periodicity. They are foreseen, they are awaited, and those who wait know that their waiting will not be in vain. The catch may vary in quantity, for there are good years and bad, but, in the main, it does not alter. At the regular time, almost to the day, the fish will be there. And if the fish are never all absent at the rendezvous, neither are the fishermen.

But this is not the only striking thing about them. These periodic fishes, appearing at one time and disappearing at another only to return the following year at the same place and at the same time, seem to be more abundant than most other fish. The species to which they belong are by far the most prolific. Enormous numbers of individual fishes arrive, often gathering in eager hosts, in shoals. Their number, their mass are in striking contrast to the shortness of the time they remain. The hosts are only passing on their way. They come suddenly, rising from the bosom of the waters, like gifts from Neptune, then go as they came, as if they returned to the depths.

The fishermen make haste, so that they may lose nothing of the harvest before it vanishes, so that they may be sure of gathering everything their nets can capture for them. It is a harvest, in truth, but one which they have neither to sow nor to protect. It comes of its own accord, it is produced and directed by natural circumstances. They must take advantage of it, when it is offered, so long as it is there. It is a moving, changing harvest as ready to give itself as to remove itself, and they must reap it without wasting time and exploit it to the full.

In their turn, these appearances and disappearances, sometimes succeeding one another in neighbouring localities, follow one another in a perfectly definite direction, governed by some invariable law. The fishermen, arranging their course of action accordingly, move from place to place in the same way. In summer they catch herrings in the North Sea, then, by degrees, following the fish, they go south to the English Channel, and, finally, secure their last catch there during the winter. Then the species disperses. It reappears in shoals the next summer, far up the North Sea, and moves according to the same seasonal rhythm, finishing the cycle as it did the winter before. In the same way, in the rivers, we see shad or salmon leave the estuaries to which they came from the sea, and gradually make their way upstream, as if striving to reach a definite goal. We gain the impression that these species of passage are also travelling species, and that the first characteristic is a result of the second. If they appear in this way, at a definite date in each locality, the reason seems to be that they gather in troops, that each year they start out upon a long journey which brings them at the same time to the same places, and that they move successively, in series, through all the places where the fishermen are able to get at them. In other words, they are migratory. Each year they undertake a great migration. A sort of periodical cosmopolitanism seems to govern their comings and goings. Like troops on the march, proceeding from stage to stage in a definite order, following that order with only slight variations.

So we come to distinguish two categories among the fish which are customarily caught. One is that of the species which are caught all the year round, which, consequently, seem always to live in the places where they are caught: these are the " sedentary " fishes. The other is that of the travelling species, which are caught now and again, only at definite seasons, not throughout the year. These make up for this disadvantage by their extreme abundance when they do appear, and they yield the best catch. These are the " migratory " fishes.

It is inevitable that we should compare them with animals other than fishes, with the migratory birds, which also make regular and periodical journeys. Living in the air, dwelling as we do in a terrestrial environment, we may follow the various stages of their journey directly. Each year, in spring, the swallows arrive, go back to their nests, fly around our houses during the summer and leave again in the autumn. We see their bands forming, grouping, and finally flying away, only to reappear the following spring. We know where they go, to warmer countries where our icy winter never goes; they avoid it by travelling south. So too, when the cold weather arrives we see bands of other birds, also migratory, go through the air towards the same goal. From time to time, they alight, in a few places, almost always the same places, they come down, then off they fly again; and the sportsmen, who wait for them in these favoured places, take advantage of their momentary presence to shoot them.

The resemblance to the migratory fishes is as remarkable as it is clear. We have only to transpose to the waters, in which our powers of sight fail us, what we see and observe on land, and the result is identical. It has therefore been concluded that these movements of fishes are those of journeying bands which at regular times of the year cover vast distances always in a definite direction. They apparently regularly visit certain chosen places, where the fishermen have only to await them.

But what a difference in numbers, in bulk, compared with the birds! The travelling groups of birds are to be counted by tens, sometimes, at most, a few hundreds. The hosts of fishes are to be counted by millions, by billions. In an average year, the North Sea alone yields between 300,000 and 400,000 tons of herrings, which means five or six thousand million separate fish. The shoals which traverse the North Sea are great enough, strong enough, compact enough, to leave behind them, in the fishermen's nets, this monstrous contingent, and still to remain enough for the fishermen of the Channel, and to form new shoals the following year. The immensity of the sea, vast enough to shelter such hosts in its depths, leaves them free to come and go from the surface to the abyss, without opposing to them, in spite of their huge size, anything which can set bounds to their movement or arrest their progress. The ocean, which is vaster still, has space enough to contain them all.

Consequently, up to the middle of the last century, fishermen and naturalists believed (and many still consider) that these periodic seasonal fishes migrate in the same way as birds, but on a larger scale. Their troops, it was said, collect in vast numbers, each year. They begin by forming groups in some place which serves as a place of departure, then rouse themselves and set off, like an invading army, for the goal which they must reach. On their way, they detach flank guards, which increase the extent of the invaded zones. They cross the seas without halting, showing themselves first at one place and then at another at various stages of their journey. Finally, when they have reached their objective, those that are left of them disperse and come together again the following year to form a new army and fill the ranks with new recruits.

All this is supposition, for no one has ever followed these mighty hosts all the way. But none the less, these suppositions agree so fully with the experience of the fishermen, that they were long accepted, and still are accepted, as the nearest approach to the truth. There is, it is easy to credit, the reality of this long journey, starting from a single centre and gradually extending and broadening as it gets farther and farther from the starting place. The imagination follows with interest the course of these huge troops of swimmers which the eye can never see, all making for their goal, striving their hardest to reach it. The mystery of it all, the magnitude of the phenomenon, hold and rivet the attention.

Theoretically, the positions of these armies and the route they take on the march have been fixed. Some species, the cod and the herring, are supposed to winter beneath the ice of the Arctic Ocean, then, in spring, to move southwards. Their forces move forward and, on their way, split up into secondary bands, which break off in different directions, some towards the western coasts of Europe, others towards the eastern shores of the United States. All, although divisions of one and the same army, are caught in different places. Others, like the tunny, take the opposite course. They spend the winter in the warm waters of the sub-tropical Atlantic, then, when spring comes, move towards the north, where conditions of existence become more bearable at that season, and break up into two troops. One goes up the Atlantic, the other enters the Mediterranean and goes all the way along in a periplus which extends as far as Asia Minor and the Black Sea. So, all the fishing grounds gather their expected harvest at the regular time each year.

II. The imagination is stirred at the idea of these vast assemblies, their concentration, their setting out, their gradual breaking up. It follows them along their way, sometimes in deep water, sometimes on the surface, swimming in eager cohorts. It goes with them in their invading ardour, in their irruption into spaces which had hitherto been unoccupied, upon which their troops suddenly and invincibly impose their domination and the power of their numbers. Pursuing and pursued, they drive back creatures weaker than themselves, or destroy them and make them their food. They are hunted in their turn by creatures more powerful than themselves, the great predatory creatures of the seas, sharks, dolphins, even by sea birds, which attack them unceasingly and without mercy. The shoals of sardines and anchovies are exploited by the tunnies which find in them an abundant and easy prey. The shoals of herrings are often discovered by the flights of birds above them which swoop down and pick them up. This continual struggle for food, with its continual succession of devourers and devoured, because of the multitudes that are concerned in it, takes on a keenness and intensity seldom observed elsewhere. Over the surface of the sea, when a shoal passes, the cries and swoopings of the sea birds and the leaping and activity of the fish themselves produce for a moment a burning agitation which the silence and tranquillity that went before by no means led us to expect.

The imagination, after having called up such visions, is

led to ask itself the reason for these assemblies, these movements directed, with such precision, in an invariable and perfectly definite direction. What urges on these bands, what cause is strong enough to act upon such a multitude, constant and tenacious enough to begin again year after year, to repeat the same gesture each time without the slightest variation? The migration is a riddle, a mystery. It faces us with a problem, that of its origin, its direction and its different ends. The inquiring spirit has plenty with which to occupy itself here.

The first stage, in our attempt to find a solution, consists in recognizing the route taken, in taking marks of the armies travelling through the waters of the sea. Authors of days gone by made a sort of rough map, based on the times of appearance of each species in its favourite localities; but they had not actually observed the course they so marked out. The fishermen to whom they referred had only vague information to go upon. Something more definite was needed, more exact measurements, direct observations. Modern science has taken up this necessary work of preliminary inquiry. Oceanographical cruises, patient laboratory work have gradually produced some order out of the chaos of detail, and separated the real and exact from the fictitious and imaginary. This work is going on. By degrees, light is being shed upon this darkness, and we are coming nearer to the truth.

The results that have been obtained, which are now both considerable and definite, are not always favourable to the theory of great journeys over the seas, of long peregrinations made, stage by stage, over immense spaces during several consecutive months. Such swimming bands have not been found all along the course ascribed to them, beginning with the point of assembly and proceeding to the place where the band is supposed to break up. Shoals of fish are seen to present themselves at their regular stations at the accustomed times. They appear, stay for a time, then disappear. But, in this disappearance, we do not see these bands move on still in formation, go elsewhere, and betake themselves to the localities denoted by the accustomed order of succession. Rather, many of these stations seem to have definite categories, specialized races as it were of fishes, which they alone can offer. The migration would have to be of an unheard-of complexity, if it grouped in this way such diverse races, and kept them in exact position throughout the journey.

Nowhere do we observe the prodigious preliminary gatherings which would allow of such vast dispersals afterwards. Nor do we find any trace of the returning hosts which we should expect if there were a reassembling the following year, or the passage of fry and of young fish destined to form the contingents of the future. On the other hand, observations corroborate in many cases the existence of several separate and distinct centres of cohesion, not one only where the whole species gathers in one block. There is multiplicity, not unity.

But observations further agree about something more important, the physical condition of the waters in the places of rendezvous. Although only a limited area of sea or stream, at the time when the fishes come there, each of these exhibits special qualities, which are found at this particular moment only, not so well or so completely either before or afterwards. During the year their water undergoes various physical changes, several of which are especially noticeable when the fishes appear. Either the temperature, the chloridation, the acidity, or dissolved oxygen for the respiration, or other circumstances which vary and take another form; but certain of them, always the same, are particularly noticeable when the fish arrive, and disappear when they have gone.

The rendezvous now appears under another light. It is the consequence of a temporary harmony between the creatures concerned and the conditions of the environment in which they live, and this harmony takes on a degree of absoluteness which makes it of the first importance. It controls and determines. The appearances of the fish are not governed by chance; they do not come about solely of themselves, with only date or custom to determine them; they are determined in some other way. They occur only in the degree to which this exterior compulsion is satisfied, for the force at work is that of external circumstances.

They do not act alone, and the harmony is continued in a deeper degree. To the compulsion exercised by the environing medium and by inorganic Nature, there is added another, arising in the interior medium, in the living flesh of which these creatures are made. Most of these fishes, when they show themselves, have arrived at a special moment in the history of their vital processes, a moment that is always the same for each species, whose coming must necessarily bear a relation to external conditions. If one is absent, the other fails, and vice versa. The rendezvous have a double compelling power, external and internal. Most often, the internal compulsion is that of the reproductive function; the fish are seen at the time of sexuality, and go away when that period is past. In other cases, depending upon nutrition, it summons the fish subject to it to places where, for the time being, prey is more abundant. Other vital activities may also play a part from within. But all, whatever they may be, and although they follow laws of their own, are unable to come into play except when they are in harmony with those of the exterior environment. They have to come together, to be brought face to face, to harmonize, before they can produce their result, which is the presence in numbers of the fishes they bring together. Over everything there is a precise determinism, outside which nothing happens. There is neither chance nor phantasy. Things have their law, and are arranged only in accordance with this harmony.

In the face of these facts, these relations which it has discovered, modern science has given up the old belief in huge migrations. The elements of grandeur and immensity change and take other forms. We discern them no longer in long journeys of innumerable hosts through the masses of water that cover the habitable globe, but in a co-ordination between the blind forces which traverse all exterior physical environments and the actions which develop in the internal environments of bodies endowed with life. The former surround and distribute; the latter perceive and receive. The ones profit from the others, and when their understanding is accomplished, when their coming together is most perfectly realized, then, for the time this harmony lasts, the manifestations of life are at their highest intensity. Such is the power of Nature, which brings together and maintains periodically, to take away again and maintain anew, without

9

ever exhausting, those marvellous resources of matter and energy which it employs untiringly.

III. Setting out along these lines, science finds something new in what seemed an unpromising subject. The migratory species of fish are not the only ones which travel, for most of the sedentary fishes do so also. Their movements take place within a smaller area, they are more definitely bounded, but they take place none the less, also determined and directed by the need for the establishment of a harmony between certain functions and certain circumstances. The carp about to spawn in a pond, come and gather in those places where warmer water and thicker vegetation afford them greater satisfaction. This we find to be paralleled almost everywhere.

We find in polymorphous nature, a regular sequence which starts with these simple, almost elementary cases, and gradually comes to an end in definite, complicated migrations. In the first class we have the genuinely sedentary species. We call them " sedentary," but this does not mean that they remain always in one place, for these fishes, in fact, do move. Although they are localized in definite places, these species move in different directions, and are able to form groups to accomplish the same vital action together. If the lake carp gather in a warmer zone to spawn there together, river carp move still more markedly. When the time for spawning comes, they leave their usual hiding places and go in a body to the lower reaches of the streams, where the water does not flow so swiftly, and is warmer. These places are often some distance away. Thus from time to time, they make little journeys, miniature migrations, without ceasing to be sedentary, for they always remain near their accustomed homes. But they give evidence of a faculty for changing their abode, which would, if carried out on a larger scale, be a real migration.

Next come those fishes to which we may give the name " seasonal." Normally they live dispersed in the waters, but come together and form groups or shoals at certain periods, especially when the time comes for them to reproduce themselves. Their reunion at a fixed date, in many localities, but always the same ones, is a signal to the fishermen. As they often have to cover considerable distances in order to come together in this way, they make real journeys. But though these differ from those of the carp only by their greater extent, they are still kept within the bounds of their home waters, and never go beyond them. The fresh water species remain in the rivers and the salt water species in the sea. Their move is only a provisional one, a periodical one in the direction of those parts of their domain which, at the moment, are the most favourable. Such are the herrings, the tunnies, the anchovies and the sardines, fishes that pass from one place to another, whose capacity for travelling, though sometimes considerable, does not take them out of their normal environment.

But there are species which do go outside it. Possessed of faculties of adaptation which others do not possess, and provided with the power to go beyond the accustomed limits, they frequent alternately and at regular intervals, fresh water and salt. Such are the salmon, the shad, the eel, and the sturgeon. These are actual migrants, in whom and for whom the word " migration " has its fullest meaning. When these fishes go from the sea to a river or from a river to the sea they really emigrate. They change, so far as may be, their surroundings and their situation completely. They make long journeys, which last for months, which take them hundreds, sometimes thousands of miles. In them, everything reminds us of the migratory birds flying from one hemisphere to the other, leaving the cold lands for those that are warmer. Like the birds, they cross considerable spaces, counting on finding better conditions for the vital action which is all-powerful within them. They are " migrants " in every sense of the word.

The swallow of spring, leaving the tropics to come to us, moves in a transparent, light-filled air, and its eyes can see from afar the landmarks it seeks. The salmon is not so well off. When it begins its pilgrimage, its home is in the depths of the sea, with still water all about it, uniformly dark and cold. It must pass beyond this first home for which it was made, and go into waters that are not salt, flowing waters in which day alternates with night, warmth with cold. It must go up swift-flowing waters which are moving in the opposite direction. It must fight against contrary currents, make its way over obstacles and rocks, and keep on constantly towards the higher reaches where its spawning places are, the goal to which it has been constantly drawn. Yet, despite these difficulties, despite the barriers which the migratory bird knows nothing of, it undertakes this long and difficult voyage; devotes all its energies to that voyage and finally reaches its goal. It has gone the way its ancestors went before it; and this way, traced in the moving, changing waters of a river, opens before it as surely and clearly as if the fish had previously surveyed it and taken its bearings most minutely. The force which drives it on directs it accurately.

What is this law, this controlling force, at once imperious and assured, which issues its commands with the full certainty that it will be obeyed? Here is another riddle, even more complex than the last. It is not only a question of deciding the changes and chances of a journey of adventure, but of finding out what is, in the creature itself and around it, the source and the nature of the vital force which produces such a result. One is effect, the other activating cause. If the one surprises by its momentary greatness, the other, although we can only realize it by experience and some deduction, is still more calculated to surprise us. The salmon, in its difficult journey up the stream, keeps stedfastly on its way. It tries to prevent itself from ever falling back, as if it hearkened to some interior voice which ceaselessly cried to it to go forward. It has within itself some impulsive faculty, whence it draws the secret of its activity. The species has a genius of its own which, taking possession of it at the proper moment, drives it forward implacably along the way that it must go.

These dumb fishes, with their tight-closed mouths and their big open eyes, are as though they had seen and yet could tell us nothing; their face seems a mask. But, none the less, if we look hard enough, it does give us some sign of the animation hidden behind that immobile mask. Much has been said and written about fishes. For ages they have excited the keenest curiosity. Their action, so varied in its extent and in its countless manifestations, so perfectly adapted to its surroundings, seems to be the consequence of a series of remarkable adjustments. These children of the waters behave, in their own realm, as masters to whom all things submit, even lifeless things. When they journey, they do so with certainty, with precision, as though they well knew the road they travel and what they appear to wish to find on it. The perfection of their conduct surprises us, to such an extent does it reveal an ordered foreknowledge and a definite choice.

So we are inclined to judge the fish as though it were one of ourselves, as if we were judging our own actions. We attribute to it a faculty of foresight which shows it where it is going. If the migration is directed towards places rich in nourishment, we say that the fish makes this journey in order to feed the better. If it moves towards the places where the spawning takes place, where eggs and fry find more favourable conditions than the fish themselves, we say that parental care is responsible for the journey, knowing whither it must go and how it must behave in order to achieve its end. Only, these actions of the fish, however perfect they may be, cannot be ascribed to a reasoning intelligence, so we pronounce the word "instinct" and go no further. The remarkable fullness of these manifestations of nature gives this idea an appearance of greatness with which we are inclined to be satisfied. Then we bow down before this unknown power, this mysterious, even mystic, force, before this "migratory instinct" which is supposed to lead the creature to its destiny, and that is enough for us.

But I find myself unable to stop at this point. I insist upon knowing more. Nature, that is so much of Nature as we can reach, is open enough, ready enough to allow the scientist to search out, and, beneath the grandeur of first appearances, to delve down to the means whereby those appearances are produced and governed. There is a dynamic force behind the externals in the living world; beneath form and attitude there is action. It is to them that we must go.

CHAPTER II

I. THE trout stream flows between banks alternately rocky and grassy. I often go and sit upon those banks, when my business or my leisure give me the opportunity, and, watching the stream flow past, I try to discern in it, beneath the sparkling water, the forms and activities of that life with which it teems. My feelings both as a naturalist and as a fisherman conspire to take me there. I discover my trout; I watch them; my eyes follow them on their way.

Before me, at my feet, the transparent water allows me, in spite of the current and the depth, to recognize, here and there, the details of its bed. In some places the water flows smoothly, its mass undisturbed. In others it breaks with great force upon the rocks, splitting up into tiny fragments, and becoming speckled with foam. Elsewhere, over deep holes and abysses, it rolls in eddies and whirlpools, and I can see nothing but the broken water of the surface. This is where the largest trout are to be found; they are there though we cannot see them, keeping watch, ready to pounce upon any unfortunate prey that comes within their reach. The rocky bottom, strewn with stones and fine gravel, is sometimes bare, sometimes covered with rich and luxuriant vegetation. The long, supple crowfoot (Ranunculus) raises its head there, in waving tufts which the water rocks to and fro like a giant's mane. Nearby, the Pond-weeds, the Starworts, the Plantains lift up their stems, their leaves, and the water, covering and passing over them, makes them quiver incessantly. Aquatic plants these, which, like their counterparts on land, provide shelter for a whole community of tiny creatures. If I pull one of them up with a grapnel, to see what it contains, I see, moving about among its leaves, insect larvæ, fresh-water shrimps like tiny specimens of the sea shrimp, little molluscs with a brownish shell, all of which serve as a foundation for the meal which the large trout love. Fishes less strong than these, minnows, loach and even troutlet, among the submerged growth feed upon these; they, snapped up and caught in their turn, serve as nourishment for the larger fishes, the more powerful trout which pounce upon and devour them.

This is not the only form of nourishment. The ordinary provender often includes other delicacies, aquatic insects which leap out of the water and then fall back again, land insects which the wind has carried over the water, and cast into it. These are drowned and carried away by the current. The trout throw themselves upon this new prey as though it were manna fallen from heaven to satisfy their appetites. They would rather have it than any other, preferring it to that of their own world, and they gorge themselves upon it. " The trout are biting," the fishermen say. So keen is their fondness for this kind of food that the best bait is that which is made to counterfeit it, made of flies and insects either natural or artificial.

Throughout the summer, the trout gorge to their hearts' content, finding all round them in the water or the air as much as and more than they need. They have no settled home, and they concern themselves solely with securing food. They establish themselves for a time in one place from which they can keep watch and then leave to find another, farther up or down stream as circumstances alter, turning out the first occupants, if they are strong enough. This continual search after nourishment goes on all the time, except when it is discontinued for a while after some excess, or when an unusually hot day drives the fish to cover. The only thing in the world for these intrepid devourers, these insatiable gluttons, these indefatigable hunters, raiders of high degree, is this constant giving chase and the continual watchfulness it necessitates, the eternally repeated motions of a body which darts forward, of a jaw which snaps and a throat which swallows.

The year advances; summer is followed by autumn, and then the large trout begin to lose this magnificent appetite. Their favourite food is still as plentiful, as varied, and as desirable. The manna from the skies may sometimes be less abundant, but there are plenty of little fishes. Yet, in spite of this abundance, there is not so much keenness for the chase. Hour after hour, the trout stay motionless at the bottom, or look for a shelter and pay no attention to what is going on around them. They are still the same creatures and their shape is still what it was, but their ways have altered. Fly-fishing no longer gives the same results; the trout hardly bite at all, or not at all. They are only to be caught with nets, drawn about their lair.

If now I examine the fish that are caught, or dissect them, I find that an internal change has taken place in them, corresponding to the change in their outward demeanour. These trout are becoming genetic; sexual glands are developing in their bodies. Small until now, these organs, the testicles of the males and the ovaries of the females, are becoming larger and more compact than they were. From week to week, each new time we dissect them, we see them grow, lengthen, thicken, in the abdominal cavity in which they are situated. The sexual elaboration is beginning, the first stage in a series of modifications which will become still more marked as autumn progresses and end in the ripening of eggs or sperm, and ultimately in the act of reproduction, in spawning beneath the water, on the bed of the stream.

But we are still far from this final stage. First, the creature will undergo a greater change, and that change will take place gradually. As we can see for ourselves, the fish is no longer the keen hunter it used to be, always on the move, always ready to seize its prey. It seems to have new interests with which to concern itself. It looks for hollows under the rocks or in the banks, away from the light; instead of swimming about incessantly it sometimes rests upon the bottom. Many take advantage of the slightest increase in the amount of water in the stream to go and place themselves in the midst of the current, heads to the source, as if they wished to be bathed by a water fresher, more constantly changed. They even try to go up against the stream, moving from one shelter to another, and so to reach the spots where the water flows more swiftly. Sometimes they go up the little tributaries, into which they would never have gone during the summer, and there establish themselves, finding the wherewithal to satisfy their new desires, the desire for shade and for water that is limpid and flows swiftly. They care little that there is not much depth in these narrow brooks, provided they find there the other qualities they seek. To secure these, to possess themselves of them, the trout go up towards the source, seek regions of a higher altitude, do not hesitate to go even to the highest they can actually reach.

In the case of the lake trout we observe this impulse even more clearly. When the proper time comes, they endeavour to leave the calm, deep, almost slumbering, waters in which they have lived and hunted their prey during the summer. They make for the sea or the mouths of tributaries, they stay, and, when they are able, even go into running water and proceed up it like their sisters of the rivers. Evidencing their new needs in the same way, they try to find a water which is enlivened by contact with the air instead of the calm, deep water in which they have hitherto been content to dwell. Some go down the different outlets, the streams which flow out of the lake, in the hope of finding in them this swift-flowing water, this fresh water the need of which they feel so imperiously. No difficulty, no obstacle is enough to stand in their way. The same impulse urges them all onwards, or at least, all that are capable of yielding to it, and carries them to their goal.

The seasons move on and autumn begins to give way to winter. The nights become longer; the days are often darker; the waters, near the source, become colder and more swift. The trout grow fatter and continue to increase in weight. Sexual elaboration continues; their reproductive glands constantly assume a greater size and weight. Their bellies widen out and swell like a balloon. In the males the nose changes its shape, the lower jaw becomes longer towards the end and curves like a little hooked beak. More agile than the females, they are the first to reach the upper reaches of the streams. Their colours change; streaks of orange, patches of rose or purple, appear upon their bodies and mingle with their old black spots. Then the females come, already grained, full of eggs now almost ripe. They have changed colour too, but not so much as the males. The two sexes, now brought together, waste no time in pairing. The process of gestation is nearing its end. The process of reproductive elaboration, begun several weeks before, has now reached the point in which the sexual elements have attained maturity. Sperm and eggs are ready to play their part. The spawning is about to take place.

Having reached this moment of their existence, on the eve of accomplishing the most important act in their lives, the act which maintains the species and by which future generations are founded, the trout seem to be concerned with absolutely nothing else. They devote all their activities to it. Nothing else seems to matter. Hitherto, they have still gone after any prey that might offer, but now that they are ready to spawn, they no longer eat; they are seized by a sort of reproductive anexoria which forbids them to take any nourishment. The genesiac excitement reaches its height, doubtless encouraged by the hormones produced in the sexual glands now on the point of maturation. The males busy themselves about the females, come and go around them, engage in love combats. Henceforth, they will pay no attention to anything else. In this dull season, in this water which is already chilly and in which one would expect sentiment to be frozen and die, their passion takes possession of them, drives them onwards, warms them, and produces this state of animation.

The trout are not satisfied with hovering about the bed of the stream. They rub themselves against it, go here and there, touching it sometimes with their bellies, sometimes their sides. They look for places strewn with small gravel, where they can, by suitable movements, hollow out a sort of hole and rub themselves more adequately. With strokes of their caudal fins they scatter the little pebbles left and right. By repeated, almost feverish beatings with their pectoral and pelvic fins, they disperse the mud, stirring it up and mingling it with the water which carries it away. The places thus hollowed out and cleared are clearly to be seen in the bottom of the brook. They will be the spawning places. The fish construct them and arrange them, and very soon make use of them, thus bringing to an end, by a mating in the swiftly flowing stream, the journey they had undertaken.

So, at last, the wedding takes place. In November, December, sometimes later still, beneath the cold running water, over those spawning places which they seem to have made with the express intention of using them as nuptial chambers, the females enter upon motherhood, casting forth the huge burden of their eggs. This they do at intervals, throwing it off in pieces, twisting and turning as they rub themselves against the bottom, so painful their maternity appears to be. They strain every muscle the better to press out their eggs. These are as large as peas, and their bellies contain them by the thousand. The fish strive to get rid of them. They throw them out with a sharp, rapid motion through the genital orifice situated beneath the belly, beside the anus, and just at the beginning of the anal fin. These eggs, like round pearls, translucid and slightly yellowish in colour, settle down all over the bottom of the spawning place. The mother, feeling easier for the moment, rises, moves away a little distance, then returns to lay still more eggs, when a new crisis of muscular pain tells her that the time is ripe for another expulsion. It is a real confinement, in which the mother, with water all about her, aided only by the contraction of her muscles and the pressure of her body upon the gravel of the bottom, nevertheless succeeds in giving birth to the great mass of offspring she has engendered.

The males do not leave the females; they accept the responsibilities of fatherhood. Each time a mother takes up her position, the male which has succeeded in approaching her, scattering his rivals for the time being, acts exactly as she has just done. When, after laying her eggs, she rises and moves away, he, in his turn, stops over the place she has left, rubs himself against the bottom and contracts his belly, throwing against the eggs a few drops of his milt, which is white and creamy like milk. Thus is fecundation accomplished, on the bed of the stream, outside the bodies of the two mates.

In spite of this separation, the males show as much eagerness, as much ardour and animation as those of land, although on land the actual union is much more intimate. They busy themselves incessantly about the mothers who are laying their eggs; they watch eagerly for the slightest sign of expulsion, and chase one another away so as to be alone at the desired moment. In their hurry to satisfy themselves more speedily and more completely, they even jostle the female and hustle her out of the way if she seems to take too long. It is a genuine case of rut, which seems astounding in these creatures, in this water, at this season, for it is as ardent, as passionate, as rich in desire as that we know elsewhere.

When the act is completed, the intense excitement subsides completely. Exhausted by the efforts they have just made, by this extreme expenditure of all their vital energies, the trout become inert, as though annihilated. The current takes them and carries them away. They let themselves be borne along without offering much resistance, and, in a practically passive condition, go back along the way by which they came so painfully a few weeks before. They go and lie on one side, under the rocks, in the hollows, and renew their strength as they rest, recover from the results of their exertions and their losses, and so pass the winter. Little by little, as the fine weather returns, they recover their appetite and their keenness in searching for prey, resume their former habits and return to their haunts in deeper water. Resuming their individual life, their normal method of securing nourishment, they have finished the task which their reproductive life, subject to the law of the conservation of the species, compelled them to undertake and to carry through.

The conservation of the species is, in fact, now assured. Up stream, in the place where the spawn was shed, now abandoned by the parents, the fecundated eggs lie motionless, little balls of life mingled with the grains of sand in which they were laid. Beneath the life-giving chilly water of midwinter, continually and abundantly renewed, they develop, and in them takes shape the embryo which will later be born. The creatures which have engendered them have no longer any function to perform; any care which they might give would be superfluous. All that the eggs need is water, and the stream serves as a womb; upon the river bed they take shape and their organism assumes its bodily form. The water, of itself, possesses all the required properties. Nature arranges things in such a way that the eggs, when this series of episodes comes to an end, are just where they ought to be.

II. When we consider a series of successive events like this, which goes on for several weeks, almost the whole autumn, we cannot help marvelling at its profound logic. From the very beginning, everything seems to combine and proceed in such a way as to produce the most satisfactory result. An intelligent being, capable of reason and foresight, would not proceed in any other way. So we tend to consider the course of events as though some such influence really were at work, and to regard it in our own way, taking into account their essential purpose. To all appearance, the trout set off on a wedding journey, which takes them up to the spawning places where they will produce offspring. The motive of this journey, the force which urges them onwards, seems to lie in the necessity of attaining this end. In order to make it, they change hue and colour; they put on a wedding dress which they never wear at any other time, a dress which, more brilliant and more sharply patterned in the males, helps them to attract the attention of their future mates. The first to arrive at the rendezvous, they wait there for the females, then join with them in preparing the spawning places, the nuptial bowers in which the eggs will be laid. Their love guides them to the suitable places and keeps them there. The reason for this behaviour is in the necessity for assuring to their offspring the most favourable conditions for life. It is a behaviour inspired by perfect foresight, by unfailing care, which arranges everything in such a way that complete success is assured. The reason, the only reason, for this liveliness appears to be the determination to make sure that the eggs are well and truly laid.

But though we may realise the purpose of all this; if, from my place upon the bank of the stream, I can guess what is happening and foresee what will happen, it is certainly hidden from the trout themselves, which remain immersed in the water incapable of feeling anything except that which affects them at the moment. Completely unaware of what they are undertaking, they seem, none the less, to be perfectly well aware of the results that undertaking will have, for they never make a mistake; they do exactly the right thing at the right moment. Their movements are always exactly suited to the needs of the moment. What reason have they then within themselves to make them act always in the right way, to give them the very same advice that I should give them if I were in a position to offer it? Who is their counsellor, and to whose voice do they listen, in that cold swift-flowing water in which they move, that they persevere in their efforts, and never give up? What genius is their guide, so mighty, so categorical in its commands that they obey it so completely?

There is at work an unknown factor which is at once both surprising and disconcerting. Whilst we wonder at its power and precision, we ask ourselves how it comes into being and, especially, how it is able to accomplish its end. This unknown factor stirs our curiosity. We may stand before it, content ourselves with looking at it, remarking upon it, lauding the excellence of those supreme laws of nature which control the unconscious; but we cannot help feeling the desire to discover how those laws succeed in governing action. We should like to understand what these fishes do to achieve such success, cut off, as they are, in the water. The knowledge they display is so much beyond the capacity of such creatures that we try to discover the mechanism of an action so well adjusted. Does it reside in a particular psychism, handed down from generation to generation, an innate self-contained instinct, which obliges and constrains apart from any other cause? Is it related to some extraordinary gift of foresight, which lets the fish know what the future eggs will need, compelling it, still more surprisingly, to do what is necessary to make all the necessary provision? This subordination of the needs of the individual to those of the species, this personal sacrifice, are they the consequences of some unescapable interior command, or do they exist for other reasons? The riddle of this miniature migration devoted simply and solely to spawning is sufficiently freely propounded for us to look in every direction for a solution.

At first sight we might conclude that everything is a matter of simple chance, and that it is consequently useless to give an explanation for something which does not possess one. Trout in love, it might be said, going about their stream, seek to mate, and it is pure coincidence that we should find them gathered up-stream; they might just as easily be down-stream. But when we come to examine the facts of the case, it is not so. There is no fortuitous coming together. Every year, at the same period, that of spawning, the trout exhibit the same changes of behaviour and follow the same course. This natural phenomenon is constant and invariable; it recurs at exactly the same times, and always comprises the same succession of identical actions. There is, therefore, a definite law about it, a determinism, a relation between cause and effect. It is this cause we must discover.

Now, at this period, the trout are not the only things that change. The water in which they swim about, the current which bathes them, change likewise. When the summer heat comes to an end, the stream grows colder, increasingly so as autumn gives place to winter. The light is not so strong; the nights lengthen; the days, often cloudy or misty, are only moderately bright. The submerged plants, the meadows beneath the water, lose their foliage and leave the bed of the stream barer. But in these swift-flowing waters, the dissolved oxygen, without which the fish cannot breathe, alone does not change; it may even increase in quantity, since the lowering of the temperature allows it to dissolve in a greater proportion.

Through these changes, both internal and external to them, the trout follow the same road. With one accord they go up stream, to the more swiftly flowing water. They go towards the more strongly oxygenated water. Modifications of temperature and of light being very much the same in both lower and higher reaches of the stream, it is not so with the oxygen. Nearer the source, where the water is colder, swifter, more whipped by the air, where the broad stretches of fine gravel which are fitted for the depositing of the eggs are to be found near foaming waterfalls, the oxygen is dissolved in greater quantity. The trout make for these reaches. Later, in the height of winter, it is often the same in other parts of the stream, and the water of the lower reaches is equally cold with that of the upper, and hardly differs from it in that respect. But, during autumn, when the trout are developing the germs which will later fructify, the water nearer the head of the stream is the richer, and, on their way there, they come to places where they find this life-giving oxygen in greater proportion.

The trout do not breathe very easily. I mentioned this fact when dealing with the water in which they usually live, which contrasts with that in which most white-fleshed fishes live. They require from their environment a degree of oxygen greater than that which suffices for other fishes, sometimes even twice as much. They must, all the time, find in the water round them at least six to seven cubic centimetres of dissolved oxygen to the litre, whereas the carp family are satisfied with half as much, three or four cubic centimetres, or even less. So, in order to live, to get on comfortably, to prosper, they try to find swift-flowing, clean, limpid water, like that of the mountain torrents and the streams that flow between rocks of granite. Only there, thanks to the unusual quantity of dissolved oxygen, do they find and secure their physical well-being. In any other environment they would fail.

This state of affairs is even more accentuated when the time comes for them to lay their eggs. The requirements of their respiratory system are more demanding at this period. Then the sexual glands begin to develop, the two ovaries in the females and the two testicles in the males; the development is rapid, and throughout it up to the stage of maturity, these organs continually enlarge. There is no resemblance to what happens in land vertebrates, in whom the corresponding organs always remain practically the same size. The ovaries of the mother trout, when she is nearly mature, account for a fifth or a sixth of the total weight of her body. In a trout weighing two and a half pounds, they weigh from ten to fourteen ounces. Two or three months earlier, when sexual development was only just beginning, they weighed only a fraction of an ounce, hardly anything in proportion to the whole. In eight or ten weeks, they take form, grow, come to completion.

This short space of time is sufficient for a tremendous production. Think of an abdominal tumour capable of growing in three months in such a way as to form a mass of flesh equal in weight to a fifth of the body which contains it, and you will have a picture of what happens in the trout about to bring forth young. No other pregnancy, no other gestation, approaches this either as regards volume or capacity. Further, the trout is no exception among the fishes; most others can do as much. There is not much difference between the females and the males in this respect, although the development is not quite so marked in the males. Their testicles, though not so large as the ovaries of the females, are also of ample size at maturity.

It is not difficult, therefore, to understand the change in the behaviour of the trout, seeing that such an elaborate development takes place in its own organism. We now see why it becomes so heavy, why it so frequently becomes inert, and why it is eager for rest. We need only think of the inevitable consequences which such a swift and ample proliferation would bring about in other creatures. Now we understand why the trout suffer from troubles of nutrition, why their appetite grows less and disappears, why they seem almost to be disgusted at the sight of food. It is due to the compression and disorganization of their digestive apparatus caused by the continual growth of the sexual glands. The trout become unwell, after a fashion, and their illness, though it is normal and regular so far as the life of the species and the exigencies of reproduction are concerned, none the less does not fail to affect the personal life of the individual. We see clearly that the sexual glands, in which are gathered the germs of future existences, though they are situated in the fish's body, are yet foreign to it and take up a sort of parasitic position with regard to it. These collections of germs grow upon its substance, they take form at its expense, and then control all its actions in such a way as to enslave it, turn it to their own purposes, use it absolutely that they may attain their own end.

If we cared to use medical terms appropriate to such a state of affairs, we might say that these sexual glands, in their totality, form a rapid neoplasm, and further, that their substance, instead of being composed of tissues of secondary importance, is made up of a flesh, that of the sperm and that of the ovules, in which are collected the purest and richest principles of all vitality. In this way it is easier to understand the changes which take place in the creature so affected. This substance of sexual elements demands for its development and maturation the very best materials among those of which the body is composed.

It summons them in its increasing parasitism; it receives

them as the blood furnishes them, and incorporates them in itself. The whole organism is at its beck and call. All the resources which the fish had accumulated, all the reserves of food which it had previously stored up, are moved about, turned from their original purpose, and directed towards these sexual elements as they develop, and there remain.

At last we understand the reason for the most obvious and appreciable change, that which carries the fish up the stream towards the waters where oxygen is most abundant. These new and living substances which the creature is producing within itself, require, that they may grow and increase in size, a blood which is richer and fuller of life-giving elements. Their system of respiration has need of an element essential to it which the blood takes from the water through the gills and can only secure from the surrounding water. The proportion of dissolved oxygen which once sufficed does so no longer. Henceforth, more is needed. The trout makes for those parts of the stream where it can secure this oxygen in more substantial quantities. Driven on by the exigencies of the development that is proceeding within it, it makes for such places, and obstinately endeavours to pursue a course which will result in still fuller satisfaction. It draws nearer and nearer to those places which are best able to provide what it needs. It seeks the most swiftly running water, so that it may be unceasingly bathed in fresh water, and drink it in continually through mouth and gills. It chooses, so far as it can, the most freely aerated water, that it may find in that water what has become necessary to its existence. The process of reproduction at work within it increases its respiratory needs and determines the line of conduct which it is compelled to follow. Its former well-being now seems no longer adequate; it is driven to discover a still greater well-being, and this it can only attain by changing its habitat, driven by the organic need to breathe more actively, more easily, a need which can only be satisfied by means similar to those which would drive us towards air that is fresher and keener.

Contemporary biology is well acquainted with such impulses, brought into being and directed by external circumstances. It has collected numerous examples in all sorts of different living beings, and has given them a name, *tropism*, which comes from the Greek *tropein*, which means to turn aside. Their immediate cause seems to be a differential excitation of the individual which has the effect that the influence exerted by external factors is produced more rapidly or more completely on one side of the body than on the other, so that the creature is impelled in a particular direction according to the side from which it comes. The impulsions which we find in the spawning trout belong to the categories of *branchiotropisms* and *rheotropisms*, the former being deviations brought about by respiratory influences, and the latter, deviations caused by the action of the currents. The individual, whose peculiar condition at this period has a stimulating effect upon its sensitivity, obeys both, and, guided by these impressions which it receives from outside, proceeds in the direction of those places whence they reach it, almost like a passive object, carried along by something independent of itself.

There is certainly much truth in these explanations; they do account with a certain amount of accuracy for the actions accomplished and the sequence in which they take place. But they do not tell us all the truth; they do not go far enough. In the case of the trout, the individual has his own definite part to play, since at this period he is the object of profound organic modifications. His vital machinery is transformed in a manner so complete that it is, of necessity, compelled to take a hand in the affair, in due relation to its new condition. And, as this condition affects the whole being, this is not a case of differential excitation, for the body as a whole is concerned. There is another active principle, one more uniform, more general, more complete.

We can find no more suitable term for this than *polarity*, which biologists are beginning to use in other cases, applying to these manifestations of energy a word already applied to physical energy. The spawning trout are really endowed with polarity. Under the pressure of their new organic requirements, they develop aspirations which they did not know before, or which affected them in less degree. They need water richer in dissolved oxygen and more swiftly flowing, and they make efforts to reach it in conformity with these aspirations. Their behaviour is determined by their most recent sympathies. These, leading them on, bring them progressively and in successive stages towards water which is always more strongly aerated. Little by little this demand for greater well-being, which corresponds to a definitely felt inner need, receives its fullest satisfaction as the oxygen becomes more abundant. If we carried further this comparison of a vital activity with a physical phenomenon, we might say that the organism is here obeying the law of least effort, for its needs are satisfied more easily and with a lesser modicum of expense and labour, since conditions are more favourable. It looks as if the trout were exhausted by its struggle against the current; whereas, as a matter of fact, it is the gainer by it. In that elaboration which is going on within it and which will end with the production of young it unceasingly takes the best and easiest way.

The proofs of this appetite for oxygen, the immediate consequence of a more active need for respiration, are not to be discovered only through a consideration of these successive actions but also from that of more secondary dispositions which, arising from the same cause, give it an added strength. The trout which live in a high altitude spawn earlier; they live in waters rich in oxygen; their sexual elaboration and their maturation occur sooner. Lake trout, when they are going up to higher waters, select those streams in which the water flows more swiftly and ignore the others. They often become sterile if they cannot leave the bottom of the lake and find their way to regions and torrents where, the proportion of oxygen being higher, there would be a greater possibility of spawning more effectively. Spawning takes place later when the melted snow, which is poor in oxygen, pours into the stream, in those warm periods which sometimes occur in winter, and diminish for a time the respiratory capacity of the water. The trout streams of Vaucluse, which contain enough oxygen for ordinary respiration, but cannot greatly increase the supply because of the special conditions due to their flowing largely underground, often hold back, and sometimes even stop, reproduction. We may take as our final example the trout farms, where we see the trout, collected in tanks, having no need to hunt one another since their nourishment is daily supplied to them, gather near the inlet taps which bring them water so as to benefit by its life-giving action as soon as they possibly can, and doing so the more as their sexual elaboration draws nearer and becomes more advanced.

III. So the trout set off on their wedding journey, not by chance or phantasy, not in obedience to the orders of some mysterious innate power, not by some unconscious pre-awareness of a necessary goal, but because they are compelled by nature so to do. At the proper time, each year as the seasons come round, the need declares itself, the effect is produced, and the exodus proceeds upon its appointed way until its purpose is accomplished.

It is the same for all. Longer or shorter, difficult or easy, according to the conditions in which the fish are living, or seasonal circumstances, it always begins in the same way, is carried out by the same means, ends in the same results, and is completed by the production of young. Wherever they live, they carry out this same vital ritual. Though they are scattered about the earth and have no means of communicating one with another, though they are not even conscious of each other's existence, none of them fails to behave in the same way at the same time, not because some invisible spirit dwelling continually in them constrains them to do so, but because their very organism is the compelling force. In the Alps and the Pyrenees, in Auvergne and in Normandy, in Switzerland, Britain and Central Europe, they obey this urge which drives them on with a vigour everywhere the same. And since the force which compels them is the same everywhere, the act which results from it is also the same.

They do not travel very far or for very long; they do not go beyond the fresh waters in which they live. But theirs is a migration none the less, although in miniature. It shows, better perhaps than any other, in its short and vigorous form, wherein no secondary circumstance interferes to mask the main feature, what things are really like. Since the production of young is impossible without it, it is the consequence of an ineluctable necessity which will tolerate no resistance. Further, the creature strives with all the

strength of which it is capable, to give itself up to the
purpose in view. As it develops, during the process of
elaboration to which it is devoting itself, a host of new needs
which demand satisfaction, it finds around it, in the environing water, those qualities which are able to procure that
satisfaction for it. Of the harmony thus established a
definite line of conduct is the consequence; this contact
produces a definite result. There is here no question of the
play of any innate mental powers. It is all a kind of exchange between the two environments which life brings into
contact; the organic environment which prepares and the
physical environment which directs. There is at work only
a very complete and multiform reflex which concerns the
whole of the individual, polarizing it as regards its choice
of movement, and leading it in the direction to which it
must go if it is to effect the purpose with which it is now
invested.

This reflex is not confined to the journey. Even in the
most trivial incidents it never ceases to manifest itself under
the continual influence of the external environment. The
oxydizing excitation, coming from without, makes a
definite impression upon the whole organism, and that
organism responds unflinchingly. Thanks to it, the creature
obtains every instant an immediate satisfaction which
prepares it for a further satisfaction, and makes it act in
such a way as to secure it. The journey up the stream
represents this continuous progression in terms of space.

When it has reached the spawning place the creature tries
to lay its eggs, to get rid of the sexual elements which are
now in full possession of it. The sensation of weight which
the mass produces makes it rub itself upon the bed of the
stream, press down upon it, in the hope of finding immediate relief. Its movements, its comings and goings,
indicate those places which may serve as spawning places.
The reproductive act of expulsion takes place as a result
of contractions of the abdominal muscles, and these come
into action when the excitation of respiratory origin reaches
its highest point. The creature, from moment to moment,
gradually goes through a series of progressive, related,
actions which are called forth one by the other, all, in turn,
being the inevitable effect of one great influence, that of

the environing medium and its dissolved oxygen. Caught up in this machinery it must pass through one phase after another of its vital processes until they attain their end.

In all this it behaves exactly like an automaton. The trout obeys; it does not act on its own initiative. Automaton though capable of sensation in the ordinary conduct of its personal life, it remains an automaton in its reproductive life, and does not depart from its appointed course, except as its capacity for sensation becomes keener and more specialized. This wedding journey is a migratory reflex. The wedding dress is woven of pigments excreted by the skin, for the organic over-activation to which the trout is subject produces them in the greatest abundance. The nuptial place of rendezvous, the adaptations which it necessitates, are determined by organic needs. Nothing is beyond the reach of this obligation. Everything about it is determined, realized in conformity with the needs of the moment, from day to day; the final conclusion, the producing of young, being only the ultimate outcome, the final realization.

When we look at things in this way, it seems that the creature loses in importance. Enslaved, submitted to conditions in which its personality takes only a secondary place, it seems in a measure degraded, shorn of its dignity. But this is only in appearance; on the contrary, it is enriched and exalted. Its automatism, in fact, should not be considered in isolation, but in reference to that environment which is responsible for its activities. The enslavement is only superficial. In reality, the creature levies tribute upon its surroundings, and utilizes in itself the principles which it needs for its vitality.

Strictly bounded and restricted by the medium in which it exists, it takes from that medium and uses for its own purposes all that it is able to extract from it. Although it is restricted, it profits by all the resources which it can get, and turns them to its own ends. This vital activity is a sign of its superiority. The trout in their water, making use of it and whatever it brings them, taking advantage of what it has to offer, are greater than they seem; they are possessed of all the predominance which living nature acquires over inorganic nature.

The trout has two lives, which succeed one another and take each other's place. One life is that of nutrition, and this is personal to the individual, and maintains it in its integrity. The other is that of reproduction; it makes ready the germs which are destined to become future generations. The trout in nutrition grows continually, in proportion to the amount of food which it consumes. The trout in reproduction ceases to grow, and begins to grow again only when the spawning is done. The two lives have their own peculiar requirements. They are not really antagonistic, but rather specialized, and each makes use of the individual who is the bearer of it in its own way and, in its own manner, submits him to the influence of the environment. So, passing from one to the other, there is not only a change in form, but also in methods of behaviour.

A contrast of this sort is not so clearly to be seen in the vertebrates which live on land, although it does exist in the interior working of functional changes. Specialization is less apparent in them, although it is present, and is sometimes made manifest by actions of the same type. The two lives are either not separated at all, or they are less so. To discover dispositions among terrestrial creatures comparable to that of the trout and the fish which resemble them, we must go to the metamorphic insects. In them we find the two lives distinguished, the nutritive in the caterpillar stage and the reproductive in the winged. But in these insects there are complementary differences in appearance and in structure; the individual takes up two entirely different forms, one after the other, each in accordance with its own category. There is nothing of this sort in the case of fishes; with them the only form of specialization we find is in their vital manifestations. There is no modification of form. The spawning trout is as much a trout as it was before, except in so far as it accomplishes actions which are not the same as those it used to accomplish; and it will resume the nutritive phase as soon as the spawning has been carried out. The reproductive life compels the individual to assume relations in regard to its environment which are unknown in the nutritive life.

Usually, in this picture of natural phenomena which we draw from our own observation and experience, we are inclined to consider especially that which is most ordinary and most common and to regard that as most important. We prefer to think of the trout as a greedy fish which the fisherman is anxious to catch. The wedding journey, with its varied episodes, seems something exceptional. It is, on the other hand, natural. The creature is doing what it must do, and what its structure compels it to do, just as its conformation at another time makes it perform other series of actions. But its new behaviour is not concerned with itself alone, since it is bound up with the life of the species, and it takes a form, a characteristic peculiarity, which, together with its astonishing animation, gives it a greatness proportionate to its importance. It is another life; but it is still life.

It is only in appearance that the future parents upon their wedding journey behave in such a way that we might believe them actuated by a prevision of what they have to accomplish. Such a prevision does exist, but not in them. It belongs to the covenant of natural things, which vary and change, yet are controlled in such a way that they must combine to produce the required harmony. It is in Nature herself, who has arranged everything to conduce to her own ends. Nature guides and counsels, and her counsel has the force of law. She favours her creatures on condition that they observe her rules and hear her voice. The trout hear it as they go up the streams; they obey it when they put themselves into due relation with the water that surrounds them. The action of their environment takes the place of any foresight on their part. When they go on their wedding journey they have no need of knowledge. It is sufficient for them to feel, and to allow themselves to go where satisfaction is promised them: an immanent law leads them to the place where they must go.

CHAPTER III

First Part: The Ascent of the River

MARVELLOUS, indeed: the term is not too strong. It is this word that comes into our minds when we study, successively, the various episodes which go to make up the life of the salmon. Nature, it is plain to see, is composed of marvels. Science, whose especial purpose it is to deal with facts, might refrain from using an expression which, if it were repeated too often, would end by seeming banal. But there are cases in which this quality is particularly manifest, in which that association of forms and structures, of actions and reactions, which constitutes natural life appears in a precise intensity which we do not find elsewhere, or only in disguise. We are driven to use the word, and science is sometimes driven to bestow its sanction upon it.

I. Up with my companions, as the night draws to its end, we reach the bank at daybreak on a salmon-fishing expedition. The red dawn of a March day is about to break. Little by little, the light grows stronger in the east. Over the river the darkness is turning to light; the stars are going out; and soon we can see the sparkle and the ripples of the swift-flowing water. The tall poplars that keep guard upon the banks stand out from the shadow, one after another, stretching out their leafless branches in all directions. A light, softly clinging mist spreads like a curtain, at first translucid and delicate, then becoming thicker and heavier. A feeble breeze, warmed by the first breath of approaching spring, sets the slenderest branches in motion. The noises, the murmurs, the songs which hail the dawn in summer are not yet to be heard. There is silence everywhere, repose everywhere, in this last of winter's days, save for the rustling water of the stream and, a little way off, the

34

dull sound of a waterfall tumbling from the top of some rock.

In the foaming eddies, just where the water is most turbulent, a few large fishes come and go, putting their noses out of water occasionally for a moment, diving, and appearing again. These are the salmon. They are trying to get over the fall, to pass beyond it, so that they may resume their journey towards the source. Journeying by night, they got as far as this in darkness, came up against this rocky obstacle, and it has given them halt. So they are moving feverishly in the swirling water which pours down upon them, trying to get on all the same, in spite of this unforeseen delay. Diving into the deepest eddies, turning their heads against the falling water, they bring all their muscles into play as they try to make a little progress. They twist themselves into the shape of a bow, then straighten themselves again, and, taking advantage of their slight specific gravity, helping themselves, when they can, by the face of the rock, they finally succeed in climbing the cascade, getting all the way up, surmounting it sometimes with a single bound. Having passed the obstacle, they look for a hollow place in the bed of the stream, a shelter somewhere in the bank, rest for a while, and then set out again upon their journey.

We give the name of " salmon's leap " to a waterfall like this that breaks the stream and bars the way. It is a very good name. The salmon are, in fact, compelled to get beyond it by leaping in the water, just as an animal on land would leap in the air to reach a higher place. They persevere most obstinately, never giving up, until at last they succeed in doing what they wish to do. They do not go back down the stream if their first attempts are in vain. They go on swimming about the foot of the waterfall, or somewhere near by, trying to find those places where the water is most lively and most disturbed, and stay there for several days, sometimes several weeks, as though their tenacity would not let them tire. Patiently, they await a favourable moment, a temporary increase in the volume of the stream which, by bringing more water to the fall, will open up a broader and easier way. Then, little by little, one after the other, except for occasional accidents, they succeed in forcing the difficult passage, make the leap and, with the same determination, continue their journey up stream.

But this journey, which keeps them so insistently on the way to the source, is continually beset by difficulties which they must as continually surmount. Such leaps over obstacles are often the least of their troubles. This journey, pursued with so much energy, keeps the salmon always moving up stream till they can go no farther. They begin

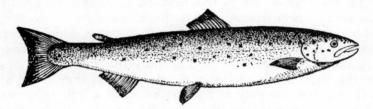

FIG. I.—FEMALE SALMON

Atlantic salmon (*Salmo salar*, Linnæus) female: the jaws are not misshapen. Much smaller than nature.

it at the estuary when they first leave the sea, and then keep on the move as though impelled always to swim to a region higher up. They have to fight against the very water in which they live and against the tendency it has to bear them with it. They swim against the stream. They can never slacken their efforts, for if they did, the water would carry them with it and take them back whence they started so that they would lose all that they had gained. They must overcome the forces which try to push them back, go to meet them as a traveller fights his way against wind, and so they must continue to progress, constantly, without ever weakening.

The little coastal rivers, whose course from source to sea very often does not exceed fifty or sixty miles, are usually easy going for them; the journey is not a long one. But it is not so in the case of the great rivers which may mean their travelling up a waterway for five or six hundred miles. Yet even these long rivers are travelled from end to end, the salmon pausing for a while when the water is low, then continuing their journey, resting under cover and taking advantage of every little favourable circumstance which presents itself. The journey may be broken occasionally, but it is never given up. The salmon devote weeks, even months, to it. Bold, determined, patient travellers, they keep on their way without faltering, without looking back, always making for the head of the stream, always straining towards the higher reaches, urged on by a force which is directed solely towards their constant progress to their goal.

This wandering wayfarer, so fond of travelling, is built in such a way as to ensure success. He is all vigour, all strength. When he bounds over an obstacle, we see nothing but a flash, swift as lightning; before he is hardly out of the water he is back in it again and has disappeared. If, taking due precautions, we get near to him as he lies in a

FIG. 2.—MALE SALMON

Atlantic salmon (*Salmo salar*, Linnæus) male: the lower jaw, hypertrophied and bent back, looks like a hooked beak. Much smaller than nature.

hollow in the bottom of the stream, resting before going on his way, we see vaguely a long body, whose colour in the shadow is easily to be confused with that of the surroundings. But if we catch him, and look at him as he lies on the grassy bank still quivering with the life that soon will be his no more, we cannot help being struck by his beauty and strength. No other fish is so exquisitely shaped.

His lines have a purity and a fineness which have no equal. His oblong body, slender without being lean, plump without being clumsy, tapers at each end; the head cleft by the deep slit formed by the jaws, the other with its full caudal fin spread out in a vertical blade. Its length, breadth and height are all properly proportioned and perfect in equilibrium so as to compose, with the trunk drawn out to a spindle, a model which other fishes often imitate, but never equal. Its fins have exactly the size and strength they need. On the lower part of the back, not far from the tail, there is the soft, flat little protuberance of the

37

" adipose fin," a second dorsal which has no rib to support it, whose presence is characteristic of the species, as of the related species also belonging to the Salmonid family, the trout, the "white fish" and the grayling. Everything, as far as outward appearance is concerned, tends to perfection, making it really a " show " fish, a fish " de luxe," worthy to be served at the most sumptuous and exquisite of banquets.

Its colours, when just caught, enhance the beauty of a form so excellent. Its belly and sides are of a brilliant, pearly white, in places slightly pink. Its back is of a deep azured grey which extends as far as the head and a little way down the sides. Brown and black, sometimes russet, markings in different parts of the body make the general colouring stand out more gloriously. The salmon in our streams so far surpasses the other fishes both as regards shape, beauty, and excellence of flavour that he seems like a king whose subjects are smaller, less handsome, less desirable than himself.

But this lord of the fresh water does not make his permanent home there. He is only a visitor, passing on his way up stream. He is like a tourist anxious to reach new countries, who leaves them when once he has reached them. He seems to travel for the sake of travelling, for the sake of the voyage, the satisfaction he gets out of it, and for no other reason.

This journey through fresh waters begins at the mouth of the river where the salmon leaves the sea. The majority of other sea fishes, if they wished to follow his example, would have to stop at this point, and would find themselves unable to get any farther. Accustomed to living in water rich in dissolved chlorides, their humoral qualities would not be able to accustom themselves to the shortage of these saline compounds, for river water contains them only in minute proportions. They would perish if they tried to keep on. Differing from them in this respect, the salmon is not in the least disturbed by the change. He can live as well in fresh water as in salt, a capacity he shares with very few other species, and he does so, when necessary.

Science has a word for these exceptional creatures which, unlike most other fishes, are able to exist in both fresh and salt water. It calls them *euryhaline*, an expression made up of two Greek words one of which means *facility* and the other *saltness* or *salinity*, and thus expresses their quality of being easily able to accommodate themselves to considerable variations in the content of dissolved salts. The sturgeon, the shad, the lamprey, the trout are euryhaline like the salmon. But the parasites which are attached to their bodies or to their gills during their existence in the sea, little crustacea clinging by their feet, are not so, and they become victims of the change. They perish very soon after the fish has begun to make his way up river.

The salmon, apparently without any difficulty, without requiring a long period of adaptation, are able to change their habitat. Their exodus being individual, they set out upon it separately, not forming shoals before they begin. They may follow one another at short intervals, but, at the outset, they do not join together. Migrating individually, the river which they all have to follow brings them together as they go up against the stream. This is the case in most European countries, so that fishermen secure none too great a reward for their efforts, and the few travellers often slip by without being noticed. But in Canada, Alaska, and Eastern Siberia, the fish are often found in very large shoals.

In these countries, the rivers, held up by ice during the winter, are set free by the arrival of spring. The crust of frost breaks up; the current rushes it along, the water-course becomes open. Then the migrating salmon-like fishes, hitherto imprisoned in the depths of the sea, arrive in great quantities to go up the rivers. They make the journey in myriads. The waters of the rivers and their tributaries are filled with a living, tumultuous host of fish which lifts them up in eddies and whirlpools. Foxes and bears, indeed most beasts of prey, then become fish-eaters; they have only to dip their heads into the water, snap their jaws, and gain a prize every time The fishermen use huge rotating machines which lift the fish out of the water by hundreds. The corpses of the dead, cast into creeks, obstruct them before they decompose. Perhaps in prehistoric times there was such an abundance in Europe and the cave man fed upon salmon. It is not so to-day.

Actually, in Western Europe and on the shores of the

Atlantic, if the majority arrive separately, or in little bands, there is a definite order about their coming. They do not all rise helter-skelter from the bottom of the sea. They come according to their size, in due season. Towards the end of autumn and during the winter, the salmon which leave the sea to enter the estuaries and go up the rivers are all of a fair size. They are often a yard or more in length and weigh thirty-five or forty pounds, or more. Splendid specimens for which the fishermen are waiting and are glad to take some trouble for. As spring approaches, these large " winter salmon " gradually grow fewer and fewer. Then the smaller fish come, called " spring salmon " because of the time at which they make their appearance. Their weight varies between eleven and twenty-two pounds, and their length from twenty to thirty inches. With the arrival of summer the newcomers become fewer and fewer, sometimes none come at all for a while and the salmon are smaller, weighing only six and a half or seven pounds. They are almost all males, whereas those who came before belonged to both sexes. These young male salmon which, in France, are given names corresponding to the Saints' days which occur about the time of their appearance, mark the end of the decrease in size. Later, in autumn and winter, the large specimens take the lead in a new progress towards the spring waters, and the same process is gone through.

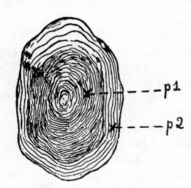

FIG. 3.—SCALE OF A SMOLT

Simplified sketch, magnified thirty times, of the scale of a smolt (young salmon going down to the sea) showing the lines of growth: $p1$, part of the scale formed during the first year: $p2$, part of the scale formed during the second year.

II. Such regularity every year, such an unusual procedure, are worthy of note. They show that the travellers act in obedience to a definite law. Not only is their journey, so to speak, prescribed for them, since it consists essentially of an ascent of the river to the farthest possible point, but the prescription extends backwards to the preparation for the journey and its start, for it decides categories and groupings, each of which appears in its due season, afterwards to disappear and return again in the same way the following year. Groups arranged in series, which do not correspond to races like those of our domestic animals and cultivated plants, or to the subdivisions of wild species. The only difference between these successive salmon is that of age.

This age is certified by their scales, which cover them with an everlasting garment, which grows as the body itself grows. When the salmon increases in size, lengthens, thickens, and so acquires a greater surface, the scales, whose number and arrangement remain fixed, have to make the necessary adaptation. They grow larger too. They do this by adding new peripheral layers which fit into each other like the rings in the trunk of a tree, and continue this process indefinitely, the last rings surrounding those of an earlier period. If we examine a single scale under a microscope we find that from centre to circumference, except for a homogeneous sector, its substance is divided into thin concentric bands, not all alike, for some are narrower than others, but, none the less, arranged quite regularly. After a series of narrow rings we have a series of broader ones, then another set of narrow ones, and so on. It would seem that the narrower series are formed during the winter, when the growth of the salmon is less rapid owing to the shortage of food, and that the broader series are formed in the summer, a period of more active growth when food is abundant. It is sufficient, therefore, to count these series on carefully prepared scales. Their number gives us the probable age of the salmon in question, or rather the time it took to grow in the sea water before the ascent of the river, since it indicates the total of winters and summers which this development has taken up.

This " scale reading ", as we call it, is really a remarkable operation, a very valuable method of research in the investigation of matters relating to fisheries. The fish itself, in its deep, moving water, is beyond our observation. All the information we can get about its existence comes to us in scraps. And these scraps of information we have to arrange and collect that we may reconstruct the whole life of the salmon in its effective continuity. Since the object of our study is beyond the reach of our senses, this reconstruction must be a mental process. We are not able to take advantage of such facilities as those offered by land-dwelling animals which we can not only hunt but breed, for we have only our eyes to help us; we cannot touch, we cannot make direct measurements. If there is anything we wish to find out

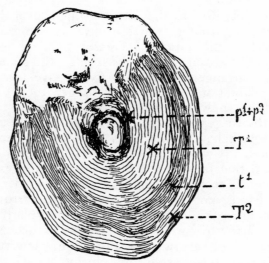

FIG. 4.—SCALE OF A GRILSE

Simplified sketch, magnified twelve times, of the scale of a grilse: p_1 and p_2, part of the scale formed in the smolt stage in fresh water: T_1 part formed during the first year's growth in the sea; t_1, part formed during the following winter; T_2, formed during the following summer, after which the fish returns up the stream. The age indicated is two years of the fry stage in fresh water, followed by fourteen or fifteen months of growth in the sea.

we must set to work in another way. As it is necessary, if we wish to make sure of a successful fishing season, to know how long the most important edible fishes take to grow, all methods of investigation have a right to be taken into account. Scale reading is one of them. It is used, therefore, not only in the case of the salmon, but for other species of equal importance, the sardine, herring, cod and others, and in books devoted to pisciculture we find considerable space given to photographs of scales and their series of annular lines of growth.

We may tell the age of these travelling salmon by the coats they wear. The largest and strongest show, by their scales, that they have grown in sea water for three or four years, or even more. Those of the spring season, which are not so plump, show only two years. The smallest of all, which we find in summer, show a growth of from fourteen to fifteen months. These differences, though they only tell us the age of the fish, are none the less extremely important.

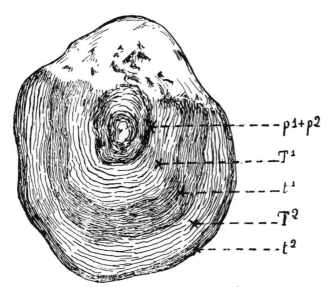

Fig. 5.—Scale of a medium-sized Salmon

Simplified sketch, enlarged eight to ten times, of the scale of a medium-sized spring salmon. This is similar to that of the scale of a grilse (p. 42) except that $T2$ and $t2$ indicate that one more summer and one more winter were spent in the sea. The total age indicated is thus: two years of the fry stage in fresh water, followed by two years of growth in the sea.

They show that the salmon, when they are about to go up stream, do not sort themselves out before they start. Fish of all ages, and consequently of all sizes, are able to leave the sea and go up the river, for the capacity to do so is not the privilege of any particular size. The rule they follow is to proceed by a decreasing succession of age and weight throughout the year. The oldest and heaviest take the lead, as though to show the way and get things started; then come the middle weights of spring and, finally, the small summer salmon. After which, the following autumn and winter, the big ones appear again, and so on from year to year with a regularity which nothing ever breaks.

Each season sees the estuaries crossed by dissimilar representatives of one and the same species. But whatever the size, whatever the period, they all behave in the same way. They all set about ascending the watercourse with the same determination, the same continuity. In this respect none is behind the others. They all show the same vigour and obstinacy. This resemblance is not confined to the journey. It is to be found in the travellers themselves, for their bodies all experience the same modification, that of sexual elaboration. Their reproductive glands, present when they leave the sea, though small, begin to enlarge as soon as they reach fresh water. And they continue to grow as the individual goes farther up the river. In short, this ascent of the rivers is a genetic process; the journey is nothing but the preliminary stage of producing young.

An inevitable comparison arises here. The salmon, on a larger scale, do what the trout do on a smaller scale. Their behaviour is identical with that of the trout on their way to spawn. Like the trout, they move towards the upper reaches of the watercourse, producing within their bodies as they do so the germs destined to be spawned. There is nothing astonishing in this. Both trout and salmon belong to the genus *Salmo*, of the family *Salmonidæ*, which takes its name from them. They form two related species, *Salmo salar* (Linnæus) and *Salmo trutta* (Linnæus). There is, therefore, a reason for the resemblances between them. But the salmon make a long and complex migration of what the trout accomplish more simply and in a shorter time. Since they grow up in sea water instead of spending all their time in fresh, they have to come from the depths of the sea before they reach the river in which they will ultimately spawn. Up that river from mouth to source they have to go, before they reach the spawning places not far from those in which the trout spawn. The trout, on the other hand, have only a short trip to make; they live, so to speak, on the very threshold of the spawning place. The salmon, since they have farther to go, take a longer time over their journey.

But intention and purpose are the same in both cases. This is a wedding journey.

These migrants, in fact, will one day be lovers, though, as yet, they have not learned to know one another. Puberty is only just awakening within their bodies. When they chance to meet, they pass each other with complete indifference, never dreaming that, in time to come, their relations will be much more intimate. For the time being, they are content to prepare themselves for the wedding to come. And in face of this law of love, in face of this obligation imposed upon them by the future production of offspring, all are equal and alike, big and little, old and young. There is, among them, neither opposition nor difference: age is of no account. They all behave in the same way, and there are no exceptions.

A functional necessity of this sort, so closely tied up with the circumstances in which they dwell, is really very remarkable. The salmon enter the fresh waters and go up the rivers not because they like doing so or merely by chance, but that they may spawn in them, and because the need to spawn there drives them onwards. There is no sign of all this so long as they are still in the sea, but as soon as they reach the river it becomes obvious. Their whole existence is divided into two definitely distinct parts: one marine or *thalassic* (from *thalasse*, the sea), which is entirely given up to the maintenance of the individual, to the nourishment and development of the body; the other, of the rivers, or *potamic* (here coining a term from the Greek *potamos*, which means " fresh water "), which is entirely devoted to spawning. A nutritive life of growth in the sea, a genetic life of reproduction in the river: these are the two different, successive phases of the existence of the salmon, which is forced to adopt a dual personality that it may realize its cycle fully.

The salmon are not the only fish which behave in this way. Several other species which we have already mentioned, the shad, the sturgeon, and the lamprey, also have two separate lives, one of growth in the sea and one of reproduction in fresh water. Like the salmon, they must leave the sea and go up the rivers to be able to produce young. This similarity causes us to include them all in one category

45

based upon uniformity of behaviour, neglecting their differences of shape. This is the category of those fishes which are obliged to leave the sea to shed their spawn in rivers, and constrained to migrate in order to acquire the capacity to bring forth young. This is a biological category, founded upon the special accommodation assured between

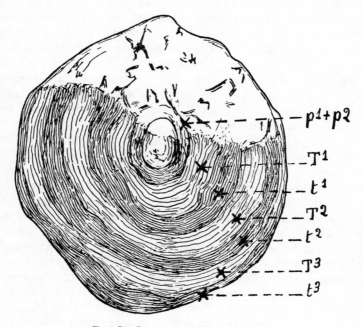

FIG. 6.—SCALE OF A WINTER SALMON

Simplified sketch, enlarged six to eight times, of the scale of a large winter salmon. This is similar to those which have been illustrated on pp. 42 and 43 except that $T3$ and $t3$ indicate that still another summer and winter have been spent in the sea. The total age indicated is thus: two years of the fry stage, followed by three years of growth in the sea. The largest salmon show one or more years more, and their lines are added to those shown above.

the interior organization of the fishes and the conditions under which they live, which favours them to such a degree, despite the relatively small number of such species, that they are able to multiply freely instead of being restricted because of the difficulties involved. These fishes go up the river in thousands. Every year, their migrations bring the fishermen the reward they anticipate, a catch of considerable value. Unlike all other fishes in this respect, and thereby quite definitely distinguished from the rest, they form, in the aquatic world, the section of *anadromous migrants*. This title, taken from the Greek, indicates that they " run up " (*anadromein*) the fresh-water streams for the fulfilment of their reproductive urge.

The anadromous salmon arrive at the mouths of the rivers to start out upon the journey which will bring them to the places most suitable for them to spawn in, and these places are often a long way off. The usual spawning places, which alone provide conditions favourable to the act of reproduction, are most frequently in the highest reaches, near the sources, at the " basin head." Every hydrographic basin, opening to the sea by the single entrance which is the estuary, is like a vast reservoir bounded and enclosed by hills and high grounds. Down from these hills in which the springs are, flow streams which, gathering at different confluents, ultimately enter the great river. The whole forms a vast network of running water, which all comes down and converges on a single outlet and loses itself in the sea. The salmon, coming in by this door, is faced by a number of different possible alternatives, going off in different directions, and as he goes farther up the stream further alternatives present themselves. Then this strange traveller adds a new complication to those which would already seem to make his journey so difficult; he will only take certain of the ways that offer, and having set out upon them he will follow them to the end, paying no attention to the others.

In every river basin there are ways that he will take and ways that he will not take, streams that he always frequents and streams which, with equal persistency, he will never go up. They are always the same; there is never any changing over from one to the other. At each confluent, as though it were a cross-roads, the salmon enter the stream which their predecessors entered before them and which their successors will enter after them; other possibilities they ignore. If, by chance, any should start up the wrong course, they soon come out again, and return to the right way. This looks almost like intelligent choice, as though it were inspired by a precise indication of some sort. They all do it; there are no exceptions. I have watched them several times. Those which go up the Loire basin never enter the tributaries of the right bank, though many of them offer easy access; on the other hand, they go up most of the streams of the left bank. The Adour gives us an even more striking example. Where it meets its principal tributary, the Gave, which rises in the mountains near by, the salmon leave the river itself and go up the tributary.

The fishes, constrained to make this difficult wedding journey, do not seem to have the freedom of action that would seem desirable. Like the pilgrims of the Middle Ages, who were eager to increase the dangers and risks of their way by forcing themselves to take certain roads and to perform certain practices, they seem to be carrying out a sort of ritual. Their speed and their capacity for leaping, which seem to open up such wide possibilities, really disguise a definitely categorical compulsion, to which they must invariably and inevitably yield. Not only does the law of their migration bring them out of the sea and send them up a river, obliging them to keep on their upward way till they reach the swiftly flowing torrents of the upper reaches, but it bids them, further, only to go up certain streams and to avoid others which are, as it were, tabu, placed under an interdict. And the fish obey.

III. What then is this force whose constraining power, in these confluents of flowing water where circumstances often seem identical on either hand, is so great that it can determine a choice so invariably observed? To all outward appearance there is nothing to show what must be done, to indicate which route should be taken. Yet the journey always takes the same course. The salmon arrive at intervals, each apparently its own master, yet they all behave in exactly the same way and follow the same road. What do they find, what signpost like that upon our roads, that they manifest a preference, so definite and so lasting?

The direct and immediate reason for their choice certainly does not reside in the fish alone. Where would he find, within himself, one strong enough to make him adopt a certain course of action? Many of the salmon, coming for the first time, cannot have any idea where their journey

will take them. Even those who have been there before
can hardly recognize the things and places they have seen
on a previous occasion. In the flowing water, often disturbed and anything but transparent, details and landmarks
are not seen; it is the water itself with which the traveller
is concerned. In his case the memory for places which we
find among land animals, favoured by the sharpness of their
vision, could find no scope even if it existed. The natural
features of the road along the river bed or of its banks, and
any sequence of memories they might evoke, can have no
effect upon a creature enveloped by the water and always
struggling against it, feeling that water, experiencing that
water, blind to everything but that water. Evidently it is
to this water, this fluid, running mass, that he must look for
guidance; he has nowhere else to look.

When the river is a single stream without any large
tributaries, as is sometimes the case, the road is plain and
the salmon has no choice. But when, vaster and more
complex, it is joined by tributaries, the question of choice
must arise, and the different qualities of the waters which
ultimately come together, now enter into the question.
They do so according to their importance. At the confluences, there is often no resemblance between the currents
which meet there; even when they are brought together in
a common bed they can be distinguished. Among these
different qualities, some are constantly changing, but others,
such as temperature and the degree of oxygen dissolved,
are more constant. The degree of their permanence depends
upon topographical considerations, upon the lie of the land,
the constitution of the river bed, its length, its steepness.
When the salmon reach a confluence on their way up stream,
they often, if not always, find there two entirely different
kinds of water, and since this is the only matter to be taken
into account, they make their choice between them.

The chief motive, and doubtless the only decisive one, is
that of the amount of dissolved oxygen. The migrants
always go where the proportion is greater. In the labour
and weariness of swimming against the current they seek
insistently for the most richly aerated waters, the waters
with the most life. They seek them out, go up them, and
leave the others on one side. And these are the only waters

they do go up, for here they find the guide they seek. They take it in their own way, as aquatic beings to whom water is the chief consideration, for it is necessary to the manifestations of their life, and they follow it tenaciously.

The basin of the Adour gives a definite example of this fact, one as clear as could be desired. In all the many different districts I have investigated from this point of view, I know none which illustrates this point more effectively. And it is very rich in salmon. In a normal year, it alone furnishes more than a third of the salmon caught in France. And its fish, which have for long enjoyed the reputation they deserve, are exported to other countries.

This basin is bounded by that of the Garonne and by the Pyrenees. It is not of any very great extent compared with the other great river basins of France. It is indeed the smallest and hardly extends over four Departments. A tiny piece of land now part of France, it was separated from the Iberian peninsula and joined to the continent by that great upheaval which set up the Pyrenees. But it still preserves traces of ages long since past. Fish of the same species are found on both sides of the chain of mountains. The same people have come to live there, with the same type of mind, the same customs and the same language, the sonorous Basque with its strange inflections, the last vestige of a dialect which formerly extended over Western Europe, and even reached Central Europe. This language is now forgotten nearly everywhere, though it has given more or less disguised names to various places, mountains, and watercourses in the regions where it once prevailed. Its territory continues into the Spanish provinces which border the northern slopes of the Cantabrian Mountains, Biscay, the Asturias, Galicia; it reaches as far as Cape Finisterre. A splendid district, green, bathed in the Atlantic mists, warmed by the southern sun, holding fast to its old ideas under its modern elegance, and combining within itself the fulness of its seascapes, the beauty of its cliffs, the ruggedness of its lofty peaks, and the delicate charm of its woods, fields, and gardens.

The river, from the mountain to the ocean, has made its bed in the shape of an arc of a quarter of a circle, a shape taken also, but in a larger sweep, by its neighbour the Garonne, whose course follows its own concentrically, and fixes its boundaries by cutting it off from the rest of the mainland. The Garonne, although it rises in the Central Pyrenees, extends, if we take into account the great tributaries on its right bank, the Tarn, the Lot, the Dordogne, as far as the Cevennes, the central plateau, and so to the continental range. The Adour, on the other hand, strictly limited to the Pyrenees and the south, remains definitely connected with Béarn and Gascony.

Its course is certainly short, but it is none the less magnificently characteristic. The breadth of the river at Bayonne and below is greater than that of the Seine at Paris and equal to that of the Rhone at Lyons. Lower still, when it is nearing its end, the current casts its waters into the sea and the rising tide casts them back again, raising considerable waves. It receives its last tributary, the Nive, in the town itself, the sources of which are in the Roncevaux pass, by which invaders have always come. Higher up the stream, not far from Peyrehorade, it splits up into two almost equal branches, one which bends round to the north and retains its name; the other, called the Gave, which goes south and west, towards the Pyrenees. The latter, itself dividing into two swiftly flowing streams, the Gave de Pau and the Gave d'Oloron, so called from the most important towns which they water, gorgeous, picturesque torrents, whose abundant noisy waters still seem to re-echo the roar of the cascades from which they fall.

The short trunk of the river has thus three main origins, three principal roots, differing both as regards quality and length. The chief branch, which bears the name Adour from its beginning, rises in the Pic du Midi range, in the high valleys of Bigorre, not far from the Garonne and the Val d'Aran; then pointing to the north before it turns westwards and begins its curve, it sets out upon a long course across Gascony. The two Gaves, more direct, come down more rapidly. The Gave de Pau imitates the Adour, and also goes off to the north, but soon bends westward again towards the ocean. The Gave d'Oloron, which is still more swift and short, comes down from the Ossau valley, and pours its waters straight into the sea without turning aside or allowing anything to stand in its way.

These three watercourses, though all offspring of the same mountain range, rising at the same altitude amid cascades and rocks, differ as regards the length and situation of the beds they have hollowed out for themselves. The Adour, which is the longest of them and is made lazy by its very length, swollen by tributaries which rise in the Gascon hills, runs slowly, and its waters are gradually warmed by the land. When they join those of the Gave, they are usually three or four degrees warmer. The Gave de Pau is fresher, swifter, clearer. The Gave d'Oloron, which runs to extremes, has the swiftest currents and often the coldest waters.

The amount of oxygen dissolved in the water corresponds to the differences of origin. Low temperatures, rocky banks, producing cascades and eddies, facilitate and maintain the solubility of the oxygen which the water borrows from the atmosphere. The Adour is always the poorest. The Gave d'Oloron is usually the best and most constantly provided. In spring, when the temperature of the water is average, I have found 5·93 cubic centimetres of oxygen to the litre in the Adour, 7·72 in the Gave de Pau, 7·89 in the Gave d'Oloron. In summer, when the more tepid water is less able to absorb oxygen in solution, the Adour has only from 5 to 5·6 cubic centimetres per litre, but the Gave de Pau still has from 6·7 to 6·8, and the Gave d'Oloron, 6·9. Finally, in winter, when the salmon spawn in water gone down to 6 and 8 degrees Centigrade, the power of dissolving oxygen being then higher, the Gave de Pau contains as much as 8·79 cubic centimetres of oxygen to the litre, and the Gave d'Oloron 8.84, thereby nearly reaching the limits of solubility.

The salmon make no mistake. Going up from the mouth of the river against the stream, they make for the two Gaves and their life-giving waters. Setting out from the depths of the Gulf of Gascony, they always seek those places where there is the most dissolved oxygen. After crossing the bar, they go through Bayonne, where, with very few exceptions, they pay no attention to the Nive, and continue their course up stream. Often they keep to their right, to the left bank of the river, for there they find an environment more favourable than that of the other bank, where the influence of the water of the two Gaves, which flow in on the left bank, is more intense. When they reach the confluence, finding there currents dissimilar both as regards temperature and amount of dissolved oxygen, the two Gaves on the one hand, and the Adour on the other, they scarcely hesitate, and even those who have gone wrong, return later. They all leave the Adour and go into the Gave. Then, a few miles farther on, at the confluence where the two Gaves themselves part company, the majority go up the Gave d'Oloron, establish themselves there and remain several months until the time comes for them to spawn.

From the deep abysses of the ocean to the spawning places in the mountains the actual itinerary which the salmon take is determined by the waters themselves, and based upon differences in the content of oxygen in solution. At first mingled and confused near the mouth of the river, then gradually becoming distinct as they are nearer the source and farther from the mouth, it is the current which is the deciding factor. The road which the salmon take, originally the same as that of other roads, little by little departs from them at the successive confluences, as at a series of cross-roads. The fishes in their ascent of the river never stray from this road, and never leave it. The lower reaches of the Adour, whose bed is the collecting place for all the waters of the basin, is only a place of passage for them. They are really making for the Gave. And the travellers make for it quite distinctly, the precision and intensity of their reflexes taking the place of landmarks and signposts. Their behaviour is controlled externally, in accordance with the progressive succession of varied conditions of environment.

IV. In this respect the salmon is like the trout, its sister species. It behaves in the same way though on a larger scale. Its great migration is a wedding journey pure and simple, a journey up to the spawning grounds, and the force which drives the fish thither is, itself, the consequence of a need for more vigorous respiration. As it goes up stream, fighting its way all the time towards the higher ground of the watershed, the creature develops its sexual glands, which grow larger and larger, and continuously builds up the substances of which they are composed. In this respect it goes farther than the trout. When it first came to the mouth of the river, the weight of its sexual glands was hardly a hundredth part of the whole weight of its body, often not so much as that. Little by little it is transformed, growing until it reaches a considerable size, developing proportions so great that the organism can only accommodate itself to them by an intensive increase in vitality.

So, respiration being the function *par excellence* of every living thing, the essential principle of vital activity being found in the respiratory system, the salmon, like the trout, makes for the places where it is assured of greater facilities for that system. Greedy for oxygen and able to obtain it from the water only through its gills, compelled to breathe more fully, it goes where it is best able to obtain satisfaction, just as, in a stuffy room, one goes to the windows and doors where the air is purer. The salmon, when engaged upon its genetic function, acts in exactly the same way. It must have oxygen, and the more the process of reproductive elaboration progresses, the more eagerly it goes in search of streams well provided with that oxygen. This necessity is its law. It drives the fish up the stream, and determines its choice, its behaviour.

There is a good reason, then, for this long and perilous journey: it is a voyage in search of oxygen. At the mouths of rivers, when the salmon gets there, it usually finds in the water into which it is now proceeding, from five to six cubic centimetres of dissolved oxygen per litre, a proportion greater than that of the sea which it is leaving. This being running water, the fish begins to move against the current and go up stream, making its way to those places whence this fresh, energy-supplying, aerated water, which it finds so satisfying, issues. The strongest eddies, the most foaming cascades, the fiercest rapids being the most favourable to this aeration, it makes for them, waits in them, and remains in them longer than anywhere else. And as it gets higher and higher the proportion of oxygen increases continually, reaching seven to eight centimetres per litre according to the temperature and the time of the year. The farther it goes the greater its feeling of well-being, so that it is encouraged to go farther still. In spite of dangers, in spite of obstacles, heedless of the former because it does not perceive them, and careless of the latter for it tries to surmount them, the salmon goes on and on, urged forward all the time by its increasing desire for oxygen to breathe. It is dependent upon its water, and seeks always for water that is more and more aerated. Producing within itself the germs of its future loves, this excess of vitality drives it forward, giving it a guide that enables it to reach its end.

There is a definite determinism about this ascent of the stream, a determinism resulting from the agreement of the interior organic characteristics of the fish with its surroundings. The former necessitate an increased respiratory activity, and this it tries to secure from the latter. It is completely polarized towards the most highly oxygenated water, in order that its breathing may be more intense. Doing on a larger scale what the trout does on a smaller, its branchio-polarity drives it forward and acts as its guide. It progresses with the utmost determination towards the freshest waters, finds what it wants in them, and behaves accordingly. Such sensations are quite outside our own experience, for we cannot live in water. When we stand upon the bank of a salmon stream, the water flows before us, but our eyes cannot discern in it the peculiar features of its composition. To find them out we have to make a very careful examination and a series of elaborate analyses. The salmon know all they need to know straight away, and the knowledge is made available to them by their sensations; they have only to follow the guidance of their sensations.

They do this; they are constrained to do this, because there is nothing else they can do. The needs of their respiratory system compel them. A creature that lives in water is in a very different position from one that lives in air, for though the function of respiration is common to both, the conditions in which it is exercised are very different.

On land, with air in which oxygen is mixed with nitrogen generally in the proportion of one in five, all living creatures have an ample provision of oxygen, because the mixture is so rich in it. Except for accidents, land animals never have to fear a shortage, or to be uneasy about a deficit which never exists. In the realm of waters the situation is very different. The oxygen which is to be breathed is found there only in solution, and the rate at which it is so dissolved varies according to the temperature (which increases it when low and decreases it when high), from $\frac{3}{100}$ per cent to $\frac{1}{150}$. One litre of air contains two hundred and ten cubic centimetres of oxygen available for breathing; a litre of water has, according to circumstances, from three or four to seven or nine cubic centimetres. This is a very small proportion, only just sufficient, and it obliges the creatures which live in the water to make continual accommodations, since those whose respiratory requirements are strongest are sometimes on the verge of asphyxiation.

The journey is governed by circumstances outside of the fish itself, that is, by the natural conditions of the place in which it must be made. It can be successful only in so far as the conditions for accommodation are fulfilled. Realising, in these future mates, the aspirations of the individual towards a more intense vitality, it consists of a progressive ascent which is continued to the very limits of the stream. There, in the mountain torrents, the highest branches of streams mounted, so to speak, against the current, close to the very summits of the mountains, the rendezvous is fixed where the salmon will soon come together to produce their young. Nature places it there, because there, in the bosom of the waters which compose it, the proportion of life-giving oxygen is at its highest. There, and only there, the marriage will be consummated, for there everything is ready, and this cannot be said of any other place.

In this respect we find that the salmon exemplify in the clearest possible manner the law obeyed by other fishes, fishes which, anadromous like themselves, spend the period of their growth in the sea, but go to spawn in fresh water. All these fishes, as they prepare for spawning and while the elaboration of their germs is proceeding within them, display a vastly increased respiratory activity which could never be satisfied in sea water. Unlike most other marine species, which are able to find all they want where they are, their needs are more intense, and since, further, they are particularly able to adapt themselves to fresh water conditions and to realize the suitability of this quality to natural circumstances, they leave the sea water, which has not enough dissolved oxygen to suit them, and go to the estuaries. There they are first aided by the dechloridation of the water which assists their respiratory processes. As they go farther and farther up the running fresh water whose content of dissolved oxygen increases gradually as they near the upper reaches, they are continually encouraged to push on, to go higher and higher still. But most of them, sturgeon, shad, lamprey, seldom go beyond the middle reaches of the river basins. The salmon, more vivacious and consequently more exacting, go farther still; the greater intensity of their respiration driving them ever onwards to the regions near the mountain tops.

CHAPTER IV

THE MARVELLOUS STORY OF THE SALMON

Second Part: The Wedding on the Spawning Grounds

I. THE salmon have reached the rendezvous. Since they can no longer go higher or farther, for, in the mountain torrents in which they will henceforth live, the water is hardly sufficient to cover them, they dash about in all directions, rest for a while, dart out again, rest again, seized by a continually increasing agitation. Now that they have completed their ascent of the stream, have actually swum upwards towards the goal where they are now assembled, neighbours in a closely restricted space, it never occurs to them to rest peacefully, or to allow themselves some relaxation. Quite the contrary. They feel that the moment for their wedding is drawing near, and, having now found the very spot where that wedding is to take place, they hasten to make the final preparations and set to work to complete the task they had begun.

But their ascent has been wearying. They have made tremendous efforts to overcome one obstacle and one danger after another. If they could have completed the whole journey straight off, their speed, which is sufficient to allow them to travel as much as twenty-five or thirty miles a day, would soon have brought them to the required place. But to keep going against the current at such high pressure for so long a time would have been impossible. Now and again they have to stop; to rest in a hollow in the bed of the stream, beneath the shelter of a tree trunk or a rock, and stay there resting·on their pectoral fins for a while, motionless sometimes for hours, sometimes for days and even weeks. Occasionally they may move away, but not for long. A few strokes of their fins carry them to another hollow, or take them back to one they had left some time before. The time they take to go up stream is made up alternately of active periods and passive periods, the former short, the latter longer and passed in a kind of languid torpor, which is not difficult to understand when we consider the intensity of the modifications which the organism is obliged to undergo. The fish is devoting itself to the elaboration of the germs. Its chief work, which goes on entirely within itself, consists in getting ready for the spawning. This is the one dominant consideration.

The journey necessitates a series of frequent and prolonged halts, and so it takes longer. There are various places where the salmon stay, varying according to the time of year and other circumstances, particularly in summer, when the water is apt to be low, tepid, poor in dissolved oxygen, and so depressing. To the fish this is a season of discomfort and pain, fortunately relieved when the autumn floods come. The time taken varies with the individual. The big heavy salmon, which arrive at the mouth of the river when it is already quite cold, in November or December, start up stream at once. They reach their spawning places the following spring or summer, and wait for the next winter before they get on with the business of reproduction. They spend a whole year, sometimes thirteen or fourteen months, in fresh water. The medium-sized spring salmon take less time and are in fresh water only from seven to ten months. As for the young summer salmon, their trip takes no more than four or five months.

These differences depend entirely upon the date of the rendezvous, for they all have the same course to follow. This date being fixed, all take care not to be absent when it arrives. The wedding is celebrated at the beginning of the cold season, towards the end of autumn and the beginning of winter, usually December and January. At this time, all these future mates, if they are to produce young, must be present in the spawning zone. In spite of the fact that they have set off at different times, some sooner, others later, upon the road which is open to them all, they must arrive together. Scattered at the outset, strung out upon this long road of flowing water, often travelling individually, or together in little groups which come together and break up again continually, they come closer together as they gradually near their goal, and remain together for longer periods. Finally, in October and November, differing in size, but not in intention and situation, they assemble in the spawning regions, all ready to fulfil the object which has brought them so far from the sea whence they set forth.

These wedding rendezvous at the heads of the streams present few characteristics that we should consider satisfactory. The torrents, girt by rocky peaks, have nothing to offer, in the severe, harsh setting which surrounds them, save swift-flowing waters, pure and fresh, save a bed made of gravel and rock which is constantly being washed away. But this is all that the lovers desire. It is sufficient and even pleasant in their eyes. The regions which at this time of the year we find forbidding are suitable and favourable for their purposes. The snow-covered slopes which surround them, the white girdle of the peaks which shut them in, accentuate in our eyes the qualities they seek and which their eagerness demands.

At the beginning of winter, the swift waters of the heights, constantly whipped up, in their eddyings and cascades, by the cold air, dissolve oxygen in a hitherto unattained degree. They sometimes contain as much as eight or nine cubic centimetres per litre, occasionally even more, thanks to a super-saturation which the cold weather allows to continue for a considerable period. The water provides the salmon, in an abundance which they have hitherto never enjoyed, with this life-giving and exciting element, and their organism seizes the opportunity which will enable it to fulfil the task with which it is charged. Ever since the salmon left the sea, a natural chain of events has brought them gradually to this ultimate point of their journey, by continually increasing their respiratory activities. Here they find their final excitement, the most compelling of all, which will put the finishing touch to the long work which has gone before. It is only here that they find it. Nature, by a cunning co-ordination of the operations which it brings into being, has attempted the seemingly impossible. Utilizing its power, its diversity, its supreme capacity for using time and space simultaneously, it succeeds and attains its end, although adverse conditions seem in league to secure its failure. The salmon, urged on by Nature, helped by her provisions, a fish lost, so to speak, in the surrounding water, completes this marvellous journey, this extraordinary romance of love and adventure.

But when it nears the denouement, when it reaches the stage upon which the last scene will soon be played, in what respect is it different from what it was a few months before, at the beginning of its journey? Once bright and lively, strong and agile, robed in blue and silver, it is now emaciated. It seems longer than it used to be, its head seems larger, for the height of its body is not so great. But though its colours are not what they were, it is still rich and glorious of hue. The blue and white have become purple and greenish gold, as dazzling, if not more so. The back and sides are adorned with carmine-coloured patches, which change rapidly, from moment to moment, from palest rose to bright red. The black spots are still there and make the colours stand out. The belly, which used to be pearly white, is now reddish yellow. Here and there, the cheeks and opercula are tinged with pure gold. Yes, the tints have altered.

"Wedding dress!" we say when we see such an alteration, and we are right, for these colours, brighter in the male than in the female, are those in which the fish adorns itself at spawning time. But it is a strange dress which, in spite of its splendour, is not a gorgeous robe put on for this very grand occasion, but a cast-off made up of the products which the organism forces to the skin so as to get rid of them by excretion. The old pearly, bluish pigments have disappeared, covered over now by other pigmentary substances of different hue. And the new dress which it acquires in this way is less expressive of the approaching wedding than of the profound process of the breaking up of assimilation, which has gradually been taking place in preparation. The colours are indicative of sickness, a sign of the intense crisis which is going on within.

Other symptoms too reveal the greatness of this organic change. In the males, the snout often becomes enlarged. The jaws lengthen, as a result of a proliferation of their bony structure, and form a sort of beak, the lower part of which, the longer, turns up at the end and protrudes in front of the upper, either rolling up underneath it, or fitting into a hole pierced in it as if by a punch. As a result of this temporary hyperplasia, which takes the form of a definite chondrostean appearance, Cuvier described them as a special species which he called *salmo hamatus*. But they are really only ordinary male salmon in which considerable organic changes are taking place.

These proliferations are doubtless due, as far as we are entitled to make such a presumption, to new humoral activities, due themselves to the completion of sexual ripening. These hyperostoses have, doubtless, no other cause, and, probably, no other significance. Yet people have tried to find a use for this beak. It has been taken to be a weapon in the love battles between the males, or as a gripper by which the females can be seized and held. There is no justification for any such idea. These temporary forms, secondary sexual characters which the creatures concerned assume in various ways, are the outward manifestations of an interior change which calls for the expenditure of considerable energy; they are the external results of the active metabolic urge which is at work deep in the tissues of the living being.

The governing impulse, continually growing in strength and now assuming exclusive supremacy, is, in fact, that of the final maturation of the sexual elements, the completion of the testicles and ovaries so that they may be able to play their proper part. The fish is emaciated, certainly; it seems longer than it used to be, but there is no lessening in the size of the organs of reproduction. On the contrary, they have acquired the preponderance and occupy more space in the body than any other organ. In spite of the emaciation, the belly, because of them and of their size, swells out and distends. In the females, the ovaries with their ripe eggs ready to be spawned often weigh as much as a quarter or a fifth of the total weight of the body. The testicles of the males, though they are not so large, still account for a tenth of the total weight. Such proportions, greater than those in the trout in similar case, have no parallel on land. These organs occupy a privileged position, and the whole organism seems to base its existence and its vital actions on its possession of them.

Formerly, when the journey was beginning, there was a perfect balance in the different portions of the organism; they could all perform their functions. The digestive apparatus was intact; the salmon, snapping up the bait, was an easy victim to the fisherman. Its flesh was full, firm, well supplied with juices. Little by little this state of affairs has altered. The sexual glands, in the course of their proliferation, have drawn towards themselves, and used for the elaboration of their germs, the active substances of the whole organism; like a parasite they have absorbed them and made use of them to the detriment of all the rest. The digestive system partially degenerates and no longer functions; if the salmon swallowed a prey it could not digest it. The reserves of nutriment with which the flesh was abundantly impregnated everywhere disappear and are absorbed by the reproductive glands. These glands are the only ones to grow, to prosper; the other parts of the vital mechanism are progressively impoverished that these may be enriched. The creature empties itself, gradually deprives itself of its own individual possessions, to fill and vivify these newcomers, which are always anxious for more and are always well served. Everything that the nutritive life of the period of growth had slowly accumulated in the body is now assimilated by the reproductive life, which is preparing to expend in one single gesture the wealth gained as the result of much sparing and effort.

In fact, the creature, in producing its germs, feeds upon itself. Though its ovaries or its testicles fill out and become firmer, its flesh becomes soft and flabby. The organism devoted to the working out of this reproductive process gives itself entirely to its task. Nothing else counts but this coming act of reproduction. The future lovers think only of their love and of the preparations that must be made for it; they take no heed of anything else. An old proverb which has a considerable element of truth in it despite its exaggeration says of a particularly devoted lover that he is happy to live on love and fresh water. This is literally true of the salmon and other fishes of the same sort. Their appetite is concerned only with the approaching satisfaction that will come with the spawning. The rest is utterly suppressed, for weeks and months. Love is supreme.

II. Then the marriage takes place. Like the trout, their smaller counterparts, going through the same processes at no great distance from them, the salmon spawn on the bed of rock and gravel which covers the bottom of the torrents. They settle down and hollow out their spawning places. The coldness of the season, the iciness of the water, interfere with them very little and do not trouble them at all. Do they not find in this water at this time of year the superabundant oxygen which so stimulates their vitality? And have they not, in their bodies, mature sexual glands whose internal secretions, acting upon the whole organism, animate it with a feverish excitement which is just reaching its paroxysm? The creature is possessed by an increasing agitation, a real delirium, which will come to an end only when the spawn is actually released. In the rivulets of pure water in these high regions where the trout and the salmon find all the natural conditions which favour reproduction, they give themselves up entirely to the same course of action, of which spawning is the sole aim. The salmon surpass the trout, both as regards size and activity of movement. When they have come together in sufficiently large numbers in the same place, they make it the theatre of scenes of extreme animation, in which, amid the silence and repose of winter, with the swiftly flowing waters for their stage, they alone are the actors.

Often the males begin and prelude. More excited than the females and less weighed down, they first set to work to hollow out the spawning places. Spreading themselves over the stony bed, they cling to it and rub themselves against it, pressing their whole body down upon it. They come back, start again, repeating the process over and over again. Not only do they press their bellies against it, but they scatter the tiny fragments all around them with sharp, repeated strokes of their fins. As a result of this pressure and of these strokes, the bed is first cleared, then gradually hollowed out. It takes the form of a longish furrow, shaped by the fish in proportion to its size, and framed by a rampart of little pebbles which have been thrown up on either side. The fish can lie down full length and dig itself in completely. This is the wedding bed, the spawning place, and the female will soon come to join him there, to cast forth the eggs which he will fertilize.

This episode takes place in a kind of frenzy. The male,

having hollowed out one nest, leaves it to go and hollow out another one near by, then he comes back to the first and deepens it, unless he decides to go and dig another somewhere else and make other hollows beneath the water which streams relentlessly above. The fishes press and push down their bellies so insistently, so obstinately, that they often rub off the scales, sometimes till they even bleed. But these accidents, these wounds, do not hold them back; they go on just the same, keeping continually at work. These rubbings, these excavations, are the only thing that matters to them. Doubtless, when we see them so engaged, it is easy enough for us to conclude that, in this final stage of sexual maturation, they are seized by a feeling of weight in the abdomen, a local irritation, which they try to get rid of by the only means available to them, that of rubbing themselves against something resistant. But there is no element of calculation, of foresight about the business, or indeed any exercise of reason at all. There is no question of the creature's instinctively preparing a nest in which to spawn. The behaviour, as I see it, irregular and spasmodic, gives evidence of nothing more than a mechanical, material attempt to find immediate relief.

The females finish off the work the males began. Often stronger, heavier, with their bellies distended by an enormous mass of eggs, they take their turn in the depressions that have just been made, and deepen them. They go and come to one spawning place after another, the weight of their abdomens making them press and rub against the gravelly bottom. Then, after several days, sometimes several weeks of this excitement, the marriage is actually consummated.

This consummation takes place in the beds so prepared. When they are engaged in making them, the lovers seek each other and mate. According to locality, circumstances, and chance, sometimes they pair off, one male to one female; but sometimes, and more frequently, each female is courted by several males, aspirants to her favours who try to chase each other away and so to oust their rivals. The larger drive off the smaller. The amorous paroxysm, the feeling of abdominal distention, gradually reach their height. The females, leaning over on one side, press down their bellies and their sides, squirm about on the bed of the torrent and finally provoke, in the abdominal wall, the reflex of muscular contraction and tightening which expels the eggs. The males, coming after them, press down in their turn, and sensing the exciting emanations of the spawn thus ejected, themselves experience similar contractions, which make them shed their milt upon the eggs in the gravel against which they are rubbing themselves. All of them come back several times. The females, ridding themselves in packets of the heavy burden of their gestation, go in turn to several spawning places; the males follow them, and eject several times the fecundating milt with which their testicles are filled.

These unions, which sometimes take place by day, but most frequently at night, last only a few seconds. Renewed at intervals, for the eggs of the female are not all ripe at the same time and the males only milt when they are with a female in labour, all follow the same course and end in exactly the same way. And, every time, husband and wife show the same eagerness. Nothing in the world matters to them but the satisfaction of their desires. One can go near them, stand beside the torrent in which their spawning places are, even kill them. Nothing will disturb them or induce them to get out of the way. The salmon, normally so easily alarmed, have now lost all fear, or rather, it never occurs to them to feel fear. Their whole organism is given up to this sole aim of reproduction; their being vibrates and quivers with love alone. The combination of natural conditions having caused them in turn to prepare for bringing forth young, for the elaboration of the germs and their ripening, they are nothing more or less than slaves to this urgent necessity. Henceforth the germs alone count. The body in which they are fashioned, which has produced and nourished them, is only a living envelope which has served its purpose when the spawning takes place.

So the wedding is consummated. The females, almost at the end of their strength, cast forth the last packets of their eggs and the males the last drops of their milt. This tremendous process of gestation terminates by the almost complete ejection of what produced it. Its large mass has entirely disappeared. Compared with what it was, the creature seems empty. It then shows itself, having no longer in its body the burden of reproduction, such as it really is, alone. Long, emaciated, almost a skeleton, muddy looking, its bones are covered with flabby, mucilaginous flesh, surrounded by a chafed skin. It is only the shade of what it was. It was the bearer of germs. It used up its vital resources to engender and mature them. Now that it has accomplished its task, and the germs are there no longer, there is nothing left but a receptacle deprived of its contents, a scabbard, still living but almost on the point of death.

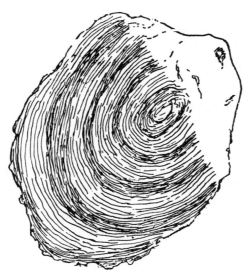

FIG. 7.—SCALE OF A KELT
Simplified sketch of a kelt's scale, showing the frayed and worn edges.

These great emaciated bodies show not a trace of the excitement which, a moment ago possessing them wholly, brought about their exhaustion. They let themselves go wherever the water carries them; they have hardly strength enough even to attempt to swim—their muscles are no use—all they try to do is to keep their heads up stream so as to receive the current of fresh water as it comes down. Most of them do not survive this condition of profound depression, of intense exhaustion, into which their amorous effusiveness has plunged them. The torrent which welcomed them on their arrival will now have none of them;

it sweeps them towards its banks, hurls them against the rocks, thrusts them into hollow places from which they cannot escape. Often they perish there; beasts of prey and birds of prey hasten to dispose of all that remains of them. Love, for them, has fulfilled itself in death.

But they do not all perish. In some districts and in certain circumstances, a goodly number of them succeed in keeping in mid-stream, letting themselves be carried away by the current, inert, almost completely passive, into deeper waters and, finally, into the river itself. Their condition improves as they are carried farther and farther down the stream, as they go back along the road up which they came in their ascent. When the opportunity offers, they snap up any prey which ventures within their reach, swallow it, and can now digest it, for their digestive apparatus is recovering its former healthiness. They seize upon any and every object that presents itself, leaves, floating pieces of bark, as though they were starving, which is hardly surprising when we consider the long period of abstinence through which they have just passed. Little by little the survivors come back to life, like invalids convalescing. Then, borne by the river to the sea, they go back to their lair in the depths, until their recovery is complete and they can again resume their old life of growth, which later will result in another ascent of the fresh water to repeat the spawning process.

There are thus two categories of salmon. The first, often the more numerous, consists of those which die when the spawning is done. The others, favoured by circumstances, go back to the sea, from which they will return again to spawn a second time. Among these latter, a few will succeed in surviving after this second spawning, will return to the sea and there grow still larger, and go up for a third spawning. But they seldom do more than this.

We know that this is so from an examination of the scales of salmon caught as they go up the stream. Those which have escaped have rough edges to some of the lines of their scales, forming what is called the " spawning mark." This is due to the rubbing of the edges of the scales on previous journeys up stream. In the great majority of salmon caught in rivers, such marks are not found, and their absence is an indication that these fish have not spawned before, that they are still virgin, and are making the journey for the first time. Among the others, often very much in the minority, a spawning mark shows that they have spawned before, have succeeded in getting back to the sea and are now on their way to spawn again. A still smaller

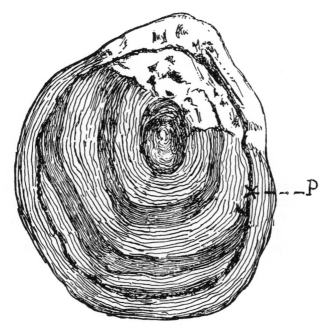

FIG. 8.—SCALE SHOWING A SPAWNING MARK

Simplified sketch of a salmon's scale, showing a spawning mark (*P*). This salmon, formerly a kelt, returned to the sea after spawning and continued growing there. The additional concentric lines surround the worn and frayed edges of the kelt scale.

minority, reduced to one or two out of hundreds and thousands, show two spawning marks. These have spawned twice and are returning for a third time. Very rarely indeed, giant salmon are found which have on their scales the signs of three or even four spawnings. More than this have never been found.

The old theory, held even today by a few people, is mistaken. Taking into consideration the regularity of the annual journeys up stream, the number of fish that take part in them, and without paying too much attention to those which died in the spawning places, it was assumed that all the travellers found their way back again, and that the escaped fish were not the exception but the rule. Each year, it was thought, had its ascent and its descent, and it was held that the salmon, every year or every two years, go up the streams to spawn, then return to the sea, come back again to spawn, and so continue several times in their lives, in a regular alternation, renewed again and again. Studies based on reading the scales, a more careful observation of nature, have proved to me the error of such an idea. Things follow quite another course. Most of the salmon are making the journey for the first time, and, in the case of the majority, it will also be the last time. A second and a third journey are exceptional. But there are such exceptions. Account must be taken of them when the question of repopulating the salmon streams arises. The veterans should be spared despite the ease with which they can be captured, and they should be allowed their chance of return.

It may sometimes happen that the travellers are brought to a halt in mid course by obstacles, dams across the stream, which prevent them from going farther. If, in spite of this, the water in such places is fresh enough and sufficiently rich in dissolved oxygen; if sandbanks and small gravel are available, an imperfect sexual maturation may take place and the spawning may be carried out, although with difficulty. When fish have spawned in a place like this, where the water is plentiful and not too rapid, they return in great numbers to the sea, recover their strength there and then return again. But those which go up to the real spawning places in the highest reaches, which reach the difficult if invigorating torrents, and, under the influence of this invigoration, exhaust themselves in effort and in combat, these, which are excellent from the point of view of reproduction and produce a plentiful offspring, will have less chance of reaching the sea. The circumstances which make them the best spawners likewise make them the most susceptible to the blows of fate, and favour them less.

III. In view of these different conditions, whose diversity and quantity mask in some measure the unity and continuity of the force which brings them into being, it is the first duty of science to recognize them, to make an inventory of them, and range them in their proper categories. In the first place we secure a carefully arranged repertory of documents and facts. But this is only the beginning. The phenomena are the phenomena of life. Instead of being separated and unconnected, they appear as a succession, as a relation, mutually determinant. Science, if it is to carry out the task it sets itself, must follow them, and study the relations between them in their proper order. It has seldom an opportunity to carry out such an investigation, for the door very easily shuts upon its researches. But sometimes, when circumstances are favourable, it is possible to grasp the golden key which opens this door, and the secret is revealed, at least in part. Life, coming upon the stage, animates and puts together again that which was otherwise broken up into fragments. The history of the salmon is a case of this sort.

We might be content to confine ourselves to mentioning facts and nothing more. But, in order that the story may be complete, we must further express these facts in their due series, see how they fit in with one another, and set them down according to their merits. Then we find that everything changes and takes on another aspect. Cold enumeration becomes a living story. We see the ascent of the river as it really is, a race to love and death. The traveller coming from the sea and entering the stream is now marked by a definite seal. Its fate is inevitable. This act, which brings about the elaboration within it of the coming spawn, consecrating it as a predestined lover, forces it into a continual state of excitation which increases as it continues. When, after all its struggles, it arrives at the love rendezvous and there its mating is consummated, the process of spawning exhausts it. When the spawn has been cast forth, the excessive vitality which has kept it going hitherto, leaves it, and, after having reproduced itself, it succumbs. After the completion of the reproductive act, the rendezvous is filled with dying, of whom many will perish, and with eggs full of life from which a new generation will spring, whose work it will be to begin the cycle again in the years to come.

Nature determines everything with this end in view. From first to last, the traveller is directed unflinchingly towards it. Prisoner of that elaboration which is going on within it and which it maintains, subject in advance to the needs of the reproduction for which it is destined, no escape is possible. It is a slave to its own needs, and these demand from it an ever more intense vitality, an ever more active respiration. Consequently, it must always go forward. A force against which it is powerless drives it on, leads it where it must go, compels it to the act of reproduction which it must accomplish, then, when once the act is consummated, abandons it and lets it perish. Lover for a few hours, not even for a day, tortured for a long period before it experiences the satisfaction of producing young, it succumbs and finally disappears, a sacrifice to the germs which issue from it, which are given shape at its expense.

If we regard this story from our own point of view, as though our own existence and our own feelings were involved, it must seem a terrible tragedy, in which dread fate and horror are the masters. The victim of destiny, the salmon is doomed to perish after it has loved. Its history is a poignant drama, compact of dangers, struggles, exhaustion, death. If our own tragedies affect only a minority among us, those of Nature affect multitudes, affect all. This history is not that of a single individual, of a few; it is the history of all. As things have been determined, there is no exception.

In this, Nature appears to go beyond all bounds; all kinds of questions 'why?' come into our heads. Why waste in this way lives which might still be of use, instead of allowing all the salmon to go downstream after they have spawned? Why this excessive exhaustion which leaves the creature helpless? Why indeed compel the salmon to leave the sea and make them spawn in fresh water, instead of allowing them, as so many other fishes are allowed, to reproduce themselves in the sea, instead of insisting on this long, difficult journey, which so often ends in a death which they are powerless to escape?

Nature herself gives the answer. The salmon, in the tragic, almost absurd, extremity of its destiny, may act as her interpreter. In it, she uncovers and reveals the depth of her feelings. These deaths of parents who have just engendered young, which are prepared, and consequently desired, by her, have not the meaning people have tried to give them. Nature is neither cruel nor wasteful. In her sight, the only thing of value is the series of successive generations; individuals are important only in so far as they assure this succession. The salmon bearer of germs, mechanically, automatically, devoting its whole existence to the production of those germs, then perishing, is itself proof of this.

Deaths and disappearances are of no account; it is the coming life, that of the offspring, which alone matters. Nature does everything in her power to prepare it, to foster it, to bring it into being. To this end she makes use of the very creatures who will transmit it. They are the instruments which she employs when she needs them, which she breaks when she has done with them. Love, in nature, is only a bait to induce the bringing forth of young. It is not an end. If it develops in torture; if it ends in annihilation, this is only a secondary consideration, the means to an end. The first consideration is elsewhere.

One must live one's life, not for oneself but for those who come after: this is the principle of natural morality. The love life of the salmon shows us this principle in action.

CHAPTER V

Third Part: The Descent to the Sea

I. THE spawning is done. The eggs of the salmon lie scattered about the bed of the torrent, mingled with grains of sand and fine gravel. Like little translucid pearls, lemon and pink in colour, at most five or six millimetres in diameter, they lie inert, motionless, in the spawning places where they have just been laid and fertilized. The spawning places, which served as a wedding bed to their parents, are become their cradles. The pure, brisk water, flowing constantly over them, is ceaselessly renewed as it bathes them. Rich in dissolved oxygen, having first poured out upon the parents its life-giving qualities, it now distributes them to the children. The environment is the same; the stage setting has remained; but the actors have changed.

The parents have disappeared. They have played their part and are now no longer in the picture. Their germs remain, alone, small, unmoving, apparently abandoned, but actually watched over and assisted. In the silence and repose which succeed to the animation and tumult of the wedding, Nature provides them with everything necessary to their development. Guardian of the elements of life, she arranges all things in such a way that this life shall be able to persist; she protects in them the series of events. The stream becomes a sort of womb. The eggs find in it, beneath a moving veil of flowing water, the aid which their weakness demands. The little pebbles shelter them. The water, constantly renewed, brings them continual supplies of oxygen to breathe. They themselves, possessing in their substance the nutritive materials they need, use those materials to shape the embryo.

There are thousands of them all going through the same process at the bed of the stream. Since each mother has laid several hundreds of them for each pound of her weight, and since the male has fertilized most of them, the swift-flowing water passes above hosts of minute living creatures which, silently but persistently, are at work building up their own bodies. The apparent quietude of things external, in the silence and cold of winter, covers an extreme activity and an animation which, though hidden beneath the translucid shell of a tiny egg buried in the water, display an extraordinary intensity. The embryos take shape in this icy water, devote several weeks to their development, then emerge, and stripped of their envelope and set at liberty, continue to fashion and complete themselves.

The emergence from the egg, in these children of the stream, takes place about the middle of winter. At the outset, the little embryo, translucid, measuring only about twenty millimetres in length, with only the rudiments of fins, and weighed down by the accumulation of nutritive material which forms a voluminous vesicle like an enormous hernia under the belly, remains inert upon the bed of the stream, incapable of movement. In the language of the expert it is called the *vesiculated fry*. Then, little by little, its organism becomes complete. The fins take definite shape and begin to beat. The skin becomes pigmented and takes colour. The ventral vesicle gradually withdraws, becomes smaller, then disappears. The little creature looks more and more like a tiny fish. It darts about, rises, falls again, then, by degrees, acquires greater strength and greater assurance. Soon it begins to swim, launches forth in mid-stream, head towards the source, facing the current. It finds new means; it grows in strength. By the beginning of spring, it has developed into an agile little creature, hardly larger than it was when hatched, but better formed, almost complete, and, on a small scale, quite recognizable as a young salmon.

The waters of spring, as they gradually become warmer, are thus peopled, in the neighbourhood of the spawning grounds, by hosts of salmon fry, swift, timid, swimming almost always in the same place, for it takes them all their time to hold their own against the current which would carry them away if they allowed it. The water, flowing directly towards them, brings them the microscopic floating creatures which, then first appearing, become their prey. The tiny mouths, open to the current, receive without any difficulty this modicum of food, minute grains of living

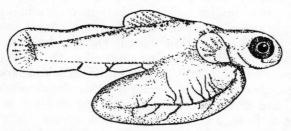

FIG. 9—FRY IMMEDIATELY AFTER BEING HATCHED

Salmon fry immediately after hatching. It has a voluminous vitelline vesicle on its belly. Enlarged four times.

paste, brought them sparingly by the water. For the whole summer this nourishment is sufficient for them. By the time autumn and winter come, the fry, flourishing upon this provided sustenance, have almost tripled their length. They are still small, measuring at the most five or six centimetres, but already they have good strong bodies, and the most important stage of their development is now complete.

The following winter, their first, interrupts this pleasant existence and condemns them to abstinence, for the icy

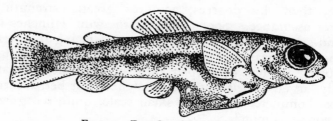

FIG. 10.—FRY ONE MONTH OLD

Salmon fry aged five weeks; the vitelline vesicle is not completely reabsorbed. Enlarged four times.

waters of the upper reaches are poor in foodstuff. But the next spring it begins again, and is continued through the summer. Still in the neighbourhood of the spawning places where they were hatched, they begin swimming about again with their eyes open for anything they can eat, facing the current, and stuff themselves with the various victims, tiny larvæ, little crustacea, which the water brings them. For companions and competitors, they often have little trout of the same age and size as themselves, but more agile, more mobile, less determined to stay always in mid-stream with their heads turned to the source. As brightly coloured as they are, but of a reddish brown instead of dark grey, the young salmon join the young trout in making up a little world of rapacious fishes, hunting down and chasing creatures still smaller than themselves. Greedy and quarrel-

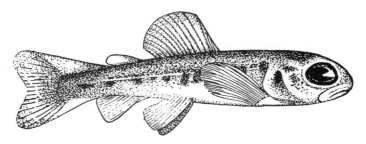

FIG. 11.—FRY TWO AND A HALF MONTHS OLD
Salmon fry aged between 10–12 weeks. The vitelline vesicle is completely reabsorbed. Enlarged four times.

some already, they hunt one another, and, often varying in size although they all come from the same spawning, the larger ones bully the smaller, and nibble at their fins.

So the second summer comes to an end. The fry then measure eight, ten, even twelve or fifteen centimetres in length, depending upon the profuseness of the food supply. The second winter begins. Then, unlike the little trout, which do not change in any way, the little salmon change colour. The brown pigment disappears in part and, in its place, the skin takes on another pigment, violet and bluish. The belly, the greater part of the sides, losing any shade of darkness, become pearly with flashes of silver. Broad azure patches appear on the sides, one after the other. Only the back retains its opacity, though it too assumes a shade of blue. The fry, which used to be a dark reddish grey, is now white and blue with gleams of pink and purple. It has become whiter and brighter. It has taken on a new appearance; it has changed, and, consequently, is about to behave in a new way.

Usually, this change of pigments occurs about the end of the second summer, and during the second winter. That is the rule. But certain of the fry experience it either earlier, in the first winter, or later, in the third year. However, the changes of colour in the case of these precocious or sluggardly individuals are the same and their consequences are equally the same. The only point of difference is in the size, the former being smaller than the average, and the latter, larger.

II. Every year, during the first part of spring, though sometimes carrying on into the second, the salmon streams are the scene of extraordinary animation. This begins abruptly, and, when it is over, does not occur again until the corresponding season of the following year. For several consecutive weeks, the waters are filled with shoals of young salmon, going down from the upper parts of the river basin on their way to the sea. These passing travellers are those who, in the spawning quarters in which they have hitherto lived, have just completed the alteration in pigment. Now that they are no longer fry, now that they have assumed the colours they will henceforth live under, they start down the stream, and their place is taken by younger brothers and sisters, a year younger than they are, who will follow their example the following spring.

Thus, each year, the salmon people go and come, newcomers taking the place of those who have gone away. The parents arrive on their upward migration and the children depart on their downward journey. But the numerical proportions are not the same. There are several hundreds of the latter for each one of the former, an inequality which is necessary to repair the losses which will inevitably occur among those which are not yet full grown.

In the salmon streams the order of going and coming is continually and regularly observed. Every year the upward migration is carried out by adult fish which will spawn thousands of eggs. Every year a compensating downward migration carries the fry which are hatched from those eggs down to the sea. Since an interval of two full years is necessary for the development of the young, the direct succession of parents and children must take an equal time. But this interval is not wasted: it is taken up by another set behaving in the same way. Each year has its upward movement for reproduction and its downward movement for evacuation. The years follow one another, identical in this respect, but differing, according to circumstances, as regards the number of those which take part in the migrations. Two years after a heavy spawning, we may expect to find a great many fish going down stream, and when the spawning has not been so productive, we find a

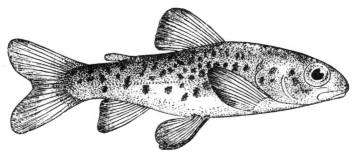

FIG. 12.—FRY ONE YEAR OLD
Salmon fry aged one year. Enlarged four and a quarter times.

corresponding decrease in the number of those which go down to the sea two years later.

These young salmon in their new colouring, are resplendent in hues so brilliant that they do not pass unseen. Called *smolt* in England, *tocans* or *tacons* in the greater part of France, and *Salmling* in Germany, the best name for them is that of *pintos*, used in Spain, and meaning " speckled, spotted." They are not very large, seldom measuring more than twelve to sixteen centimetres in length and from forty to fifty grammes in weight, but they make up for their smallness by their beauty. Their bronzed back with its blue gleam is sown with scattered black spots. Their pearly sides are adorned by ten or more large patches, one after the other, whose colour varies from the lightest to the darkest blue, broken by red spots sometimes surrounded by a lighter red. Their belly is silver, delicately shaded by

79

pink. Occasional blue tones, on the snout, on the upper part of the head, add to the beauty of the whole and give it brightness. Blue shades predominate. More resistant, they are also more lasting.

The smolt, in their splendid dress, go down the river in stages, slowly, in shoals which at first are quite small but increase at each confluence. They are not very active and allow themselves to be carried by the stream. They only bother to preserve the attitude, customary in their species, of keeping their heads turned up stream, towards the water which pours down upon them, goes into their mouths and passes through the gills. They often go down tail foremost, in a strange attitude, frisking about as they are carried along.

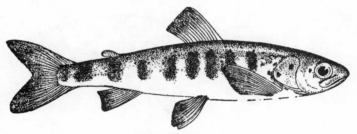

Fig. 13.—Smolt
Smolt at the time of going to the sea. Half natural size.

Where there are dams, when they come to a cascade, we may see them pass sliding over the rocks. Often they rest awhile and wait upon the bed of the stream, spreading themselves upon their bellies, keeping their equilibrium by supporting themselves on their pectoral fins, so remaining without moving for hour after hour, their heads still turned towards the upper part of the stream. Now and again, they come up to catch a fly, to snap up any prey within reach, for they are greedy and great eaters; then they fall back to their motionless waiting, their characteristic position. Unlike the young trout, which are more active and quick in their movements, they often remain inert for a long time at a stretch.

They are most active during the night. Then they interrupt for a moment their passive descent of the stream and go hunting. Their migration is very different in every way from that of those whom they meet on the road on their way to spawn. These, weighed down by the burden of germs, weakened by abstinence from food, are obliged to exhaust themselves by their efforts to swim against the stream and to get over the dams. The others have no such difficulties to contend with. They have only to let the water carry them along; they are sure to succeed without either trouble or weariness. The river in which they were born itself directs them. Helping them across any obstacles they happen to meet in the protective mass of its waters, it leads them little by little to their goal. As it annoys the parents, so it favours the children.

Finally, after some weeks of this idle descent, the smolt reach the estuary of the river. There, for the first time, they make the acquaintance of the sea. Hitherto, they have lived only in the fresh waters in which they were born. Here they first come into contact with salt water. Although the humoral qualities in their bodies prevent them from being upset by such a change, which calls a halt to most other fresh-water species, they, nevertheless, have to get used to it. They stop some time, occasionally several days, in the estuaries. They follow the tides, coming up with the flood, going back with the ebb, and, each time, they go a little farther down the stream. After this short apprenticeship, they have become sea fish instead of fresh-water fish; they set out to the open sea and bury themselves in its depths. Nothing more is to be seen of them in the estuary, their last halting place.

Nature seems to contradict herself in this respect, for, at one and the same time, she sends some of the salmon to the sea and others away from it. But the contradiction is only in appearance; its obvious purpose is to organize a regular circuit, a going and coming, carried on by different sets of travellers, one being made up of children who will grow and become parents, the other of parents whose destiny it is to produce children. In this way the desired arrangement, which entails a continual renewing, an endless replacing of losses, is brought into being. But the contradiction remains, in the means if not in the result, since the process, with equal precision, with the same success, is split into two so as to operate in dissimilar manner. How does that come about? How is the same species able, according to age, to take the same road but in opposite directions?

III. I decline to have recourse to that semi-mystical theory which, in order to secure an explanation at all costs, assumes some innate faculty of memory in the fish, some impulse which submits the fish to a mysterious but supreme tendency, of which we humans are incapable but which is possessed by the fish, so that it seems to sense the sea from afar. But where does this memory of sea water, inherited by the little fishes from their parents, reside? And how does it come into existence in little creatures who still know only the fugitive, flowing waters of their native torrent? How does this so-called genius of the species set about bringing down the fry, directing them unfailingly, encouraging them till they come to the end of their journey?

We must allow ourselves no such easy way out of the difficulty. The greatness of human thought and scientific method consists in searching, in co-ordinating, leaving the fewest possible gaps. We must, as Descartes insisted, first enumerate our facts; then, by comparison, ascertain their exact importance, the further step suggested by Buffon. So we take things for what they are and not as we would have them. In this problem of the journey seawards of the smolt, in which the offspring travel in a direction opposite to that taken by their parents, we must not be satisfied simply to look on at this flight to the sea, and be content instead of trying to see further. We must search beneath elementary appearances, reassemble phenomena which our impressions separate, and follow Nature in the movement and relationship of her parts. Then, perhaps, we shall know better.

What, in this journey towards the sea, brings together all those concerned? Why should they take the opposite course to that which their parents take? What voice do these smolt obey, different from that which guided their progenitors, which they themselves will hear later when they return, their growth completed? Far away in the mountain torrents, they can know nothing of the existence of the sea into which the water of those torrents will soon empty itself. No visitor from the sea can find its way to them against the current. Yet they all, with one accord, go down to the sea together, while the trout beside them, of the same age as themselves, stay where they are and never dream of joining them. This journey is personal to them, it affects them only, with the peculiar characteristic that it takes place at a definite time, and is every year repeated as soon as the fine weather comes.

Yet this spring is in no way different from the spring of last year when they were only a year old. They have the same waters about them, swollen with the spring rains, gradually becoming warmer in the longer sunny days. Apparently, the year before, these circumstances made no impression upon them. They continued to live in the same place, hunting their tiny prey and seeking nothing else, no other place in which to live. And now they seem to obey, or at least to fall in with, an impulse which nothing until now has given us cause to suspect. External circumstances have not changed; they have manifested themselves in exactly the same way according to the customary rhythm of the seasons. How comes it then that the young fishes behave in a different way, and all, uniformly and consistently, give up their former mode of behaviour and set out in a body on this descent to the sea?

It is because they themselves have changed, though their surroundings have remained practically unchanged. At the beginning of this particular spring, they are not what they were at the beginning of the last spring; they are not what their younger brothers are. They have just undergone the change of pigment which has brightened their colouring and altered it. The former harmony with the conditions of their environment exists no longer. A new harmony has been created in them and for them. Formerly, the abundant pigment of their skin protected them against too strong a light, against too prolonged exposure to the sun. Henceforth they no longer have this protection, or, at least, it is less complete. The long sunny days of April affect them directly, strongly, and disturb their vitality. As far as they can, they try to avoid their influence. They let themselves sink to the deepest parts of the stream, where the light is more diffused, where its force is less. They allow themselves to drift with the stream and so find their way to regions which are progressively deeper. At night, they pull themselves together, resume their activity; but by day, almost over-whelmed by a light which is too strong for them but which they cannot escape where they are, they keep on the way down stream. Finally, they reach the estuaries where their humoral qualities allow them to find their way into the sea which is deeper still. So, determined by this necessity for running away from the light, this extraordinary journey to the sea is ended, this journey which nothing causes us to anticipate, which, none the less, takes place year after year.

The salmon family shun the light. The salmon himself, the type of that family, only does what all his fellows do, though he displays this characteristic early and more intensely, even as a little fry. The trout, his nearest neighbour, also becomes whiter and his colours become brighter, but more slowly. If, young and not very big, their abundant supply of pigment allows them to dwell in streamlets into which the light of the sun penetrates with considerable strength, later on they seek darker and less sunny waters. The fine, large trout of the lakes and rivers, with their pearly bellies and pale sides, go down to the deepest waters available to them, and so avoid the effects of the strong sunlight; sometimes they go under rocks. The rainbow trout (*Salmo irideus*, Gibbons), imported to Europe and more sensitive than our native trout (*Salmo trutta*, Linnæus), goes down by degrees to the sea and there disappears. The salmon does the same, but sooner and with more intensity and regularity. In so doing, it makes normal and constant what is accidental and irregular in the case of other fishes, and so the cycle of its existence is made complete and closed.

The salmon, in this cycle which makes up its whole life, has the choice between two principal constraints; that of its intense respiratory needs and that of its desire to get away from the light. In the one case it requires about it water rich in dissolved oxygen; in the other, it wants these waters to be dark. The other qualities matter less. Consequently, it acts according to the needs of the moment, according to the diverse and successive desires of its organism. In the smolt, as it comes down the stream and later during its life of growth in the sea, the needs of the respiratory system are at their lowest ebb, so the desire to escape the light prevails and has the upper hand over the other organic necessity. On the other hand, during the process of sexual elaboration, in the salmon in process of reproduction, the needs of the respiratory system, becoming more intense, succeed in gaining control; so, although it still does its best to gain the shelter of the banks and hollows in the bed of the stream, the salmon makes the painful effort to go up the middle of streams in full light of day, so as to reach its goal in the mountain torrents. Governed by this duality of vital action, the fish obeys each force in turn. It listens to the strongest voice so long as that is in control, and obeys the other when it, in turn, is the governing factor.

So we see clearly how these creatures, in their waters, are governed and made dependent upon the conditions of their environment, like automatons capable of sensation, as I have shown elsewhere. Capable of sensation, because their senses give them information with regard to the variable states in which these conditions become effective; automatons, because they respond immediately to the impressions they receive. The environment not only contains them but conducts them. Their existence is a series of immediate reflexes and of continual compromises between these reflexes. The smolt comes down to the sea to escape from the too bright light of the waters in the stream, and is then content with a relatively low proportion of dissolved oxygen. Later, when it has reached puberty and is fit to produce young, its need of oxygen becomes more and more intense, is given the predominance, and the fish goes back to the waters from which it came. It will follow the same road in two different directions, each time finding on that same road a perfectly good reason for acting in two opposite ways.

Besides, the salmon, which pushes even so far as the depths of the sea, only does on a larger scale what is done on a smaller scale by other fishes. It introduces no very remarkable innovation. The large lake trout go up the streams to spawn in the torrents, and their fry go down to the lake as the salmon go to the sea. Their journey is shorter and less imposing, but it is of the same kind. The sea trout, acting in the same way, approach more nearly to the habits of the salmon, since in their case the sea environment has a part to play, though in a limited degree. In the case of the salmon the partially double life is regularly and completely realized. In spite of all difficulties and contrasts, Nature proves rich and varied enough to allow the young fish to build itself up, causing it to benefit from the accommodations it provides. Containing the sum and diversity of influences which are able to act, she makes use of them in turn, when the need for them is there. If the resultant behaviour seems to differ and even to be contradictory, the action which directs is single and tends always to its end.

The smolt, going down to the sea, is following its destiny. Better than in its native stream, it will find around it the abundant prey for which its gluttony makes it so eager. The young fishes, destined to go up the river again in due course, will grow, and, making allowance for losses and dispersions, they will return, strong and well-founded, to the waters from which they came. Their disappearance is only temporary. So, in anticipation of their return, their descent of the streams and rivers should be protected; they should be watched over as if they were regiments of orphans, and their number even increased by careful stocking. No attempt should be made to catch them, for this flight of theirs is only temporary; it is a pledge of the abundance of which later the fisherman may take advantage. The more fry that descend the stream, the more numerous, after a few years, will be the travellers up stream. There is a close relationship between both migrations.

CHAPTER VI

*Fourth Part: The sojourn in the sea and the
summons to return*

I. THERE is a mystery in the life of the salmon; that of its
abode in the sea during the years of growth. Many of the
episodes of this life take place in mid-stream, where we can
observe them; others are hidden in unknown darkness.
The little smolt, just arrived from the upper reaches,
reaches the sea, plunges into it, and disappears. Every
spring, shoal after shoal makes its way to the salt water,
then disappears without leaving trace. Where do these
little fishes go? How far do they journey, for they never
stay close to shore? Sometimes, in one place or another,
a few smolt are caught in the sea, near the shore, a few
weeks after they come down from the rivers, but they
disappear in their turn, going elsewhere like their brothers.
All these little fishes are lost in the immensity of the ocean,
to reappear later, after several years, during which they have
grown into large plump salmon ready to make their journey
up stream.

In the hope of finding out exactly what does happen,
various experiments have been made. Smolt have been
marked by making a cut in one of the fins, or by attaching
a small numbered label to them. Later on, those which
appear with their mark demonstrate by the contrast between
what they were and what they now are, the extent of the
changes that have been wrought in them. Small and
undeveloped when they set out, they return having attained
to puberty and of considerable size. Where did this development take place? In what part of the waters of the sea have
they grown so quickly to such a size? Where did they
find such excellent cover?

This is the riddle which the salmon propounds to us, and

it is one which we cannot solve directly by observation of the fish caught by fishermen, as we often can in the case of other fishes, for, except on very rare occasions, accidentally, as it were, they are never caught at sea. We can only arrive at the solution by a series of approximations which enable us to find out what the problem exactly is, to limit it, and finally to attempt to solve it. This is a process familiar to biologists, a sort of deduction, positive and negative in turn, by which we attack the unknown from all sides of the known, in which we make soundings wherever soundings can be made, eliminating what is irrelevant and retaining what appears to be in accord with actual fact.

In the question thus considered, the first point to be dealt with is the fact that fishermen practically never succeed in catching a salmon in sea water. If, in a very few places, an occasional smolt is caught, it is always about the time when the young fishes have just come down stream; the great majority are already far away, and the few which lag behind will soon rejoin them. If, very occasionally, large salmon are caught in the sea water, these catches in Western Europe are made off shallow places, where the tide lays bare broad stretches of sand, and here the fish is surprised on its way to the estuary where it will begin its journey up-stream. Salmon fishing proper is done in the river above the mouth, never in the sea.

Yet gear is used by fishermen which can scour the ocean from the surface to a depth of nearly a thousand feet. Within those limits, which the fishermen explore in all directions and in all sorts of ways, they find the most varied species, but never a salmon. The salmon, then, must dwell farther out at sea and in regions deeper than those which the fishermen can reach.

The second fact is equally important. This is the absence of the salmon from the rivers which flow into the Mediterranean. In Europe, the species is strictly confined to the Atlantic. Yet the waters of these rivers would be as ready to receive them as those which flow into the ocean. One of them, indeed, the Rhone, has its bed beside that of the higher reaches of the Loire, up which the salmon do go to spawn. Separated by only a mile or two, the tributaries of both have exactly the same kind of water, but in spite of this similarity and this proximity, the Rhone is deserted. It is the same with the Ebro, in Spain, the head of whose basin is near to the Cantabrian streams, which are rich in salmon while the Ebro itself has none. The absence of the salmon seems to be due to causes which originate in

FIG. 14.—Map showing spawning places of salmon in France. The shaded section shows the Mediterranean slope, where the species is not found. The rivers shown by a definite line are those up which the salmon go (or try to go); those shown by a dotted line are not regularly frequented. The black circles indicate spawning places still frequented; white circles those which are so no longer.

the sea and not in the rivers. We must seek the explanation in the Mediterranean and nowhere else.

If the superficial waters of the Mediterranean are not very different from those of the Atlantic, we find notable and extraordinary differences in the deeper zones. The temperature of the sea, off our ocean coast, goes down in proportion to the depth; below the level of from seven hundred and fifty to a thousand feet which the fishermen can reach, it remains somewhere between three and six degrees Centigrade, and does not alter except to decrease as we go down to greater depths. It is not so in the Mediterranean. At the same depths, its temperature, whatever that of the waters above, is fixed invariably at about thirteen degrees Centigrade.

Further, this inland sea, communicating with the ocean only by the Straits of Gibraltar, where the bottom is not so deep, is partially stagnant in the lowest levels. There is very little dissolved oxygen there, and very few living creatures are to be found there. The proportion of chlorides, undoubtedly, also plays a part, the Mediterranean's waters containing about thirty-eight grammes per litre of saline compounds, compared to the thirty-five grammes per litre of the Atlantic. If we remember the preference of the salmon for cold water with a high respiratory capacity, we can easily divine the reason for their keeping away from the Mediterranean. They cannot satisfy their peculiar tastes there, at least as things are now, though it may have been otherwise in bygone ages when that sea, now almost completely enclosed, was more open.

This view, which is based upon the state of affairs in the Mediterranean, corroborates the evidence provided by deep-sea fisheries. The salmon, in the salt waters of the ocean which alone are capable of providing it with a suitable home, settles far below the surface, in zones whose depth must be many hundreds of feet. There and there alone it finds the cold water, relatively rich in that dissolved oxygen of which it is so fond and which it always seeks. This water contains about five cubic centimetres of oxygen to a litre. We may assume that the smolt, on its way down from the source, does not stop near the coast, near the river from which it has come. It prolongs its journey, in distance as well as as in depth. It goes far beyond the coast and the sea near it. It goes to extremes. Coming from a mountain torrent which rushed along in the open air, it buries itself in the submarine abysses, in the great hollow depths beneath the immensity of the sea.

But these abysses are almost as vast as the ocean above them. The immensity of the surface gives us the measure of the immensity of their depths. Leaving out of account the coastal area, the Atlantic Ocean rests the whole mass of its waters upon a bottom which, for the most part, is between ten thousand and twenty thousand feet down. Where, in this huge, prodigiously immense area do the salmon finally settle down to grow and live their life of development, of preparation for the future journey up the river to spawn?

A number of further observations enables us to be more precise, more definite as regards the locality. Unlike the trout, its nearest relative, the salmon is not a fish that is always or even usually swimming; it is glad to rest. If it hurls itself upon its prey in short, swift rushes, it returns to its rest immediately afterwards. It does not keep watch in mid-stream for very long. So we must not think of it as populating the waters of the ocean with individuals swimming about persistently and continually. In the ocean, as in the fresh waters to which it migrates, it remains resting upon the bottom, motionless for long spaces of time. It seeks its prey near at hand, in its immediate neighbourhood, and does not go swimming in search of it, or track it down. This characteristic limits the extent of its marine home. It lives in those parts of the bottom of the sea where there is enough intensity of life at hand, abundance enough to suffice for a consumption of food which is by no means small, if we are to judge by the rapidity and amplitude of its growth. The deepest places, several thousands of feet below the surface, are too poor in such nutriment, and, therefore, would not suit it. On the other hand, the middle levels, rich in resources of every kind, are more favourable. It is in them, probably, that the salmon settle, to lead their life of nutrition in the sea.

This is probability and not certainty; but it is surely not far from the truth, for another peculiar fact supports and confirms it. The salmon, at the beginning of their journey up stream after their growth in the sea, plump and well-found, have a flesh gorged with fatty substances of a particular pink hue, which has given a name to a definite colour. This colour, or rather the product which brings it about, is derived from a red pigment contained in the carapace of most crustaceans. The conclusion to be drawn from this is that the salmon, when in the sea, feed mainly upon the crustaceans which live beside them, just as, in fresh water, they bite more readily at a shrimp bait than at anything else. Now the middle levels are populated, on the bottom itself, or very near to it, by hosts of shrimps of several species which live there all the time; and these deep-water shrimps are naturally red in colour while they are alive. This particular pigment, abundant in them, is not masked by any blue pigment, as is the case with the species found on the sea-shore, where they must be cooked, or be acted upon by acid before the blue substance can be made to disappear and leave the red behind. The flesh of the fish, gorged upon this prey, coloured by its colour, reveals to us the favourite food, and the place in which it is eaten.

These zones of intermediate depth in which the salmon lives are now known, thanks to the investigations of oceanographers. We know where they are and the creatures which live in them. Although they are beyond our sight, we have secured a great deal of information about them, sufficiently detailed to give us an excellent idea of their nature. We can depict and describe them, and make up in this way for the incapacity of the eye to see them.

II. The littoral, which extends before the beaches and cliffs, goes out under the sea like a vast submerged shelf, a submarine belt girding the shore. Because of its situation it is called the " continental shelf." This shelf goes out to the open sea, gradually sloping downwards until it reaches a depth of from five hundred to six hundred and fifty feet. Then, almost everywhere, it suddenly breaks off more steeply, dropping to a depth of from three thousand to six thousand five hundred feet and more to the bottom of the ocean bed. Its scarp or edge, beneath six hundred feet of water, rises sharply above the submarine abysses and dominates them, though we are unable to see it because of the thick layer of water which covers it everywhere.

These steep, even precipitous slopes, go down from the shelf to the great depths beneath, facing the water almost all the way down, and they are populated in abundance by masses of the most different kinds of creatures. Judging by the results of dredging, nowhere else, either near the coasts or on the land, is to be found such wealth or such diversity. The dredgers often bring up their large buckets full to the brim. To these depths the light never penetrates; the water is dark. Consequently, there is no vegetation and the only life is that of animals. But in this perpetual darkness, in which the very signs of time disappear, this animation, strictly confined to animals, spreads out in every sort of way in every sort of place.

The dredges bring up huge lumps of white coral (*Am-*

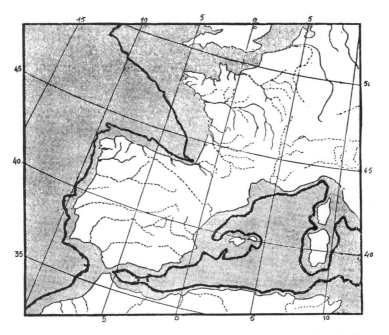

Fig. 15.—Map showing the distribution of the Atlantic salmon in Continental Western Europe. The black lines indicate the course of the upward genetic migration. The dotted lines show where such a migration is no longer found. The black band shows the places (isobath) at which the sea goes down to about an eighth of a mile or even half a mile.

phihelia and *Lophohelia*), arborescent calcareous blocks, of which the branches intertwine, interlace, and join together. They reach fields of sponges, some like leather bottles set on a base, others like finely woven gas mantles. They reap a harvest of Crinoids which, like living flowers, borne on long delicate peduncles, stretch out their denticulated arms, like so many sensitive petals. They bring up, together with these creatures which were attached to the bottom, all those, still more numerous, which move about there crawling, gliding, or swimming. Sometimes, when we examine the harvest closely, we cannot help a feeling of admiration, even of utter astonishment. One of the most astounding revelations of modern biology is its discovery, in these deep, dark abysses which used to be considered uninhabited, of such a swarm of living creatures, so remarkable and so abundant.

If we imagine the scenes and landscapes with which we ourselves are familiar transferred to the regions beneath the ocean, we may form some idea of this luxuriant life. Climb to the top of one of those towers sometimes built upon a mountain, whence we look out upon a chain of peaks rising above the valleys. Towering above everything else, we see the white snow-clad summits and the glaciers; this is the first jagged line which catches the eye. Lower down, we see the steep slopes covered with forest and meadow land. Lower still, the valleys, like the base upon which all the rest is built. We see the movements of the cattle pastured in the meadows, the birds voyaging through space with great sweeps of their wings, the tiny insects flying hither and thither. The scene is bathed in light, luminous, transparent air, which obstructs the view hardly at all. The alternation of day and night sometimes brings light to it, sometimes hides it beneath a dark sky sown with stars. The winter cold, the summer heat, the wind, sometimes gentle, sometimes violent, storms, rain, lightning, introduce a perpetual element of diversity and bring about continual changes.

Put all that aside, keeping only the framework and the supports, the line of summits, the slopes, the deep hollows. Take away the light air and replace it by water, fluid also but much heavier, whose density interferes with the view. Put out the light, do away with the alternation of night and day, the varied brightnesses of light upon the earth; replace them by a continual, complete, and unremitting darkness. Take away all the changes which continually modify the scenes to which we are accustomed, and substitute for them monotony, uniformity, perpetual sameness and an almost wintry temperature. Then you will have a faithful picture of those slopes that go down to the great depths under the sea, a picture which science paints for us and authenticates, declaring that it exists, though the eyes of our flesh are incapable of seeing it. It is there, in the sea, in regions which we can never reach, but which are accessible to the salmon, that the salmon lives and grows, the salmon born among the mountain heights. The salmon dwells not only in the high places of the earth but in the depths beneath the sea.

The smolt, running away from the light, is drawn towards these depths where utter darkness reigns eternally, and there it finds the gloom it seeks. It finds there, also, all the food it needs, better as regards quality and quantity than that doled out to it with a niggardly hand by its native torrent. It settles down on these slopes near the abyss, makes its home there. Stretched out at rest beneath the branches of white coral, among the fields of sponge and crinoids, as the cattle rest beneath the trees and in the meadows, it feeds lavishly upon the wealth of prey about it.

While the salmon are growing in stature, and developing into fine plump fish, they do not leave these admirable hiding places, these well-filled larders, in which they have only to take whatever they desire from this profusion. As they grow older, they move still lower, if they find there is anything to be gained by the change. The surrounding darkness does not trouble them, for their eyes are no use to them in the pursuit of their game. This surrounds them on all sides. Swarms of red shrimps are rising up or settling down within their reach all the time. They have only to take such an easy victim, their gustatory and auditory sensations being a sufficient guide. They are like oxen being fattened, stuffing away in the darkness.

They grow very quickly on a régime of this sort. On an average they take on weight at the rate of four to six pounds a year, a proportion double, even triple or quadruple, that of most other fish. They grow intensely, at a rate proportioned to the seasons, more rapidly during the summer than during the winter, although they grow all the time without ceasing. The salmon, in this cramming down of nutriment, consume and assimilate continuously. If their relatives of the fresh water, the trout, are obliged to content themselves during the winter with a very small ration, for the lakes and streams have then little to offer them, the sea salmon have no such troubles. The provender around them is always abundant, except for the diminution in winter which results from the changes, the reshuffling which goes on in the upper layers of the ocean above them, the reverberations of which come down to them. They accumulate reserves in their own flesh, live the nutritive part of their lives almost to excess, and so become the

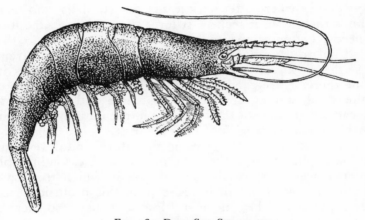

FIG. 16.—DEEP SEA SHRIMP

The red shrimp of the Atlantic abysses (*Acanthephyra purpurea*, Milne-Edwards). A little less than natural size.

magnificent fish whose succulent flesh is a delight to the epicure.

III. But there comes a time when the salmon, having grown as large as it can grow in the sea, when repletion and accumulation can be carried no further, is obliged to hold off for a while from so rich a diet and even to interrupt it. Its power of assimilation has been utilized to the utmost. Then, if circumstances are favourable, a new influence comes to bear upon it. We might say that it hears, through the ocean, a voice to which it has hitherto paid no heed. For a time it did not listen; but now the voice keeps resounding in its ears and begins to produce an effect. This influence is that of the fresh waters pouring into the sea. The voice is that of the rivers, coming down to the salmon that live on the submarine slopes beyond the continental shelf. It will put an end to their life of nutrition and summon them to the life of reproduction.

The smolt, and the corpulent salmon they later become, have not lost all contact with the fresh water. Both retain in the sea the attitude they are accustomed to take up in the streams; they settle on the bottom, their heads turned to the current that they may breathe the more easily. Now, although it is considerably less in strength as it gradually becomes dispersed, this current does run out into the open sea. The rivers do not come to an end at their mouths; their water does not at once merge completely with the waters of the ocean. Carried on by its swiftness, it pushes forward like a liquid wedge which gradually disintegrates and becomes diluted. We can sometimes find traces of it far out at sea. A certain number of the land valleys continue under the sea and form ravines in the continental shelf. The river system and the marine system are much more intimately related than they would seem at first sight.

Probably the smolt, on their way down to the abysses of the ocean, endeavour to remain near the zones influenced by the river water. They go down deep, but do not go right away, and they stay in these zones so long as they are growing up into real salmon. They remain fresh-water fish, always ready to hear the call of the fresh water. They go to the sea to get away from the light; they settle there, favoured by their humoral qualities and the ease with which they can secure food, but, none the less, they are the children of the mountain stream and its swiftly flowing waters. Although it seems to us that they have gone far away from it, they have not entirely given it up. Their delicate sensations, fitted to the conditions of their environment, afford them possibilities for which we can find no parallel except, perhaps, in the keen scent of some of our land animals, and in our own sensitiveness to imponderable perfumes which some chance wind brings to the air we breathe.

The salmon fishermen of the estuaries, who work when the fish leave the sea for the river, know that their best catches come some time after each flood water. The river waters having been more considerable, the penetrating wedge has gone farther and deeper into the ocean. The zone of influence has been enlarged. The voice of the river speaks with more insistence, and compels attention; its summons assumes a greater urgency. When the flood begins to decrease, the salmon which it has awakened from their greedy complacent state of calm repose, start on their long journey, and considerable numbers arrive to begin their ascent of the rivers.

Thus, we see, there is a definite relation between the extent of the flood waters, the life-giving quality of their waters, and the coming of the salmon. Repeated floods, sounding the call more often, improve the harvest reaped by the fishermen. The years follow one another, never two exactly alike, some favourable, others giving but a scanty yield, and these contrasts are often the counterparts of what happens in the rivers. The greatest floods, going deeper and penetrating farther, thrust forward their zone of influence till it affects the great salmon living at the lowest levels and brings them up. In European countries these floods occur in autumn and winter. Before then, there is no sign of movement from the sea; often no fish arrive at all, or else very few. On the other hand, when there are floods, and their waters have poured into the ocean the vast volume of cold water they bear, the large winter salmon decide to undertake the journey and set out upon their upward journey. Later, the floods abating, the zone of influence is not so extensive; the middle-sized spring salmon, or those of them which have reached pubescence, are the only comers. Finally, as summer approaches, when there is less water in the rivers, when it contains a still smaller proportion of dissolved oxygen because of its warmth, only the youngest and nearest salmon are affected, the little males caught in summer.

Various factors have to be taken into account. The zone of influence is only established and its summons heard by the salmon when the water possesses the life-giving, exciting quality whose action stimulates the fish deep down in the ocean. The first sign of this is an increased activity in the respiration. The fish, gorged, replete, on the point of pubescence, feels the need of more intense oxydization in order that assimilation may be complete, and it turns in the direction from which such oxydizations come. But that is all. The rivers whose waters do not contain enough oxygen in solution have no attraction for it; no fish ever go up them. Round the Gulf of Gascony, the Charente, the Vilaine, in spite of the size of their estuaries which offer every opportunity to the salmon, are never visited, or very seldom, because of their customary poverty in this respect. The fish hurry towards the Loire, the Adour, most of the rivers on the coast of Brittany and the north of Spain, whose waters, flowing more swiftly, are more what the salmon need.

These are the usual features of the return of the salmon, and we can reconstruct them in accordance with circumstances and the relations between them. But there are occasional exceptions, strange cases like those of the giants of the species, which are sometimes caught, weighing forty pounds or more, with scales showing that they have lived in the sea for six, seven, eight, or even nine years. The very rarity of such catches as this is itself significant.

From them we may presume that very large salmon lie hidden in the depths of the ocean, just as enormous trout are contained in the depths of the Alpine lakes. These are most often sterile, and cannot produce young; they have not been able to reach the torrents where the spawn is laid; their ovaries have degenerated; they are castrated by nature. It is doubtless the same in the abysses of the sea. The salmon which go down to them to live their life of growth do not all come back again for the life of reproduction.

Those which bury themselves in the lowest depths are unaffected by the zone of influence of the rivers except very occasionally. They do not hear the call which, by setting in action changes in assimilation, would render them pubescent. Lost, buried as it were, at the bottom of the places to which they have gone down, they have no encouragement to leave them. They go on growing, fattening, thickening in their gluttony; but they remain sterile, incapable of spawning, their nutritive life being all that interests them. If, occasionally, one of them, awakened by some extraordinary circumstance, comes up for the journey up the stream, the others, its former companions, of whose existence it gives evidence by its own coming, go on living uselessly in depths which they will never leave.

Here we have a series of incidents which, considered together, explain one another and confirm our theory of the usual course of events. Every year, the Atlantic Ocean receives in its depths, beyond the continental shelf, upon the slopes which plunge down to the abyss, a contingent of young salmon, still puny and small, which have come down from the fresh waters. These tiny fishes, penetrating this domain which provides them so copiously with all sorts of prey, do not go entirely beyond the reach of places which the influence of the rivers is still able to reach. Resting on the bottom, feeding to repletion, they remain turned towards the place from which they came and to which they will return when they start out once more. The food they find so abundantly makes them grow rapidly, covers them with copious fat, until they reach puberty.

Then a new need develops in them, that of an assimilation directed towards preparation for the production of young, and this demands a more active respiration. Until now they have been indifferent to the emanations which come down to them from the rivers; they now become sensitive to them. Experiencing, as a result of these emanations, the interior satisfaction of better elaboration, they move towards them, and their feeling of well-being increases correspondingly. This increasing well-being stimulates them, as it does the trout in their much more limited wedding journey, and results in their polarization. Always guided in this way, they move upwards towards the light, to the regions above. They draw near the mouths of the rivers. When they come to the fresh water, their elaboration improves still more. They enter the river and begin to go up it. Their great wedding journey has begun. Children of the stream, they had left it for a while to find elsewhere a material well-being which it was unable to give them, but they return to it to produce their young, to found families in waters like to those in which they themselves first saw the light.

IV. It is easy to go into ecstasies about the fullness and the realization of such a wedding journey, beginning in the depths of the sea and ending in the mountains. It is indeed a marvel. But the cause is more marvellous than the result, although it is always the result which most surprises us.

We consider the fish after our own likeness. We measure its action by the measure of that which we should show in similar case. But that exists only in relation to us. The fish, having no knowledge of it, does not bother about it.

My placid trout, swimming about and ceaselessly turning in their tank, actually travel a considerable distance in the half cubic yard of water which the tank in which they are imprisoned holds. But if they were free, subjected to a force which would drive them constantly in the same direction, they would cover at least as great a distance, and to some purpose.

So with the salmon. The only water they know is that with which they are immediately in contact. The only influence they feel is that which drives them to swim on and on till they can breathe more actively. They continue always in that direction, resting sometimes, stopping for a while before the obstacles they meet, but never turning back. They act in this way so long as this same influence carries them along. Nothing else matters. Blindly, they swim, go forward, and in fact cover a very considerable distance. They remain in a permanent state in which they are as much imprisoned as my trout are in their aquarium. In these vast spaces, it is always the same water, always the same vivifying action of that water, which drives them forward.

It is often thought that the salmon, after its growth in the sea, returns to its natal river to bring forth young there. Several experiments have been tried, for example, marking the smolt on their way to the sea, and finding out how many return. The results are contradictory. Generally speaking, the proportion of those returning is only a fraction, a few hundredths of the number which go down. Greater in certain places, it is smaller in others; sometimes, indeed, there is no sign of the marked salmon. Further, it is sometimes found that they make their way to other river basins near by. Examples of this sort are rare, but they do occur. These variations are explained, not only by the destruction of young salmon by sea fishes stronger than themselves, and the difference in numbers of such inevitable casualties, but by another reason connected with the submarine topography, the course taken both in going down to the depths as well as in going back to the estuaries. In both directions the salmon must cross the whole continental shelf. It is in so doing that they meet their principal difficulties.

We may take the Gulf of Gascony as an example. One of its shores, by the Cantabrian mountains, plunges steeply into the sea, and has only a short continental shelf. Depths of several hundred fathoms, even of five hundred or a thousand fathoms, are to be found not very far from the coast. The rivers, which spring from the neighbouring heights, fall straight into the ocean, and the young salmon which go down them to the sea have only a short journey before they find the shelter in which they will grow. It is consequently easy for them to return again, and most of them, making for the nearest place from which the summons comes, go back to the river in which they were born.

It is not so along the French coast. There, the continental shelf extends for hundreds of miles before it reaches the threshold of the slopes that go down to the depths. When it is time for the salmon to return, the call of the native river is not so easily distinguished, for, over so vast an area, the influences that convey that call become confused, come together or separate. The fishes make as fast as they can for the voice that is strongest at the moment, seeking nothing but immediate satisfaction. Besides those who belong to them, the rivers receive strangers whom circumstances have brought, whose numbers vary accordingly. But both natives and foreigners, children by birth and children by adoption, are accepted with equal readiness and behave in exactly the same way. All, under the guidance of the polarization of their respiratory system, urged on by the ever-increasing need for oxydization, set off up the stream and finally finish the journey together in the final excitation of their nuptials.

We may note here an interesting analogy. The inhabitants of the Basque country and of Brittany, which are rich in salmon, have long been famous as navigators and colonizers. Their sons have no objection to leaving their homeland, scour the seas, and settle down in foreign lands. When they have made their fortunes, many of them return to their native land, and end their days in the very places from which they set out. Unconsciously, guided by natural circumstances, the salmon in the animal realm present us with the counterpart of these human wanderings. The child of the niggardly, but limpid and life-giving mountain torrents, it does not find in them the subsistence it needs. It goes down to the sea, feeds there, grows fat there, but it cannot bring forth young. Its most noble function is placed under an interdict. That it may fulfil that function it needs the pure, swift waters which it can only find in the mountain streams. So the salmon goes back. Retracing its course along the road it has already taken, it returns to spawn, to found a new family in places like to those in which its parents and its ancestors founded theirs.

If there is anything remarkable about this similarity, its interest is to be found in the cause that determines it, rather than its conclusion. The salmon has neither memory nor foresight. In its little brain there is nothing to tell it how it should behave. It has only sensations, immediate reflexes. But that is enough. Nature, herself, takes the place of intelligence and reasoning power. The harmony which she establishes between her creatures and the circumstances with which she surrounds them is all the guide that is needed. She creates this fish with a more than healthy appetite, and then enables it to subsist in spite of the difficulties usually placed in the way of those whose demands exceed their resources. She makes use of its distaste for the light, and the humoral qualities of its temperament, to drive it to the depths of the sea. She employs its respiratory activity to bring it back to the swift-flowing waters in which it had its beginning. In order to direct it she polarizes it. She behaves towards it like an imperious but reasonable counsellor. The creature must obey; for, if it did not, it would perish and disappear.

The story of the salmon may be a lesson and a model to us. In its complexity, it shows how precise is the government of Nature. It reveals to us the marvellous power, the continual establishment of harmony, a fitting together of circumstances always supreme and beneficent. In Nature, nothing stands alone; everything holds together, is interrelated. All things work towards a common end, and, finally, are conjoined in that end.

CHAPTER VII

I. I AM very fond of what are called the byways of history, of rummaging through old archives, ancient documents and family papers. And, I think, rightly so. In the faded pages of such relics we have the direct traces, the immediate imprint, as it were, of what life used to be. In them we see our ancestors as they really were. History proper is often a show, a chronology, sometimes a tissue of conjectures; we find reality more clearly expressed in its byways.

In our day, certain species of migratory fishes seldom appear upon our dinner-tables. But, as old papers show us, it was not so in bygone centuries. All through the Middle Ages they were a usual article of diet. They were so abundant that sometimes there was an over-supply. Once, in most salmon countries, it was understood that labourers should have salmon two or three times a week at least, so plentifully stocked were the neighbouring streams. Several towns, proud of their wealth in this respect, had a salmon on their coat of arms. Still further in the past, our pre-historic ancestors carved on the walls of their caves the outlines of this fish, which they used to catch in the river that flowed past their rough houses. Everything goes to prove that in Western Europe up to the most recent times there was a profusion of salmon which stands out in striking contrast to the shortage of that fish to-day.

Another species, more remarkable still, has undergone the same fate: this is the sturgeon (*Acipenser sturio*, L.). The giant of our fresh waters, it was often six feet and more in length; its weight could be reckoned in scores and even hundreds of pounds. The firm succulent flesh of the sturgeon was greatly appreciated. Formerly, at those state banquets at which the guests sparkled with precious stones and wore magnificent clothes, though they had no spoons and forks, and used to bite their food or tear it to pieces with their fingers, one of the principal dishes often consisted of a huge sturgeon cooked whole, served on a great pewter or silver dish. Four pages brought it in to the sound of trumpets, set it down on the table that it might be suitably admired, then carved it. Other servants handed round, in vessels of precious metal, the spiced and perfumed sauces which gave it seasoning. Such was the magnificence of former days; it has now been replaced by a different kind of ostentation, which, in its turn, will doubtless be succeeded by another.

The sturgeon has almost entirely disappeared from our country. Today it is caught, and in very small quantities, only in the Rhone, the Gironde, or the sea near the mouths of these two rivers. Very occasionally, it appears in the Loire. But its practical disappearance is of quite recent date. The fishermen of the lower Rhone, of Arles, Beaucaire, and Avignon, even so far up the river as Valence, used to catch sturgeon every year as late as the second half of the last century. Many of them had special nets, appropriately fashioned to catch such lusty fish, and used them in spring and from April to July, when the fish were going up stream. About this time, at Agen on the Garonne, sturgeon fishing always afforded a satisfactory catch. But that is over and done with. The fish is now only caught in the Gironde near the sea, by Bordeaux, and rarely higher up. This falling off is now almost complete, in contrast, not only with the wealth there used to be, but with that which there still is, of the sturgeon and its near relations in Central and Eastern Europe.

Fishermen are excellent as observers. But their observations are sometimes cut short, for they have neither time nor means to repeat or prolong them. Their judgment can concern itself only with things of the moment, not with things the knowledge of which demands long and careful study. Consequently their associations of images and ideas do not go beyond the most immediate factors; they do not look far beyond them. Finding their interests adversely affected by the falling off of the sturgeon fisheries, they have attributed its cause to circumstances which are really only incidental, whose very novelty seemed to the fishermen sufficient reason for its effectiveness. They noted the synchronism, and took for consequences what were actually nothing more than coincidences. So the fishermen of the Rhone attribute the disappearance of the sturgeon to the coming of steamers, and declare that this fish cannot bear noise; they say that the vibration of propellers and paddle-wheels was enough to put the sturgeon off its ascent of the river and send it back to the sea. Yet exactly the same sort of noise, even more intense because river traffic there was intensified, has not prevented the sturgeon of the Gironde from frequenting that estuary, which is sufficient to show that the real cause must be sought elsewhere.

So with the salmon. As the fish have grown fewer everywhere since bars and dams have been built across the streams, and as everybody can see that these obstacles make it more difficult for the fish to get up stream, the increasing shortage of salmon has been attributed solely and directly to this cause. Fishermen are only too ready to believe that it is so. They forget the damage, the altogether disproportionate destruction they wreak themselves, now that the transport of fish has been so greatly facilitated. The salmon used to be consumed where it was caught; very little was exported. Today the very contrary is true, and the fishermen are encouraged to work more intensely. They never consider for a moment the fact that many streams which are not dammed, such as the Vilaine, do not contain a single salmon, while others, like the Seine, which are dammed so often that the fish really cannot succeed in getting up them to spawn, have salmon in their estuaries. The decline is due to other causes besides the dams which are regularly brought forward as the one reason why fewer salmon are caught in these days.

The fundamental simplicity of Nature is hidden, almost always and nearly everywhere, by such a complexity of detail that first appearances often prevent us from seeing the reality. They lead us to reality, but only on condition that we take them all into consideration and follow them wherever they lead. The causes of the present decline of the salmon fisheries are not limited to the obstacles placed in the way of the fish by dams over which they cannot pass, or even to the wastefulness of the fishermen. There are others, chief among which is the necessity of living in a water rich in dissolved oxygen. Formerly, most of our rivers were filled with swift-flowing water, and the salmon were glad to frequent them. Today many of them are largely polluted, and their water, whilst good enough for the majority of sedentary fishes whose needs are not so great, are incapable of satisfying more imperious needs like those of the salmon family. These streams, once peopled by the species going up and down it, are now, so to speak, out of bounds.

The case of the sturgeon is different though the result is the same. This giant fish, like the salmon, leaves the sea and goes up the rivers to spawn, but instead of continuing its journey to the highest reaches, it does not go beyond the lower, where the bed of the river is broad and deep. There, at the spawning period, in spring and the beginning of summer, each female, an imposing matron of considerable size, accompanied by a sort of harem of males smaller than herself, settles down in a hollow in the bottom, beneath a considerable depth of water, and makes an alcove in which to bring forth her young. She must be able to find such a niche to rest in, where she definitely settles down and lives for several weeks, in order to eject the enormous mass of eggs which her body contains by the hundred thousand. If she did not, her spawn would be scattered abroad, her males would be dispersed, and the spawning would come to nothing.

Formerly, in the Loire, the Garonne and the Rhone, the females had no difficulty in finding such hollows, where, keeping perfectly still while the eggs were ripening within them, and surrounded by the eager attentions of their males, each lodged and completed the process of gestation. Today these spawning places have disappeared nearly everywhere. The canalization of the rivers, the dredging carried on in order to facilitate navigation and to protect the fields from floods, have covered most of these hiding places with sand or gravel. The prospective mothers do not know where to stop and settle. They shed their eggs by chance, and these eggs fail to be fecundated, and are barren. The process of decline sets in, and things are very different from what they used to be. Ultimately complete disappearance is inevitable.

But this disappearance is relative. From time to time, a few odd specimens appear from other places and show what the profusion of bygone days was probably like. And it is variable, more or less pronounced according to locality and circumstances. But it is none the less real, and often made more rapid by immoderate fishing. The final result is everywhere the same. It amounts to a restriction of births. This is the ultimate reason for the decline of migratory fishes. Those whose task is reproduction can no longer dispose of the spawning places they used to have; if these still exist, the fish cannot now reach them; perhaps they have been destroyed and there are no others to take their places. There is less spawning, perhaps even none at all, and the number of fry decreases, fewer and fewer go down to the sea, and, consequently, the number of those capable of producing young becomes less and less. We find ourselves faced by continually decreasing numbers, and as things get worse from year to year, sooner or later the species will disappear. The decline is complete. Its essential cause is a crisis of natality.

II. From the economic point of view these losses must be considered very serious. Except for those who are immediately concerned, fishermen, amateur and professional, the general public knows very little about them. These migratory fishes were a source of food; they are replaced by other food products, and the demand of the consumers takes another direction. But this substitution does not make up for the loss, which can never be repaired. It means the disappearance of a foodstuff, of a natural resource which used to be abundant, but which now is either lacking altogether, or available only in very small quantities. Moreover it costs us more than the labour of getting it, that is to say, of the fisherman.

If the sedentary fresh-water fishes, obliged to take their nourishment in that water and at its expense, cannot increase their numbers beyond the limits of a localized nutritive cycle, the migratory fishes, salmon, sturgeon, shad, are not limited in the same way. The greater part of their nutritive life is spent in the sea. There they grow and develop, there the main part of their lives is spent. They come back in hundreds of thousands, their hosts encumber the streams as they have always done, and as they still do in certain privileged places, without upsetting the equilibrium of nutrition in those places. From the economic point of view, they are particularly useful to us. They grow and fatten in the depths of the sea; they provide us with a food that costs us nothing. When they go away, when their numbers decrease or when they disappear, this disappearance, following upon such abundance, is so much loss to us and there is no corresponding advantage to counterbalance it.

We shall do well to try to find a remedy. The streams are still there; their waters flow as they have always done. Only the hosts that used to populate them have vanished, and their absence is due to a fall in the birth-rate. It must be to the birth-rate, then, that we should direct our attention. Science has two means at its disposal; it can assist Nature by preserving the spawning places, making access to them easier, and by favouring reproduction in the natural way, or it can take the place of this, making use of that faculty of fishes which enable them to be fecundated from outside. Fertilized eggs are prepared, fry are obtained, reared, then put into the watercourse so that they can go down to the sea. This is an artificial process of reproduction designed to take the place of the natural process which, for some reason or other, does not take place.

One of the most interesting operations which have been undertaken to facilitate the journey of the salmon to their spawning places, and to assist their natural reproduction, is that of constructing, through the dams which obstruct the salmon streams, passages which serve to make the bed of the river still continuous. They are called " ladders," a very good name for them since they enable the fish to climb the obstacle and go beyond. They take various forms. Unfortunately, their success has not always come up to expectations. The salmon often stop at the foot of the ladders and make no attempt to get up them, or, if they have started up them, they turn round and come back again. This is because a strong fish swimming against the current can only succeed provided a number of preliminary conditions are satisfied; it needs room to move, an easy approach, and enough breadth as well as depth. Most ladders are deficient in these respects. In many cases a simple by-pass, a channel made in the bank, would give better results.

Pollution of the water offers a still more difficult problem, for in the case of the salmon and all the other *Salmonidæ*, it takes a peculiar form. Most often it is due to the presence of dissolved organic substances, which, present in too great quantity, favour the rapid development of the lower forms of plant growth, bacteria, and filamentous fungi belonging to the group of *Saprolegnia*. These, suspended in the water, by their breathing absorb the oxygen dissolved in it, and deprive the fishes of it to that extent. The proportion of oxygen falls to a very low ebb, and only the species whose respiratory system requires very little, like the *Cyprinidæ*, carp, and rudd, are able to exist in it. The salmon family can no longer do so; their needs in this respect cannot be fully satisfied. Neither the sedentary trout, nor the migratory salmon are able to exist in waters like these, which have become doubly asphyxiating, for the vegetation not only absorbs oxygen, but sets free oxycarbonated products.

Such polluted waters have become very common in these days, now that manufacture and industry have developed to such an extent. The waste products cast into streams by paper mills, sugar mills, tanneries and the sewage of large towns, contain large quantities of dissolved organic matter. Without any complementary pollution, without the actual poisoning of the stream, the proportion of dissolved oxygen progressively decreases all along the stream as it goes down to the sea. White fishes (*Cyprinidæ*) and others are often able to put up with it. But the salmon family disappear and never come back.

The decline in the birth-rate and the decadence which follows it having once set in, it is often difficult and sometimes impossible to improve matters by suppressing the causes. The economic importance of industry is so predominant over every other consideration, that there can be no question of sacrificing it so that the local fishermen may be sure of their former success. We must look for remedies elsewhere. We can do our best to lessen the difficulties set up by obstacles of various sorts, and we can, further, protect the processes of reproduction and make up for anything that is lacking in them. The streams frequented by the salmon are not all affected equally. Some, by reason of their situation and for similar reasons, are not affected by the development of industry and will, doubtless, continue to escape its influences. We have only to preserve them, to safeguard them, and guard the road they offer to the fish. When they have become nurseries of abundant fry they will help to maintain a population of growing salmon in the depths of the sea, which will provide for future journeys up the stream again.

The creation of reserves is not in itself sufficient. We must also increase production, and so make up for the natural deficit. The processes of reproduction by artificial fertilization offer us the means, and the salmon lends itself to such processes admirably. Individuals of both sexes are caught and parked, when they are just reaching sexual maturity. They are kept in tanks, in good running water. There they continue their elaboration, complete it, and become ready to produce young. Then the females are taken to a tub to lay their eggs, and then the males to shed their milt upon the eggs. Fertilization is thus effected by those responsible for raising the fish, and the eggs are placed in apparatus, in incubators where they develop, are hatched, and produce fry. These, in their turn, are put into suitable waters where they will find all they need for their existence, though those who ought to have produced them, and who would have produced them in former days, can no longer go there because of the obstacles in the way. Artificial reproduction has taken the place of natural reproduction now that the latter is no longer possible. Not only does it take the place of natural reproduction, but it produces better results by " manufacturing " (a picturesque but, none the less, exact expression) a greater number of fry.

The essential thing is to produce as many as possible of these fry which later will go down the river and, by increasing their numbers, increase also the numbers of the salmon which are engaged in growing at the bottom of the sea. The goal is the maintenance of this marine population, which comes from fresh waters and is destined to return to them. Our principal efforts should be directed towards raising more fry for this purpose.

The decline of the migratory fishes can be checked even if it cannot be altogether arrested. Man conquers Nature. To make better use of Nature, to obtain from her advantages in an ever-increasing degree, he extends the activities at his disposal in all sorts of different ways. The means which he employs are sometimes contradictory in their multiplicity, and it is difficult for him to make them all work together to the same end.

The rivers, we have said, are moving roads, and, if they contain fish for us to eat, they bear upon their surface boats which men can control. The salmon streams formed by the mountain torrents produce energy in their waterfalls, and this we wish to capture and to utilize. Many factories, which need a good supply of water, are built on the bank of a river and then pollute it by their waste matter, if they have not installed plant for the recovery of their by-products. The large towns of to-day, vast agglomerations unknown in former times, the days of the greatness of the migratory species, throw into the rivers on which they stand the sewage they are only too anxious to get rid of. Modern industrial civilization, using both land and water to get out of them something above and beyond the harvests secured by cultivation and breeding, frightens away the creatures which used to live upon these lands and in these waters. It surrounds itself with a void so far as animal life is concerned.

Here, in one of its many forms, but not the least important, we see the conflict between industry and agriculture. The attempt to secure complete utilization of resources is attempted in both, but the processes differ and sometimes conflict. There arises a competition between the factory and the farm in which it is often difficult to hold the balance fairly. We must reconcile the contraries. The power of Nature enables her to do so in the long run, because she has time at her disposal; but we humans, weaker, more limited, more in a hurry, cannot hope to attain success in the same way. We have to devise all sorts of measures, to keep making choices, trying to choose the lesser evil every time.

Greatness and decline; sometimes greatness again, then

a new decline, perhaps ultimate disappearance; it is not only a few species of fish which suffer from changes and chances like those in man's own history. It is so throughout Nature and her many parts, between which there is continual conflict, resistance and exchange, a never-ending search for equilibrium. Some win and others lose; sometimes only for a while, sometimes for ever. From these inevitable conflicts, there springs general agreement, the universal equilibrium, always being discovered and rediscovered, always capable of transformation and always being transformed. Greatness on the point of collapse, decay that may yet be arrested: and, as one generation succeeds another, life itself, as time goes on, weaves of both greatness and decay that moving, changing material which it unfolds continually in all its varying forms.

CHAPTER VIII

THE SHAD AND THEIR LOVE OF WARMTH

I. Spring, the season in which Nature gives new life to her children, is not only a season of renewal for the creatures of earth, but equally for those of the waters. It is the time when many fishes make ready for the coming spawning. And other species, which have not been seen before, make their appearance at this season only to disappear again when the spawning is completed. We call them the "seasonal" species.

Such an expression exactly indicates their principal characteristic, that of appearing, of giving themselves to the fisherman, only at one definite season, always the same. Like the salmon, they come from the sea where they have grown up and return to the sea when they have spawned. The fry, which come from their eggs, will go down to the sea in turn, when they are strong enough. Consequently they may be described as migratory, since they make quite considerable journeys between the sea and the fresh water. And they are anadromous also, since their migration is always directed towards the spawning in some stream.

Every country in the world has such species, and their coming is eagerly awaited by the fishermen, who hope to catch many more fish at that time. Almost everywhere in Europe these seasonal species begin to go up the water-courses as soon as the severest part of winter is over. Since their migration takes place mainly in May and June, appropriate names are given to them in different places. The shad, for example, are known in some places as " May fish." In summer, about July, their number grows less, they quickly become fewer and fewer, until, finally, there are none left. Next year, in the same rhythm, the process is repeated.

Our spring migrants may be put into three classes: the lampreys (*Petromyzon*, Linnæus, and *Lampetra*, Gray); the sturgeon (*Acipenser*, Linnæus); and the shad (*Alosa*, Cuvier, and *Paralosa*, Roule). The lampreys may be recognized by their cylindrical bodies, long, supple, elastic, like the eel, but with brachial slits opening visibly at the sides of the neck, and with mouths without jaws which open in a broad contractile sucker. The sturgeon is a large, powerful fish, quite different in appearance. Its head is covered with a thick bony structure, and its trunk armoured by bony plates arranged in longitudinal rows. The shad form a contrast to their companions, for they are much more like the type of fish to which we are accustomed, with oblong bodies, and the usual fins, like many of the sedentary species they meet on their migrations.

The *Alosa* belongs to the family *Clupeidæ*, one of the most common of all families, the most abundant and the most important from an economic point of view, for it includes the herring, the sprat and the sardine, with several of the related genera, which are found in most seas. Everywhere, the frequency of their occurrence, the ease with which they can be caught, and the excellence of their flesh, put them in the first rank among the produce of the seas. They are all recognizable and characterized by the regularity of their bodies, and by their trunk, which gets more pointed towards the head, forming a ventral keel with scales that stand out like dogs' teeth. The back has only a single fin, high, not very long, supported by supple, flexible rays, which is set about the middle and the highest part of the body. At the back, the caudal fin, large and forked, shows by its fullness that the fish has a remarkable capacity for vigorous activity. The *Clupeidæ* are rapid swimmers and open-water fish.

The shad of Western Europe belong to several species, which can be rearranged in three principal species, each having its own particular domain, a place which it seems to prefer. The largest and strongest (*Alosa alosa*, Linnæus), which sometimes reaches twenty or twenty-four inches in length and four to six pounds in weight, mainly frequents the great rivers which flow into the Atlantic—the Loire, the Garonne, the Adour, the Tagus, the Guadalquivir—and goes down as far as Morocco; it is not so common in the Mediterranean rivers. The smallest (*Paralosa fallax*,

Lacépède) rarely exceeds ten to twelve inches in length and half a pound to a pound in weight; under the names of twait shad, or small shad, it is caught in abundance, in its season, on the Atlantic coast and especially in the English Channel. Finally, a species of medium size (*Paralosa nilotica rhodanensis*, Roule) goes up most of the rivers that flow into the Mediterranean. It is plumper than the twait shad, almost as big as the large shad, and often migrates to places very far from those at which it leaves the sea. Its ascent, first of the Rhone and then of the Saône, may take it as

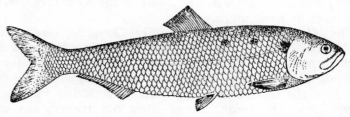

FIG. 17.—ALOSA ALOSA
The large Shad (*Alosa alosa*, Linnæus).

far as the Vosges, so that it crosses France almost completely from south to north.

The shad is a choice fish of remarkable quality, both because of its succulence and its frequency, and fishermen have employed all their ingenuity in constructing appliances with which to catch it. In the case of the twait shad, which is not very large, the usual means is the hoop-net manipulated by hand. To catch the large shad, the apparatus becomes more elaborate. Large dipping nets are used from a boat, either singly, or fastened to a net which partially bars the stream. Drag nets are also used which sweep the bottom of the river, picking up everything they come across. Then there is a contrivance which is a clever combination of methods. It rotates, and is fitted with a pocket which goes in and comes out alternately, picking out the fish on its way up. These appliances are still more elaborate in the Rhone, where they are worked by a sort of paddle which the current keeps continually moving. In these " tourniquets," for this is one of the names given to this apparatus, the net turns of its own accord and nobody is needed to manipulate it.

The shad, with such a reception in store for them, begin to appear at the beginning of spring, sometimes a little earlier, sometimes later, according to place and circumstances. In the south they arrive about February, but they do not come so soon if winter is prolonged, if the river waters remain cold for longer than usual, and at a temperature lower than that of the sea water from which they come. It is quite obvious that the time of their arrival at the

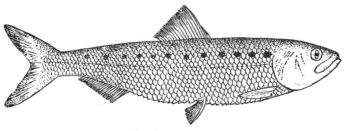

FIG. 18.—PARALOSA FALLAX
The Small Shad (*Paralosa fallax*, Lacépède).

estuaries bears a definite relation to the degree of heat in the water. This is the factor which determines the different times at which they appear, whether early or late, whether steadily or with interruptions. Usually, the fish begin to go up the rivers somewhere between the second fortnight of April and the middle of June. Then the spring warmth is definitely making itself felt.

The shad are deep water fish. They swim all the time when circumstances are favourable, never resting, or only for a short time. As soon as they reach the estuaries they set straight off up the river against the stream.

All genetic, their bodies already possess the rudiments of sexual glands, and these soon grow and develop. Their migration is a wedding journey, the pledge of a coming spawning. Like the salmon, they only undertake and complete it in order to produce young. Like the salmon, too, they have two distinct lives, one of growth and nutrition in the sea, and one of spawning and reproduction in fresh water. The first, which is the longer, lasts for several years; the second and shorter, only a few weeks.

We know where the shad live in the sea. Fishermen trailing their nets over the continental shelf, particularly in the deepest and most distant parts of it, near the edge of the submarine abysses, occasionally catch them. So do the coastal fisheries and nets. Like the majority of the genus *Clupea*, the shad live at medium levels, coming and going between the surface and a depth of from six hundred to a thousand feet. They do not seem to go lower. During their life in the sea they swim above the plain of mud which forms the bottom of the shelf, where there is no light, but a great many animals of every sort and size, and there they find all the food they need. Their mouths are small and have no teeth, but they snap up those among the fishes which swim about them which they can digest, and traces of these fishes are sometimes found in their stomachs.

This life of growth in these half-depths where there is no light, is spent in intensive feeding, in a continual orgy of food. As in the case of the salmon, the result is that their flesh is filled with fatty substances which form a reserve which will be drawn upon later when the time comes to spawn. The duration of this life varies according to individuals and especially according to sex. It is shorter in the males who spend from two to five years in the sea, and longer in the females who stay four, five, or even six years, sometimes more. The longer it lasts the more the growth is accentuated, and the larger the fish become. So, when the time comes to go up the rivers, the males are usually not so powerful as the females and can be recognized easily by their small size.

By reading the scales I have been able to calculate the length of this period of growth in the sea. We find on their thin, transparent plates, concentric lines of growth cut by sinuous transversal lines. The possibilities for assimilation and alimentation being less in these fish during the winter, the growth at that period, not only of the scales but of the body as a whole, is less or even at a standstill for a while. This temporary stoppage can be told by its effects. There is either a smaller deposit or none at all. The demarcation is shown by an annular line, the " winter ring." The number of these rings thus gives, fairly approximately, the possible number of winter absences. It supplies a sufficient basis for calculation.

The period of puberty arrives. Then the shad, like the salmon, leave their abode in the sea, approach the coast, find out the estuaries, enter the streams and go up them. But they never think of pushing farther, of going right up to the mountain torrents. They prefer the lower and middle reaches of the rivers or their principal tributaries. They are good swimmers, and as they require a considerable volume of water around them, they prefer streams that are both broad and deep. There they settle and go up against the stream. Like the salmon, they do not feed on their journey up stream but live upon the reserves they have accumulated in their own bodies.

During this journey the sexual elaboration becomes complete and reaches maturity very quickly, in a few weeks or at the most two or three months. During this time the reproductive glands become hypertrophied until they weigh a fifth or a sixth of the total weight of the females, and an eighth or a tenth in the males. Then during the second half of spring the spawning takes place in midstream. The eggs, small, many in number, surrounded by an enveloping membrane which the water swells out, become heavy and fall to the bottom. When they hatch, there come out of them agile little fry, which, during the following summer and autumn, the current will carry to the sea, where, in their turn, they will live the life of growth. Their parents, like the salmon, become slack and lean when they have spawned. They have used up all their reserves of food in producing germs and have had nothing of consequence to eat as they came up the stream, so now they have neither strength nor power of resistance, and most of them perish, the victims of the reproductive process of which they have just been the agents.

In this respect, the shad again remind us of the salmon, but on a smaller scale. If the time they spend growing in the sea is more or less the same, that of their journey to the fresh waters, devoted to the genetic or reproductive life, is much shorter. Not only is it shorter, but because of its shortness, it is different. In a few months, the shad arrive, go up the stream, spawn: in a few months, their fry are hatched, grow, and go down the stream. It looks as though they cut down to the shortest possible limits their stay in fresh water, or tried to do so. If they are like the salmon in migrating, they are different from them in other respects. The salmon appear to be fresh-water fish, whose alimentary system takes them to the depths of the sea. The shad, on the other hand, appear to be sea fish, whom necessity takes to fresh water so that their reproduction may be hurried through as quickly as possible. And if

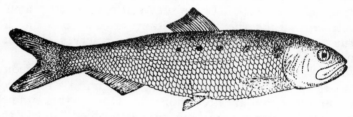

FIG. 19.—PARALOSA NILOTICA RHODANENSIS
The Rhone Shad (*Paralosa rhodanensis*, Roule).

this necessity reminds us of the salmon because the needs of the respiratory system play a great part in both, it departs from it in so far as the shad is further affected by considerations of heat or cold which do not affect the salmon in the least but are of great importance to it.

II. Shad fishing is extraordinarily uncertain. It is subject to such frequent variations that we may fairly say that, to a shad fisherman, no two days are alike. Sometimes abundant, sometimes the very opposite, then picking up again, it does not seem to be governed by any rule. The fishermen, at their wits' end, do not know what to do. In one place they just miss a splendid catch; in another a carefully planned course of action leads to no result. In their search for excuses they find explanations in all sorts of coincidences, a storm, a slight flood, a wind that is too strong or that blows from the wrong direction.

If the shad were really capricious it would be hopeless to attempt to understand them, but before we give up the riddle, let us look at the matter from every point of view.

Direct experiment in an aquarium is impossible in this case, because the shad are unable to live if they are kept in one place for any length of time; sometimes they die in the net the very moment they are caught. We must try some other method, especially the experimental observation which is so familiar to the biologist. As occasion offers we set to work to discover what are the actual circumstances and try to discover the time and the place at which they can be studied individually and consequently with greater precision. It is then Nature who makes the experiment. Elsewhere these factors work together, so that it is difficult to distinguish the effects of one from the effects of another, but when we isolate them and discover the value of each one separately, we are able more effectively to find out the part each plays and its relative importance.

We soon find indications that the temperature of the water seems to affect the shad in some way: the seasonal journey up-stream takes place in the spring when the water of the rivers becomes warmer and its temperature rises above that of the sea. Again the migration begins earlier in the south than in the north, and if winter is extended beyond its usual period, it is correspondingly delayed. But warmth is not the only factor of importance. There are several accompanying factors to be taken into account from which it must be isolated before we can come to a definite decision. The ascent of the Rhone gives us the clue.

In this river, the tourniquets, the automatic devices used by the shad fishermen, are set in all those places where, for century after century, the shad have appeared with the greatest regularity. In Provence, near Avignon and Beaucaire, they are put out along both banks. On the other hand, farther up stream, near Valence, the tourniquets are placed only near the right bank and never near the left bank, because the fishermen know that the shad never go there. Both banks look exactly alike; there appears not the slightest difference between them, either as regards the nature of the bed or of the bank itself. None the less, the fish obstinately insist upon keeping near one bank and away from the other. I was struck by the strangeness and persistence of this phenomenon and made up my mind to study it and find out the reason for it. My studies taught me that the water along the left bank is usually colder than that on the right, the difference often reaching two or three degrees.

The cause of this unusual disparity where uniformity might be expected is to be found in one of the principal

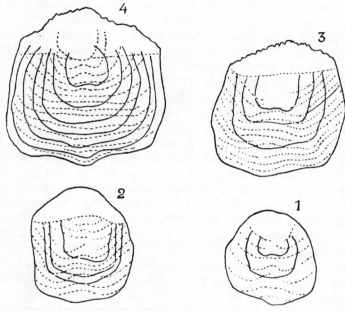

FIG. 20.—SCALES OF THE LARGE SHAD

Diagram showing the constitution of the scales of the large shad (*Alosa alosa*, L.) by stages of growth. The concentric lines are the *winter lines*, doubtless indicating the interruptions of growth caused by the winter season or preparation for spawning; the wavy dotted lines give the phases of the scale's extension. 1, scale of a small male, showing three winter lines, and doubtless indicating that the fish is three years old; 2, scale of a large male, four years old; 3, scale of a small female, also four years old; and 4, scale of a large female, seven years old. Four times natural size.

tributaries of the river, the Isère, which joins the Rhone on the left bank, a few miles above Valence. It brings a considerable added volume of water to the main river, but this does not at once mingle with that of the Rhone. To begin with, it flows side by side with it, and so passes through the town, going down quite a long way before the two waters gradually mix. Since this water comes from the glaciers of Dauphiné, it is colder at the confluence than that of the Rhone, which has been warmed on its way from the lake of Geneva. Consequently, near Valence, the river is warmer on the right bank than it is on the left. The shad, keeping always near the former, show that the temperature of the water has a very important influence upon their behaviour.

This phenomenon attracted my attention, and further investigation showed that it was everywhere the same. In their journey up the river, the shad, above Avignon but before they reach Valence, come within reach of tributaries like the Cèze, whose water is sometimes three or four degrees warmer than that of the Rhone. At the confluence many of them turn aside, leave the main stream, and begin to go up the tributary. Again, at Lyons, many of them, when they are not hindered by the dam, leave the Rhone and enter the Saône, which is warmer. Once again, in another basin, that of the Garonne, we find at the confluences of its most important tributaries, the Lot and the Tarn, eager hosts of shad going up these warmer streams and leaving the bed of the main river, whose water has not had time to get warm since it left the mountains. The same is true of the Loire and the Adour. The tributaries which do not rise at so great an altitude are often warmer than the river they join, and the shad discover this fact and go up them, gathering in considerable numbers before the dams and never thinking of returning down stream.

We see, then, that the shad are fond of warmth. The temperature of the water exercises a decisive influence over the course of their migration. Their whims and fancies are such only in appearance; actually they are governed by a principle which we can only appreciate with the help of a thermometer, though the fish experience its force directly in the water. This law has a reality and a precision of its own. The life of the shad is governed by its demands and the various episodes in that life are determined by its variations.

The migration begins when the river-water, which is poured into the sea in the estuaries, is at a higher temperature than that of the sea. It is more intense when the variation is great and less when the difference is small. In the course of the journey up stream, subject during the spring to frequent changes of weather, in which the temperature of the water varies from day to day, sometimes from hour to hour, the shad progress and form groups when the water becomes warmer, and stay near the bottom, separately,

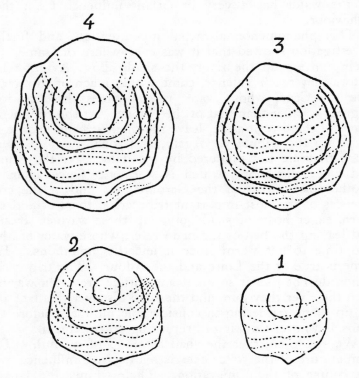

FIG. 21.—SCALES OF THE SMALL SHAD

Diagram showing the scales of the small shad (*Paralosa fallax*, Lac.) in the same manner as those of the large shad (on p. 122), enlarged about eight times. 1, scale of a small male, two years old; 2, scale of a large male, three years old; 3, scale of a small female, four years old; and 4, of a large female, seven years old.

when it is colder. Their sexual elaboration too depends upon this thermal determination. It is more rapid when the temperature rises and is checked when it sinks. Finally, to complete this series of phases so controlled, the final maturation and spawning are governed by the same action of heat. The spawning begins at a temperature of seventeen or eighteen degrees Centigrade, but if it is to be successful, it needs a temperature rising to twenty-two or even twenty-four degrees. The interval between seventeen and twenty-four degrees is, so far as the shad are concerned, the caloric margin *par excellence*, the thermal optimum in which the improvement in organic well-being, in that work of interior elaboration which is devoted to the preparation for spawning, reaches its fullest extent.

This desire for the sensation of greater well-being guides the shad; leads them to the place where it can be most fully satisfied. It is not affected by questions of nutrition, for these creatures, in the process of gestation, have lost their appetites; they have ceased to feed and are living on their reserves. It alone directs their migration, driving them unfailingly to places where the water is warmer. I used to give the name " thermotropism " to this condition. That is the term used by biologists in similar cases. But this expression is not sufficiently exact, since it is concerned only with the externals of the phenomenon. There is something more than this, something internal. The organism as a whole is concerned in it, the functions of assimilation no less than those of reproduction. The general sensitivity has a part in it, not a single specialized sensation. Just as the genetic salmon and trout are polarized towards a wealth of oxygen in solution, the shad are polarized according to the lines of thermic force which reach them from their environment. In this phenomenon the outside energy acts through its caloric radiations upon an organism all ready to receive them and take advantage of them. The creature moves towards them one after another, in conformity with an existing influence which prepares it for the next and still stronger influence. As they progress, the fish makes in their direction. It possesses a thermo-polarity which guides it and sets it in motion.

Thus the shad brings to the problem of migrations for the purpose of spawning a new feature which we do not find in the salmon. The salmon is only sensitive to dissolved oxygen; temperature makes no difference to it. The intensity of its respiratory processes alone controls and directs it. It is not so in the case of the shad which, although its needs are similar, has not the means to satisfy them so

well, because its capacity for dealing with variations in oxydation is slighter. Constrained to find in some other way the
source of energy which becomes necessary to it, it secures
it from heat. It must have calories to facilitate the preparation for its function of reproduction, to bring about the
intimate changes which accompany it. The fish takes them
from its environing medium, receiving them through the
whole surface of its body. As plants require heat before
they can bloom and produce fruit, in short, before they can
bring forth young, so do these fishes. Again, the succession
of seasons, with those alternations of temperature which,
in plants, fix definite periods for the accomplishment of
these vital processes, affects the fish in exactly the same
way. The shad, in this mode of behaviour which is
unknown to the salmon, provides a model which is very
largely copied by other species in their migrations.

Plants, attached to the soil and unable to move towards
the heat they find so desirable, must wait until it comes to
them. Fishes, free and capable of movement, are in a
better position. They can go to places where they can
more fully satisfy their need of it. Having become more
sensitive to the thermic action of their environment than
they were before, they seek the most favourable zones in
that environment. Animals of variable temperature themselves, but powerless to produce within themselves the sum
of calories necessary to their interior elaboration, they take
what they lack from the outside. They go to those places
where they can borrow more completely and more freely.
They go, in other words, to favourable water, strive to get
nearer and nearer to it, to settle there, to stay there, and
finally to accomplish the actions for which they came.

The shad pass through the phases of growth in the depths
of the sea, where, scattered and unsettled, they devote their
vital energies to nutrition and growth. They are content
with the proportion of dissolved oxygen and heat which
they find in the water surrounding them in these places.
Then puberty with its special needs comes upon them and
develops in them a more intense, more exquisite sensibility.
The organism needs a higher proportion of oxygen, and
even more, of heat. The environing water is no longer
sufficient, no longer adequate; it must have another, with

greater life-giving qualities. Then, if circumstances allow, as in the case of the salmon, this new environment to affect and summon them; if the influence of the warm fresh water makes itself felt in the depths in which the shad live, in spite of the fact that it is considerably weakened by distance and dilution, the fish perceive it and go to those places where they find those qualities they seek progressively more intense. Then the shad go to the estuaries into which these waters flow, and up the rivers.

The shad, which have hitherto been dispersed about the sea, now gather and form groups. They come together in shoals which the streams form into columns. The males are more precocious, and they arrive first, the females coming after them. All, as they find the favourable water of which they are in search, proceed to develop germs within themselves. Each shoal is made up of individuals which have reached the same degree of this elaboration. It breaks up and comes together again, according to the variations of the qualities which it seeks and which are suitable to it. Finally, the spring waters become warmer and warmer, and under their influence the maturation reaches completeness. The spawning is accomplished in a final gathering of reproducers collected in great numbers. And the shad, summoned from the sea to attain this end, thus complete their seasonal exodus.

The migration of the shad, like that of the salmon, has its determining factors, a categorical imperative of its own equally efficacious, equally compelling, though of another kind. The intelligence comes from outside the organism, and the sense of direction is also externally controlled. The environment constrains; the creature obeys.

CHAPTER IX

THE great herring trawler out in the open North Sea is about to haul in its nets. The sun has hardly risen. Beneath the dull grey sky, over the greenish water with its gloomy bluish-green waves, behind the misty distance, the light is so pale, so leaden, that the heavy dawn seems to lag, as though it could not bring itself to clear up. The boat, tossed by the swell, labours and rolls. But the sailors, rough, hearty fishermen, set to their hard work with a will despite the penetrating chill of the October morning, despite the spray which covers their oilskins. They haul in their long expanse of nets, almost four miles long, and with it the herrings caught in its meshes.

Last night, before it was dark, the skipper carefully marked the place where he meant to work. The opalescent appearance of the surface of the water, the way the foam that capped the waves persisted, the gulls diving every now and again, and here and there a number of dead fish, made up his mind for him. For there, without doubt, waiting at the bottom was a large shoal of herrings which would come up as darkness fell; the water, made greasy by the mucus which rose from the shoal and spread over the surface, was itself an indication of the presence of fish. So the skipper had given orders to put out the net which spread out, all through the night, like a huge vertical wall with fine meshes, was to arrest and capture the fishes of the shoal as they went their nocturnal ways.

He had been right. The net when it came up was laden with herrings. Their brilliant gold and silver sparkled in vast sheets of light, as they were brought out of the water. Occasionally, a sharp shifting of the tackle, a tightening and stretching of the ropes, produced an effect like a shower of sparks among the fish suspended at the water level. In the dull, greyish light, the warm, bright tones and reflections of the imprisoned fish give a note of brilliance.

Little by little, as the work goes on, the herrings are heaped up in the boxes into which they are turned as they are released from the net. They accumulate by tens and hundreds of thousands. Soon the hold is full, the deck overflowing. Then the net is hauled in and, its task completed, the trawler goes back to the port at which it is registered and there discharges its cargo. On its way it meets other trawlers, which have also done their night's fishing and are going back to the harbours from which they came. All of them, their work accomplished, having gathered their harvest from the sea, take it back as quickly as they can to the places where good use will be made of it. Then they will set out again, and go on in the same way throughout the fishing season, until the herrings come together and form shoals no longer but disperse and disappear.

It was the beginning of summer when this fishing boat began its arduous campaign, with its continual going backwards and forwards. It has taken no rest, and the men have had no respite except for the few moments that may be needed for urgent repairs to the vessel. It has never stopped loading up at sea, discharging on land, then going out and loading up again, like a tireless machine devised by man to exploit the living wealth of the sea. To begin with, it went up the North Sea, off the coast of Scotland, where the shoals then were. By degrees, with the approach of autumn, other shoals were discovered farther south where the fishing was then more profitable. Finally, with the coming of winter, they go still farther down towards the Channel, which they finally enter, and that will be the end, for in January there will be no more shoals to fish.

If we consider these regular variations, repeated each year without any alteration except in the number of fish caught, it seems that they represent a movement of the fish from north to south. The shoals first appeared in the northern parts of the North Sea, then moved southwards little by little, entered the Channel and disappeared. Fishing smacks, which must follow them along if they are to exploit to the full the possibilities open to them, are forced to join the shoals in the north and go down with them to the south.

If we judge only by the general course followed by the herring fisheries, it seems that we can only come to one conclusion. The herrings must be active migrants. Writers of former days described this migration as even more extensive than it would appear. According to them, the herrings left the Arctic Ocean in the spring, forming great columns rising from beneath the icefields and making for the south. One of these swimming armies, they said, goes over towards America. Another, moving towards Europe, enters the North Sea and there breaks up into smaller groups and parties, thus forming the shoals which the fishermen exploit. This migration was supposed to end in the English Channel. There the herrings parted company, going back separately to their home in the Arctic regions from which to set forth again some months later, after forming new groups.

Today we know that this view has no foundation in fact. There is no such migration. Not only has one never been observed, but the facts that have been ascertained definitely contradict such a theory. The herring shoals are mating groups, gatherings of future parents making ready to spawn, and, in fact, actually spawning, which break up when that end has been accomplished. Each district, each fishing ground, often has its own particular type of fish, proper to it, quite obviously belonging to it, fish which are not found elsewhere. The remarkable thing is, not that we find such a diversity, for we find the same sort of thing in several other species of fish, but that we should find it related to that sort of regular succession which has given rise to the idea of a great journey undertaken in common. What are the forces at work upon the herrings which produce such a result?

The herring's scientific name is *Clupea harengus* (Linnæus). It belongs, like the shad, to the family *Clupeidæ*, and has their external characteristics, a long, oblong body, a large and well-forked caudal fin, the single dorsal fin planted on the middle of the trunk, the pelvic fins set back behind the pectorals, the broad, thin and easily detachable scales. When we see it in the fish shops, most of the scales have already disappeared; the body, despoiled of its robe, seems dark blue and leaden grey in hue, and the general appearance is dull and dead. It is very different when the fish, alive and in its wedding dress, is taken out of the sea by the fishermen. Then, its scales, brightly coloured, sparkle with the warmest reflections. The golden hue of the top of the sides and of the head gives the dominant tone; enhanced by the darkish green of the middle of the back and heightened by a few scattered bluish dashes which contrast with the rosy silver of the belly. The fish casts brightness all about it, so glorious and sparkling are its colours. But when it is out of the water its glory seems to fade, fall away and vanish. In a short time nothing is left of all its splendour.

The question was often asked: Where does this fish live during the intercalary period between the fishing seasons? Its disappearance, apparently complete after the last days of the fishing season at the beginning of January, seemed to confirm the theory that it returned to the Arctic Ocean to prepare there for the next migration. This idea has been confuted, for some years now, by the experience of the fisheries. Their extension to regions formerly never touched, and their greater capacity, enable the fishermen to find herrings and to capture them throughout this inter-mediate period. We now know where the fish hide and what they are like.

The herring is a cold-water fish. It lives in the northern zones of the Atlantic Ocean, and never goes down to the temperate zones; its southern limit being somewhere on a line with the space between the estuary of the Loire and that of the Gironde. It lives only in the ocean, and is never seen in the Mediterranean. It frequents the water which covers the deep parts of the continental shelf, not far from the slope that leads down to the abyss, and gathers in certain definitely favoured places where circumstances provide a nourishment more abundant and more easily secured. Its existence is rather like that of the shad, a repetition in northern regions of the habits and behaviour of that fish.

Judging by the enormous number of individual fish which go up the rivers to spawn, the shad must form a large part of the population of the sea. But the herring surpasses it. The North Sea alone furnishes in an average year four hundred thousand tons of this fish, representing between five and six thousand million fish. This catch is only a fractional part of the total, for however perfect the nets, they allow more fish to escape than they actually capture. But the figures are sufficient to give us an idea of the extraordinary numbers there must actually be. If the ocean is vast, if the immensity of its habitable world confuses us by its huge extent, the creatures which it welcomes, and provides a home for in numbers proportionate to its size, increase and multiply in such a way that they leave no part of it unoccupied.

Some species are niggardly and rare; their members, few in number and dispersed, are nowhere frequent. Others, on the other hand, whose needs are either not so great or more easily satisfied, are able to adapt themselves easily to the circumstances in which they find themselves, and rapidly increase in numbers. The herring is one of these. It multiplies in swarms. If, during the period when it goes off in search of food, it is to be found everywhere in those regions which it makes its home, its abundance is made clear at the time of puberty, of reproductive elaboration, for then individuals, become genetic, come together and form groups. It is in this way that the shoals are formed.

The species becomes gregarious. The shad, living in rivers not so spacious as the sea, is forced to gather within a limited area. But in the herrings the gathering in shoals in open sea is spontaneous, it is a preparation for the spawning. The sexes attract one another and associate in bands. As far as one can see, the genetic elaboration brings about the elimination through the skin of substances, whose enticing emanations, dissolved in the water, carried along by it and perceived by the senses, contribute to form and maintain such groupings. Like certain birds and mammals, the herring, at the time of spawning, becomes a sociable being. The societies it forms, necessarily suspended in the waters of the sea, are these shoals, which the swarming species forms in the vast ocean, bringing together individuals by the thousand and the million. They are genetic assemblies, concentrations for the purpose of spawning, and they break up afterwards when the motive for their existence no longer holds good.

The shoals of herrings move, go and come in every direction, sinking to the bottom during the day to escape the light, rising to the surface during the night, when they get caught in the nets. These immense troops, made up of individuals formerly scattered but now grouped together to prepare for spawning in common, move like a single body, leaving none of their members behind. Sexual elaboration progresses during these comings and goings in which the sexes are mingled. Soon the moment for spawning approaches. The shoals are then often quite near the coast. The eggs are expelled by the females and

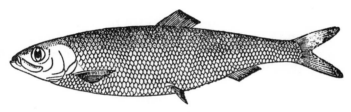

FIG. 22.—HERRING
The Herring (*Clupea harengus*, Linnæus).

fertilized by the males. A little smaller than those of the shad, measuring between a millimetre and a millimetre and a half in diameter, each of these germs swells out the membrane which enwraps it, and makes it mucilaginous, so that it sticks to its neighbours and becomes attached to various objects at the bed of the sea. Each female produces them by tens of thousands, so that the shoal, when spawning, leaves behind it billions and trillions of eggs, all fertilized, all producing, after a few days, lively fry all ready to grow and develop later. So the swarm begins, a swarm so mighty that all the disappearances and losses later will not have much effect upon it.

When the spawning is completed the shoal breaks up. Since there is no more reason for the fish to keep together, there is a general dispersion. The herrings set off greedily in pursuit of their prey; they go back to the deeper zones in which they will live until the next period of sexual elaboration, when a new concentration will take place. The existence of most of them is thus passed within a limited area, and there is no movement beyond its bounds. Far from there being extensive migrations and long journeys, the herrings lead rather a restricted, almost confined existence, though the sea lies open before them, journeying only for short distances from the open sea to the coast, and from the bottom to the surface.

The astonishing thing about them, since they are inclined to be more or less sedentary, is the show of migration they present in their trips from north to south, followed by the fishermen. The extreme mobility of the shoals, which appear and disappear for no apparent reason, gives an appearance of truth to the commonly held theory that they are migratory. There is something surprising, disconcerting about this phenomenon, which often calls for all the experience and common sense of the most skilled fishermen. There is often a relation between their presence and that of certain definite qualities in the water, especially a less marked degree of salinity, but that is about all we know, partly because of this very mobility which often prevents the observer from being sure of the places and depths in which he must get to work. Consequently, opinions and explanations are numerous and diverse, as is usually the case in such circumstances, where every theorist can point to a few facts which seem to prove his case.

In my opinion, the most satisfactory method of finding one's way amid all this confusion is to proceed by the comparative method, considering mainly the principal factors in the various phenomena. We have not far to look for a basis of comparison. The shad are fish of the same family; like the herrings they have definite spawning quarters to which they feel they must go to be able to spawn. The shad offer on a larger scale the very phenomenon that the herring exhibits in lesser degree. When we compare the herring with the shad we find that they behave in much the same way, presenting identical phenomena carried out in the same way; but they make up for the insignificance of their behaviour by the excessive multiplication of the individuals concerned in it.

There is no difficulty in noting the chief episodes in the

life history of the shad. It is sufficient to recall what I have
mentioned in the preceding chapter. These fishes have two
successive lives, or two successive phases in their lives, one
in which they have no fixed habitation, that of growth, and
one devoted to reproduction. The former is one of isolation
in the sea; the latter in fresh water when the individuals
are brought together. When they pass from one to the
other, the shad leave their homes in the depths, go first to
shallower waters, then towards the coast, enter the estuaries,

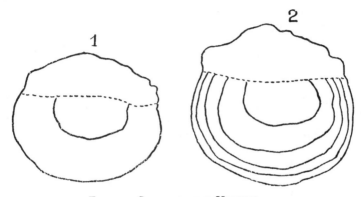

FIG. 23.—SCALES OF THE HERRING

Diagram showing the construction and the growth (probably in annual stages)
of the herring's scales. The concentric lines are the *winter lines*, showing
preparation for spawning. 1, scale of a small fish, two years old; 2, scale of
a large fish, five years old. Enlarged eight times.

and go up the rivers until they reach the spawning places.
In this change of environment they are guided by two
organic needs which polarize them, both of which originate
in the individual as functions of its sexual elaboration and
the preparation of the germs which it will later produce.
One is that of more active respiration, and the creature
satisfies it by going into waters which are only slightly
saline, or not saline at all. The diminution in chlorides
increases the proportion of dissolved oxygen, and facilitates
the respiratory processes. The other is that of a relatively
high temperature. The organism satisfies this by securing
from its environing medium the calories which are indispensable to it. The shad, controlled in this way, behaves
in accordance with circumstances, and make the necessary

accommodation to them as far as the modifications brought about in its body allow. The water which is favourable to its spawning is river water.

Now let us compare the herring with the shad. These fish are of the same family, performing the same acts on a smaller scale. Like them, they begin with a life of growth near the spawning places where were deposited the eggs from which they were hatched. This life is prolonged and continued in deeper water. Then comes puberty, followed by sexual elaboration with its organic needs. The herrings, less exigent than the shad and accustomed to cold temperatures, feel especially the need for a more active respiration. Their sexual elaboration takes them by preference towards those parts of the sea where the degree of salinity is slight, and brings them out of the deep water, up to the surface and the shore, even inducing some of them to seek out the estuaries and enter them. But they go no farther. Their needs are less than those of the shad, though they are of the same kind, and they keep the fish in the sea. This is where they continue to find the water that suits them best.

The North Sea, the principal centre of the herring fisheries, is a vast reservoir open at both ends, that is, at the north and the south, through which it receives currents of a different nature. Through the northern entrance, which is the greater, come the cold waters from the Arctic Ocean, weak in salines, the content of which may be as low as thirty grammes of chlorides per litre, sometimes even less. Through the southern entrance, the narrower, the Straits of Dover, come waters from the Atlantic Ocean, which are often quite warm, and always relatively strong in salines, amounting to as much as thirty-five grammes of chlorides per litre. The waters of these two currents, borne onward by their own movements, affected by the tides, mingle in very varied ways, differing according to locality, depth, season and year. Together they result in a rotary circulation round the reservoir, with numerous eddies all the way along, in which the sheets of water flow across and across one another, then come together again, the main direction being determined by the Arctic waters because of their greater volume. These Arctic waters, even more powerful during the warm weather because of the melting of the northern icefields, are strong enough to force their way throughout almost the whole sea until they approach the Straits of Dover.

The herrings, at the period of puberty, find themselves confronted by these sheets of water. Hitherto of no certain abode, scattered and dispersed over the whole sea bottom, they now begin to feel the needs occasioned by the development and proliferation of the sexual glands. The water they find favourable is that of least salinity. As they become aware of its influence they collect in it, form groups in it, the shoals in which they elaborate in common the germs which will be later spawned. The movements of these sheets of water, forming secondary, localized eddies, take them suddenly in one direction or another, keeping them longer near the coast where the favourable water stays longer. The seasonal progression of the water summons the herrings from their isolation, incites them to come together from north to south, to form shoals, and then to spawn. It is not the shoals which move southwards, but the water which favours their formation. Extending, little by little, to the south, it gathers to itself, in one place and another, according to the incidents and divisions of its advance, all the individuals which are capable of spawning.

Now that we have compared the herring to the shad, this seems to be the most acceptable explanation of the shifting of the fishing grounds. The herring is a seasonal fish which spawns every year. The main time for this spawning comes, as in the shad, towards the end of spring and the beginning of summer. The herrings which have arrived at puberty, whom circumstances then allow to come under the influence of water favourable to their development, are thenceforth capable of spawning. But these circumstances, affecting others only in a more tardy fashion, from north to south progressively, arouse their desire for reproduction in exactly the same way, form them into shoals, and by the time they reach the last, those farthest south, in the English Channel, autumn is at an end and winter is beginning. The search for food seems to affect them very little.

The herring shoals are temporary groupings, mobile and variable like the influence that brings them about. They form, break up again, separate and come together again, as this influence changes. They represent so many passing centres of attraction, dispersed in space and distinct in time. The favourable water summons them thither for a moment and forms into groups the genetic herrings which happen to be living in the places where it appears in its erratic meanderings. Like the shad, which are sometimes massed together about their spawning places when circumstances are favourable, sometimes dispersed when circumstances grow less favourable or temporarily non-effective, then grouped again if changed conditions bring about their return, the herrings in the sea act in the same way.

" Shoal water " the fisherman calls this favourable water, assuming that the water bears the herring along with it *en masse*. " Shoal water " we may say also, but only when we realize that these sheets of water act simply by attraction, and that their action is limited to the gathering of individuals already present, though dispersed before that water reaches them. The water does not convey the fish; it summons them to itself.

Formed in obedience to an external force, these shoals behave like giant automatons with myriads of heads. Among the individuals composing them, the action of one is at any given moment that of all the others. The whole shoal moves in a piece, like a single, huge, multiple creature. Sometimes in summer we may see swarms of tiny insects above a pond or a brook in a favouring current of air. These flying hosts change their form, lengthen or become shorter, move away as a body, then come back and stay together until the moment when the motive that has brought them together, that of reproduction, is fulfilled. There, on a small scale, we have the counterpart of a shoal of herrings. Replace the tiny insects by the larger fishes, the air by water, and you have the shoal, itself as changing, as moving, quivering as utterly with one single but universal purpose.

CHAPTER X

THE VICISSITUDES OF THE SARDINE FISHERIES

THOSE who only know the sardines well enough to be able to recognize them decapitated and swimming in oil at the bottom of a tin, can have no idea what the creature is like when it is alive in the sea in which it is caught. Even those who see the fish whole at the fishmonger's, sprinkled with salt to keep them from going bad, surrounded with ice, or packed in tubs, know as little about them. To know them as they really are they must be looked at immediately the net containing them is drawn from the water. The fisherman takes them, throws them down, piles them up at the bottom of his boat. Then the glorious iridescence of their colours can be properly appreciated. They are Nature's jewels.

Not that their colours are either many or varied. They are only two, sky-blue and pearly white. The blue covers the whole of the back and the upper part of the sides, enhanced by a slight tinge of gold near the head and cheeks. All the rest is white. If there is nothing very striking about these shades, they make up for it by the very splendour of simplicity. In this modest little creature they bring together the two essential colours of the vast spaces of the sea; the blue of the depths and the white of the foam that tips the waves. Not only do they combine these two colours, but they enhance them by giving them a sparkle, a brilliance, a softness which we find nowhere else. No enamel has shades so gentle, so bright. When the fisherman, hauling his net out of the water, brings up to the light of day the sardines hanging from the meshes like pendants; we might well say, as we look at them, that these are no common fish, but glittering jewels which the fisherman is piling up in his boat like a magician finding treasure in the sea.

Let us go to Brittany in the summer, to one of the little fishing ports that lie so snugly on the coast. Every suitable morning, at the first flush of dawn, these ports send out to sea their flotillas of little boats, each manned by two or three fishermen. They hoist their sails, manœuvre to catch the wind, use their oars, to be the sooner at their work. Setting out in file, almost one behind the other, they spread out as they reach the deeper water, and gradually disperse a few miles from the shore. The skippers watch for their marks, the places where on previous days they had their best fishing. They scrutinize the waves, the wind, the slightest sign. When they have made up their minds they haul down the sail, anchor, and cast out their net. It is coloured blue so as to be less easily seen. They spread it out like a wall, a floating wall, and its meshes are especially fine so as to make sure that very few fish escape. As the sardines usually keep far down in the water, beyond the reach of the net, the fishermen entice them upwards by throwing out *rogue*, a bait which breaks up into tiny fragments which, going down little by little, attract the fish to the place from which it was thrown out. The clever fisherman distributes his *rogue*, cod's roe or linseed flour, by throwing it first on one side of the net and then on the other. The obedient sardines, the victims of their appetites, are caught in the meshes as they dash forward to get to the other side.

When the number of sardines thus enmeshed is great enough, and the net grows heavy under their weight, the fisherman pulls it in, hauls it into his boat, takes off the fish he has caught and then puts the net back again into the water to catch some more. This he continues to do until he thinks he has caught enough for the day. Then he hauls up his sail again, and goes back to harbour. Since most of his companions do as he does, at the same hour on their own boats, almost all come back together, forming a returning caravan, which gradually draws close together as it nears the harbour. This return to port as the sun is setting, with the sea sparkling with purple light, is one of the most delightful sights the ocean has to offer us.

This goes on in Provence, Languedoc, Roussillon, all round Spain, the coasts of Italy and Northern Africa, almost the whole year round, with a few breaks during the winter. Sardine fishing, with that of several other species which are much of the same type, the sprat and the anchovy, is one of the most lucrative kinds of fishing, for it provides the fishermen with the greater part of their livelihood and is the catch most easily secured. As in Brittany, most of the little fishing villages on the coast have a number of boats specially devoted to it. Nowadays, these often have a motor instead of a sail and oars. But in those countries where the sea is warmer than in Brittany, the fishermen seldom need to use bait. The sardines are more abundant and ready to remain longer in the waters nearer the surface. There is no need to bring them up; they come up of their own accord. The fisherman has only to put out his net. If he meets with good luck and is sufficiently experienced, if he has cast his net at the right place, the sardines, coming and going, are caught without more ado. The net simply collects the fish.

The sardine, *Sardina pilchardus* (Walbaum), to give it its scientific name, frequents the temperate waters of Western Europe, showing a preference for the warmer and calmer zones. Like the herring and the shad, it belongs to the family *Clupeidæ*, and, though tiny, seldom more than eight inches in length, it has all the characteristics of that family. It is an excellent swimmer, remains in midwater all the time and never seeks to rest. Its shoals, like those of the anchovy (*Engraulis encrasicholus*, Linnæus) which closely resembles it in size and habits but differs from it by its much larger mouth and rounded belly, are ceaselessly on the move and never settle anywhere. The fisherman experiences the consequences of these habits, for he has to deal with a fish which moves about swiftly and is never in the same place twice. The sardine fisheries have their good times and their bad, from one day to another, from year to year. But as it is the most lucrative of all fishing, and as the professional fishermen count upon it to provide them with the greater part of their livelihood, it is the more disappointing when anything goes wrong. When this does happen it means misery and distress to those who live by the sardine fisheries, an economic crisis which could be avoided by more careful regulation.

The Mediterranean is less subject to such vicissitudes than the ocean, especially off the coast of Brittany which is too near the northern limit of the sardines. Its waters, even during the winter, are often peaceful, and the surface is warmed by the sun. The sardines find there a regularity, a uniformity which the ocean, more disturbed and more quickly chilled, does not and cannot offer them. People have often sought the reasons for the crisis in the sardine fisheries of Brittany. They can be discovered by comparison with the experiences of the Mediterranean. We have only to study the behaviour of the species there to find out what initiates and directs that behaviour, to understand what happens elsewhere.

I have followed this sardine fishing on the spot. I have gone with Breton, Spanish, Provençal fishermen in their

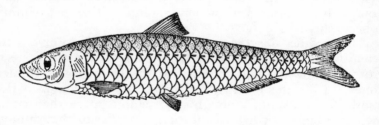

FIG. 24.—SARDINE
The Sardine (*Sardina pilchardus*, Walbaum).

boats. I have gathered a scientific harvest beside theirs. I have learned by their experience and by my own. The result agrees with our conclusions in the case of the shad and the herring, except for certain variations.

Sardine fishing, off the coast of Nice and Liguria, goes on almost throughout the year. Even in the middle of winter, in December and January, they are caught and sold, heaped up in great baskets in the streets. A few days of calm and warmth are all that is necessary, and this is quite usual in this part of the world. With the coming of spring the fishing moves westward towards Cannes and Toulon. A little later it reaches the Gulf of Marseilles and then Sète, at the end of the bay formed by the Gulf of Lions. Thereafter, fishing is in full swing all along the coast of Provence, and continues throughout the year until, with the gusty winds of autumn, the weather begins to turn cold again. Then its field shrinks, as if it turned back upon itself towards its point of departure. The fishing gradually becomes less successful and productive. It breaks off, going back from one district to another, until it arrives at the place where it is active longest. Sometimes, periods of fine weather produce a temporary return to the zones deserted during the winter, but results, as a rule, are insignificant compared with the splendid catches of the summer.

When we consider this course of events it looks as though there were an annual movement of the sardines along the coast of Provence, a migration in two directions, one, going from the east to the west; the other, returning in the opposite

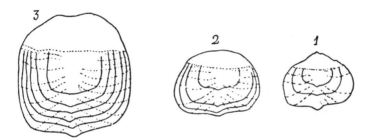

FIG. 25.—SCALES OF THE SARDINE

Diagram showing the construction of the sardine's scales and the (probably annual) stages of growth. The concentric lines are the winter, preparation of spawning, lines. The radial dotted lines show the extension. 1, scale of a small sardine, three years old; 2, scale of a medium-sized sardine, four years old; 3, scale of a large sardine, six years old.

direction to the point of departure. It seems as though this point, near Nice and the Ligurian Gulf, contains in its waters a population of sardines, rich enough, abundant enough, to become a centre of expansion and dispersion. At regular fixed seasons the fish seem to leave that part of the world and set out upon their journey, returning to it when the journey has been accomplished.

It is the same on the other side of the Gulf of Lions, where there is a movement which, beginning at Sète, extends in the direction of Roussillon and Catalonia. There we find an identical succession, this time from south to north. The Catalan fishermen, and those of the Balearic Isles, often find sardine to fish for even in the middle of winter, and anchovies too, when no success is to be hoped for off the coast of Languedoc. Then, as the warm weather approaches, both sardines and anchovies appear in the north in greater and greater numbers. As spring advances the fisheries are more and more busy, and remain active throughout the summer and often for part of autumn. Then the backward movement begins, and goes southwards, there reverting during winter to the usual state of affairs. The impression we have is that of a double migration, carried out regularly every year, with an outward movement from south to north and a return in the opposite direction, which has the effect of collecting, in the middle of summer, the hosts of travellers at the head of the Gulf of Lions. This district, with its great sandy beaches near the estuary of the Rhone, seems to be a centre at which they gather during the summer, which attracts to itself, during the warm weather, the cohorts of migrants, sending them away again later when the cold weather begins to make itself felt.

But when we examine things more closely this impression changes, especially if we study the behaviour of the sardines in the course of this supposed migration. The first thing we notice is the sensitiveness of these fishes to temperature. It is particularly striking. The appliance which the fishermen of Provence prefer to use, the " sardinal," and the mode of its employment, make this very clear to us. It is a long net, stretched out vertically in the water like a wall, fitted with hawsers attached to buoys by which it can be let down to different depths. If the sardines are near the surface it is anchored about their level; if they stay near the bottom and will not come up, it is lowered to them. If we take the temperature of the water we find that the fish seldom come up to the surface except when the water there is not below twelve to thirteen degrees Centigrade. If it is any colder the fish are few, and they are never found at all when it falls below ten degrees. In the middle of summer, during the long calm periods when it is very sunny, if the temperature of the surface water goes above twenty-two to twenty-three degrees, the fish run away from these zones which are now too warm, as they did when it was too cold, and go down to find a temperature that suits them better. Then the " sardinal " is lowered by its hawsers so that the fish can still be caught.

The sardine, then, like the shad, loves warmth. The

species is only able to attain its fullest vitality when it finds itself in waters of a definite temperature. There is a caloric margin over about ten degrees, between thirteen and twenty-three Centigrade. Above and below these figures the vitality of the sardines is affected and impaired, and they go down to find more acceptable conditions. Their thermic optimum keeps them between these definite limits.

The species is not only sensitive to temperature, it is also affected by the currents, by sudden alterations in the waters of the sea. The experiences of fishermen show that the sardine is particularly likely to appear, and in large numbers, when the " Levant current " approaches the coast. This current is a dependency of the great circuit which carries back the warm waters of the eastern Mediterranean to the western Mediterranean, before emptying them into the Atlantic Ocean through the Straits of Gibraltar. Near the coast of Provence it flows from between south and east towards north and west (hence the name commonly given to it), striking the shore line obliquely. It spreads out during calm periods, but contracts and goes deeper when the cold north-west winds blow, especially the mistral. The temperature of its water, even in midwinter, is rarely below twelve or thirteen degrees, rising according to the season. The sardines follow this current and live in it. Its waters are the most favourable, as regards thermic optimum, that the species can have. Any current coming from the open sea is a good current, the sardine fishermen in Provence say, and every current coming from the land is bad. The first is that which has the water which brings to the coast and so to the fishermens' nets an abundant contingent of fish; the second is that of cold winds, which keep the fish away.

The old Legend of the Maries of the Sea, handed down from generation to generation, from the earliest days of Christianity, among the fishermen of the Camargue, symbolizes while idealizing the story of these currents which come from the east and make up the wealth of the sea shore. The saints of the legends, bringing the Divine Word, came with them from the east, borne over the waves in a little boat without sails or oars. " Saints, Queens of Paradise, sovereign mistresses of the bitter plains of the sea, you swell our nets with fish when such is your good pleasure;

but to the host of sinners bewailing at the doors of your church, if it be peace they need, with peace do ye fill them." (From *Mireio*, a Provençal poem, by Frédéric Mistral.)

The sardines are indeed creatures of the current, like many other of the floating animals, large and small, which abound near them, of which they choose the smallest for their food. Far from having a fixed abode near the shore, such as we might expect from the usual course of the fishing season and from some temporary circumstances in their manner of find-

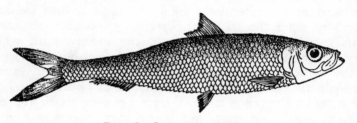

FIG. 26.—SARDINELLA AURITA
The Allache (*Sardinella aurita*, Cuvier-Valenciennes) belonging to the family *Clupeidæ*, like the herring, shad, and sardine.

ing food, their main hosts live in the open waters of the sea, and their essential habitat is a moving one. From it, as circumstances decide, little groups detach themselves. The current carries them to the coast and the fishermen make the most of them. In spite of their abundance in certain cases, these bands are only a fraction of the whole, and they cannot be considered as the whole species. This, which is pelagic, has its real home out at sea, and there most of the individuals which compose it are born, grow, and die. We have only a minority near us in those places where the sardines are actually caught. The fishery belongs to the coast, but not the sardine itself.

Having laid down these premises in accordance with the facts, the rest is easily deducible. The region about Nice, where the coast falls rapidly to the greatest depths, receives in full measure the whole volume of this favourable water which spreads over the surface of the sea. The mildness of the climate enables it to retain for a long time, even during the winter, a relatively high temperature. Consequently, the sardines stay in this water, not only the adults whose growth is almost complete, but also the little ones, the fry born out at sea a few weeks or a few months before. The current bears them to the coast, and there the fishermen catch them and sell them as especially delightful titbits. The " poutine " so highly thought of, whose delicate, dainty bodies fill baskets in the fish-shops during the summer, is only this young sardine, carried by the current from the high seas, then brought to the coast, where it will soon come to an untimely end, where the fishes of prey—whiting, bass, and the rest—soon put an end to any which the fishermen have failed to catch.

With the coming of spring the influence of the climate extends westward to the neighbouring districts, which do not enjoy such excellent shelter. Then the favourable water does not lose its warmth so quickly, as it comes nearer the shore and rises to the surface. Consequently, the sardines appear there more frequently and stay longer. This climatic action, manifesting itself in successive stages, begins in the district about Nice, and gradually extends westwards. The fishermen get busy and their catch increases, the improvement becoming more and more noticeable towards the head of the Gulf of Lions. Niggardly and uncertain during the winter, when it must be favoured— and this rarely happens—by a long period of fair weather so that the favourable water may preserve its thermal qualities as it does at Nice, the harvest becomes abundant and regular. If, apparently, we have a great host of migrants going along the coast from east to west, journeying when the good weather is favourable, things are quite different in reality. There is a succession of thrusts by echelon from the open sea towards the land, according to the season, not an unceasing migration along the coast in a continual mass.

The sardines, loving the warm currents, bound by the limits of their thermic optimum and consequently stenothermic—if we may use in relation to them that word which, derived from two Greek words, ' stenos ' narrow, and ' thermos ' heat, is given to those creatures whose vitality is confined within a small caloric margin—have a type of life that is at once simple and complex. Sedentary when in their favourite waters, where their movements are confined to the hunting down of the nearest prey, they move with those waters and are continually borne along by them. This is where they make their home, where they live, and when their home moves they are carried along with it. Those whom such a thrust brings near the shore only stay there if the climate allows their water to retain its warmth; otherwise they go down deeper and return to find elsewhere the qualities which are necessary to their well-being. So they show themselves in the fishing grounds and remain there only in so far as the climate gives them a guarantee, and we see this deep-sea creature expose to the climatic conditions of the land those of its hosts which circumstances have brought

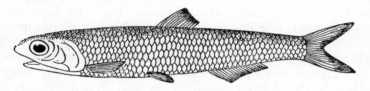

FIG. 27.—ANCHOVY

The Anchovy (*Engraulis encrasicholus*, Linnæus), typical of the family *Engraulidæ*, closely related to the *Clupeidæ*.

out of their way to the shore. Their moving home having brought them there, the local climate accepts them or rejects them, as circumstances permit, and these vary according to locality and time of year. It opens or closes to them the approaches to the coast, in this automatic voyage which brings the sardines from the open sea in relays of independent groups.

The action of climate extends even farther. Not only does it graduate the appearances on the coast in a series of echelons; it is often the cause of a remarkable diversity. In calm, warm summers, which allow favourable currents the easy access which assures the fishermen a successful season, the momentary agreement between the thrust of the currents and the state of the season fills the nets and loads all their meshes. On the other hand, a bad, rainy summer with frequent cold winds and rough seas considerably restricts these arrivals, drives the sardines away, and keeps them out in the open sea, in deep water where they like to be. No two years are alike; some afford a copious harvest, others are poor and unprofitable. If we make a graph of the annual catch we find that it takes the form of a series of saw-toothed angles. There are poor seasons in those years when climatic influences are unfavourable. If several such years come together, the fishermen have a very hard time, for which they can only make up by adopting improved methods and going out to sea to look for the fish which the shore rejects. This sometimes happens off the coast of Brittany.

These are not the only crises. There are others which result from an excessive abundance, from too great a catch. The harmony between the current and the weather being only too complete, the sardines arrive in great numbers, so great that nobody knows what do with them and the price goes down, since there are more fish than are needed. Although different, these difficult periods, which have the same result, have also the same cause. Both depend upon the changing condition of the fish. A species of vast numbers, essentially and completely pelagic, which happens as though by accident to find itself near the coast, which is sensitive to every factor which brings about a change in the moving water in which it is accustomed to live, it sends its hosts, its shoals, everywhere this water allows it to go. From the fisherman's point of view it is seasonal and alterable; but, actually, it is constant, uniform, and unchanging. An open sea species, only its detached hosts find their way to us, when circumstances happen to be favourable.

CHAPTER XI

THE SENSITIVITY OF THE MACKEREL

THERE are various kinds of fishing, and all of them have their devotees; but I know hardly any that is more delightful, more interesting, or more fascinating than fishing for mackerel with a trailing line. It is more than simple fishing; it is navigation too. It must be done from a boat, going at a good speed, under sail. One has to keep an eye on one's boat, one's course, one's lines, without forgetting any of them. Fertile in incident, both great and small, it sometimes affords, when successful, a reward beyond all expectation. In the proper season, during the summer, all round the coast, but especially in the Channel where this fish abounds, there are many mackerel fishermen. Both professionals and amateurs show an equal keenness.

We must set out early, while it is still quite dark before the break of day, and go straight out to the open sea. With the morning breeze behind us, with our two sails well filled and a foresail set, the boat makes a good speed. We choose our course in such a way as to cut across the tidal currents. The mackerel, which have voracious appetites, like such places; they snap up the prey which the currents bring them. When the dawn breaks we put out our lines and begin to fish. Far off we see the long barrier of the chalk cliffs, crowned by the deep green of woods and meadows, broken by the dark gold of sandy beaches, all shaded, enveloped, softened by a light blue mist. Around us boats like our own are also putting out their lines. The sun rises, gradually creeping up in the sky. The sea rocks us with its smooth low waves. There is every hope of a fine day.

The lines are stacked in coils, each with its hook. We weight them with a fairly heavy piece of lead to prevent them from floating on the surface. We bait the hooks with silvery strips cut from the skin of a belly of a mackerel caught the night before and kept for that purpose. Then we throw them over the side, holding them away from the boat by rods. The speed of the boat under sail carries them along and raises them so that they do not go down vertically but obliquely, and, with their baited hooks, search the higher levels of the water. The shining, pearly bait, which we can see quite easily, is carried along swiftly as the boat moves on and attracts the mackerel, which snap at it and so are hooked. The turnings and twistings they then make are felt on the line, whose end is held in the hands, and we pull it up, take off the fish, re-bait and throw in again without any more delay than possible. On a good day, though we may have three or four lines out at once, we may have to haul in, clear the hook, and throw back the line again almost all the time. The mackerel we have caught themselves serve to attract others, since we use the skin of their bellies for new bait. We have also to keep an eye on our sails and our course. We are very busy, in fact, and the morning advances rapidly with our catch gradually piling up on board.

Sometimes there is a few moments' calm to give us respite. We stop for a moment, eyes keeping a lookout in all directions to see if everything is all right. When we look down at the fish we have already caught we see a combination of splendid colours, made more splendid still by the dancing reflections cast by the waves, reflected again by the sails. The mackerel are really most attractive fish, superbly dressed. Spread out side by side in different attitudes and before they have lost their freshness, they display the glory of their adornment in all its beauty. Their back is like a mosaic; upon a ground of blue, with flashes of greenish and purple gold, are straight or waving bands and patches of a brown that is almost black, all enamelled with spangles. The pink sides flash with silver. The pearly white belly, soft and smooth, has in places a touch of all the colours of the rainbow. The head, blue on the upper part, is golden on the cheeks, and retains that colour as far as the beginning of the sides. The fins, light and delicate with their clear rose or grey shades, in no way hide the firm, robust lines of the body.

These glittering, sparkling colours only last an instant.

Bright and vivid when the fish are taken out of the water, they quickly become dull and faded. The air dries them up and soon effaces them, leaving only a sort of leaden hue in their place. Strangely enough the water has the same effect. If I lean over the side to try and catch a glimpse of the mackerel in the sea in which they live, I sometimes see one of them coming up from the depths below. All I see is an oblong body, a dark, mottled back, a whitish belly, and nothing else. This coloured firework, which the fish is when it is taken out of the water, does not exist in the very water from which it is taken; it is only for a moment that it puts forth all these flames of every colour. When it is in the air it is the play of light which gives it its

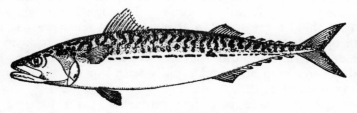

FIG. 28.—MACKEREL
The common mackerel (*Scomber scomber*, Linnæus).

iridescence, its metallic sparkle, through the still damp skin. It must have this bright light before it can show itself. Then the air destroys what it has itself created; it first illuminates, then gradually extinguishes, the brightness it had produced. The mackerel is clothed in a splendid dress, but only for a moment.

Italian fishermen call it *Ariolo*, *Auriolo*, and the Provençal fishermen, *Auruou*. These two words come from the Latin *varius*, which means mottled or striped, because of the stripes and patches which cover the entire back. From this root we have the diminutives *variolus*, *variellus* and *varellus*, in Low Latin, with the same meaning. From this last expression, transposed into the northern dialects, we have *Makrele* in German, *maquereau* in French, and the English *mackerel*. It is a strange coincidence which gives to these apparently different words, one of them the name of a fish and the other that of certain illnesses the symptoms of which are cutaneous patches, mackerel, *variole*, *vérole* (smallpox) the same origin and the same meaning, both based upon appearances.

The mackerel, in the important family *Scombridæ*, which is found in profusion in warm and temperate seas, occupies a position like that of the sardine in the family *Clupeidæ*. It is one of the smaller members of the family, usually measuring between nine and twelve and a half inches in length, rarely exceeding fifteen to twenty, but making up for its smallness by its numbers and its ubiquity, both qualities in the living world often going together by a sort of compensating equilibrium. If it does not attain the giant dimensions of the large *Scombridæ*, like the tunny and the albacore, which may be as much as six feet or more in length, it has at least all the principal characteristics of the family, those which have made for its existence: a strong tapering body, well rounded, constructed for speed; the caudal fin, broad and full, well spread out like a fan and clearly forked, attached by a narrow peduncle; the pelvic fins attached to the trunk beneath the pectorals and a little in front of them; the dorsal and anal fins prolonged towards the rear by little blades one after the other called pinnules, which continue them till they come to the tail. These different peculiarities are so marked in it that its twice repeated name, once for the genus and again for the species (*Scomber scomber*, Linnæus), has been given to the family as a whole and provides the term used for classing all the others.

The morning passes. The weather shows signs of change, as is often the case in the Channel during the warm summer weather, when one often has a delightful early morning, a stormy noon, and a temperate, delightful evening. The slight mist which got up at dawn has grown thicker. Rising little by little from the sea, it has turned into a cloud which hides the sun. The light has grown dimmer and more uniform. The wind has changed. A damp, cold breeze, blowing from the open sea, catches the sails. The temperature goes down a little. This is immediately reflected in our success with the line; we catch fewer fish. The slight cooling of the upper layers of water, caused by that of the air, is enough to make the mackerel go deeper, to take them back to the depths. We have to clew up a sail, manœuvre a little, and slacken the speed of the boat, so that the lines will go deeper and reach the fish again. Then we begin to catch fish once more, but not so many.

The clouds pile up. The breeze increases and becomes gusty. The rain begins to fall, a few drops at first, then heavily; it covers the waves with its hurried drops, smooths them out. Then we might as well pull up the lines and go back to port, for there will be no more fishing today. There will be no more bites. The tiny quantity of fresh water that has fallen on the surface of the sea, and mingled with the salt, has been enough to keep off the mackerel and send them down nearer the bottom. Even in the evening when the rain has stopped for several hours they will stay below and will not come up again. The peace and darkness of the night will be needed to bring them back, so that the fishermen may again have opportunities equal to those of the day before.

The species is sensitive to both temperature and salinity. It is not only stenothermic like the herrings, but also stenohaline. It only frequents those waters which have the highest proportion of dissolved chloride salts, and keeps away from others, even for short periods. It is only fully alive in waters which are relatively warm and strongly saline, and in this respect it is like most other members of its family. A sensitivity of this sort, carried to such a high degree, localizes these fishes. It looks as though Nature withdraws from them with one hand what she gives with the other. She gives them swiftness, strength, a digestive capacity which enables them to make full use of an appetite which is always keen; and she cuts down their power to enjoy these qualities by preventing them from entering certain kinds of water, and making them come away from others as soon as circumstances cease to be favourable.

Thus they are restrained and kept within certain bounds. Their sensitivity to cold makes them seasonal. They reach the fishing grounds during the summer and leave at the beginning of winter, as soon as the surface of the sea begins to cool. But instead of behaving like the sardines and staying in the water which is favourable to them though going out farther to sea, the mackerel go down to the bottom more or less where they happen to be, and stay there for the winter.

In the Mediterranean during the summer the species is only caught, whether by line, by seine, or by ordinary nets, in the higher regions of the water, near the coasts; trawls, which drag the bottom, catch none. But it is different in the autumn. Then it is surface fishing which produces no result, and the trawlers gather a harvest of the mackerel which have gone down to take shelter at the bottom.

It is the same in the English Channel and in the ocean. The mackerel was once a fish that could only be had at certain seasons. It was only caught in summer, and could only be found in the shops at that period of the year. But the recent extension of fishing with drag-nets, with boats

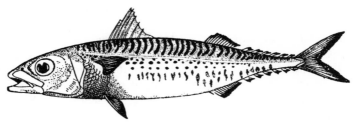

FIG. 29.—COLIAS MACKEREL

The Colias Mackerel (*Scomber colias,* Risso) is a species found in the Mediterranean and the warm zones of the Atlantic, which possesses a swimming bladder which the common mackerel has not.

larger than those of former days, using larger appliances which drag at a lower depth, enables the fishermen to catch mackerel in midwinter in the depths which they have made their winter quarters. The species, while seasonal, is practically sedentary, and never moves very far.

Where do the mackerel go in winter? The question used to be asked, and it was answered by a theory of migration which made them winter in the northern seas, which they were supposed to leave in spring. They emigrated and returned. But today we know that such a voyage is not in fact made, is not even attempted. If in winter the fish leave those places where they spent the summer, it is to withdraw to the relatively warm waters of the depths, not to go northward. They are content to reach the calm, quiet zones which cover the bottom of the continental shelf, and there they wait for the surface of the sea to become warmer with the return of warm weather. Like the herrings, the principal move they make, and that only for a short distance, is from the bottom of the sea to the surface, from the open sea to the coast. They do not go far beyond the shelf.

This short journey, caused and directed by the seasonal warming of the surface waters, follows a definite course. Beginning earlier in the south than elsewhere, it gradually extends. The fish appear by echelons in the upper layers, as the season affects the different waters in turn. Hence, as in the case of the sardines and for the same thermic reason, it looks like a migration. But this is only in appearance. In reality they simply rise by series to the fishing grounds in a pseudo-migration. It is nothing more or greater than that.

The mackerel, however, differ from the sardines and the herrings in one respect. They are stenothermic like them, but they have an additional sensitivity which takes them from those places where salinity diminishes, even in the least degree, by admixture with fresh water. They are stenohaline like all the *Scombridæ*. They like the purest water, and it is there that they must be sought. One must either use a boat to catch them or take up one's post on some point of the shore, a cape, a jutting rock, or at the head of a bay where the currents come from the open sea. They like such water, and move with the following tides. In it they find at once the completely saline water they prefer and a profusion of tiny animals on which to feed.

All these things together constitute a very extraordinary mode of behaviour. Their sensitivity pushes them to an extreme versatility which is only equalled by that of the fresh water roach, and it is this which makes the fishing of them so interesting and fascinating. Very impressionable, distrustful, and greedy, the fisherman never knows whether he will have any luck with them, or whether their distrust will get the better of their greediness. He meets continually with the unforeseen. They fly at the least provocation; the slightest disturbance, the slightest change in their accustomed surroundings, sends them off at once to the darkness of the depths where they believe themselves more secure.

A shining, moving bait attracts them best. Their behaviour reminds us on a small scale of that of the giants of the family. They have the same tastes, the same way of returning; and if we reproduce their behaviour on a larger scale we have exactly that of the Tunnies.

CHAPTER XII

THE WEDDING OF THE TUNNY

I. I STILL remember how astounded I was when I first visited one of the sheds in which the tunny nets are hung up to dry. It was in Sardinia. The fishermen had just caught and imprisoned in the " death chamber," the last division of the net in which the fish had been caught, several hundred tunny fish. They had proceeded to kill these enormous fish, to slaughter them *alla mattanza*, to use the words of the Italian fishermen, seizing them with hooks and piling them up in lighters. They had carried the fish to land and then unloaded them. And in this shed they had hung the fish by the tail to empty them, to drain away the last drops of their blood. After which the sailors, galley slaves of the sea, had gone back to the net to get it ready for action again, and the workmen, the scum of the earth, were lighting fires and getting ready the utensils in which to make preserve of the flesh of these same tunnies when they had been cut to pieces.

Since that time I have seen the same sight several times, in Tunisia and in Spain. Each time I have felt the same surprise, the same fear. It is like going into a charnel house. One feels as if one were passing through a torture chamber. These great hanging bodies, some of which are much taller than a man, set out in lines of hundreds, the blood draining from them and red pools forming along the ground, give one complex poignant sensations. *Il bosco*, the grove, the forest, is what these fishermen call the shed in which they collect their corpses. A forest in truth, of which the closely packed, squat trunks, without branches or foliage, are made of all these dead things. The bodies are allowed to drain several hours; then the fishermen take them down, cut them up, soak them in boiling brine, and put them in boxes.

When the catch has been good these scenes are repeated

every three or four days. There are piles upon piles of fish. The tunny net, called *almadraba* in Spain, *armacoe* in Portugal, and *tonnara* in Italy, is a great appliance, proportionate to the size of the fish it is devised to catch. It stretches out in the sea for hundreds of yards. Definitely fixed in the place frequented by the tunny, it is divided into successive compartments like a gigantic hoop-net. The fish go into it one after the other, and from one section to another, collecting ultimately in the last, the death chamber. Since they cannot escape from it, for the bottom of this compartment is a solid floor of rope with very strongly woven meshes, it is the end of them.

I have described the tunny elsewhere. I mentioned its great size, which sometimes exceeds six feet in length, its weight which is occasionally more than six hundred-weight, its strength, and its speed which is made more intense by its projectile - like shape. But what use to it in this net are its swiftness and its strength, since it has allowed itself to be caught? A superb fish, it used to roam the seas, putting to flight all the other fishes and fearing only the sharks which were still stronger than itself. And here it is imprisoned, bound for the slaughter-house. The net which is able so to imprison it is indeed an unrivalled marvel of ingenuity.

Nevertheless, such a net has its limitations. Its great size restricts its use, which is only possible in certain places and in certain circumstances. It can only be set up near the coast where the tunny is accustomed to come. There must be a considerable distance between one net and another, so that one does not interfere with another. Finally, even the strongest net can only be used for a short season which lasts five or six weeks, beginning always with the second fortnight in May and ending with the first fortnight of July. Before this time the net is anchored ready near the shore, so that the early comers are not neglected. Afterwards it is taken up again, and not put back until the same time next year.

The largest tunny nets in the western basin of the Mediterranean, where tunny fishing has been practised for centuries, are found mostly in Sicily, Tunisia, and the south of Sardinia. During the greater part of the year, in all these districts, hardly a single specimen of this species is to be seen, and that very occasionally. Then, suddenly, at the end of May, they arrive in a host, all swimming along the coast in the same direction, and it is then that they are caught in the nets that have been put ready for them. At the beginning of July, just as suddenly, they disappear and are seen no more. They can be followed on this retreat which is made in the opposite direction to that in which they came. Indeed nets are specially set out to catch them on it; then they disappear, and there is no more sign of the fish until spring next year. Names have been given to them according to whether they are coming or returning.

The fact that the fish is regularly present or absent at definite fixed periods, and that it is always found in certain places, going in the same direction, from west to east on the way out and from east to west on the return, has long made the fishermen believe that this was a case of migration. Connecting their observations in the western Mediterranean with other observations in the eastern Mediterranean, and beyond the Straits of Gibraltar, they concluded that the tunny came from the Atlantic Ocean. There, they thought, it lived most of the time, penetrating, by the Straits of Gibraltar, into the Mediterranean to spawn, passing through that sea from end to end, from west to east, returning to its true home, the ocean, as soon as the spawning was done. This is a very old idea, which has been accepted generally without much change since Aristotle.

When I began my studies of the complicated migration of the salmon between the sea and the rivers, I wished, for the sake of logical comparison, to find a counterpart to this in other migrations equally important but strictly confined to the sea. I chose the tunny for this comparison, because the journeys made by this fish seemed to me to be as extensive as those of the salmon, though confined to the sea, since they were supposed to begin in the Atlantic Ocean and to end east of the Mediterranean, even in the Black Sea, afterwards returning to the place whence they set out. I had my choice of three districts frequented by these migratory tunnies and furnished with tunny nets, the Gulf of Cadiz beyond the Straits of Gibraltar; the western basin of the Mediterranean; and the eastern basin. I chose the western basin because it was easier to get at, and because the species is more regular in its attendance there, both coming and returning.

As usual, I began by visiting the place I had chosen, prospecting for suitable regions in which to make my researches, and I realized at once that the imagined return to the Atlantic was only a myth. As the learned Italian ichthyologist Pavesi had already declared, the Western Mediterranean basin does not lose its tunny. It has, in fact, a definite autochthonous population of tunny fish, which gives every appearance of permanence. The old migratory theory had been made for those districts where the tunny

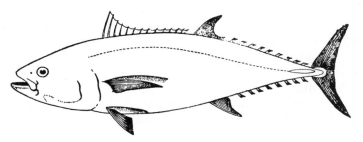

FIG. 30.—THE TUNNY
The common or red Tunny (*Thunnus thynnus*, Linnæus).

nets are used; it took no account of the places which the fish constantly frequents.

The western basin of the Mediterranean is shaped like an irregular quadrilateral. Its northern side, the smallest, is formed by the shores of France and Liguria; its southern side, the longest, by the shore of Northern Africa; its eastern side by the Italian coast, and its west by that of Spain. The upper eastern angle is formed by the Gulf of Genoa; the western by the Gulf of Lions; the lower, eastern one by the broad channel, across which is Sicily, giving access to the other Mediterranean basin. As for the lower western angle, it takes the form of a corridor between Spain and Northern Africa, which becomes progressively narrower until it ends in the Straits of Gibraltar.

But this is no more than the outward, superficial aspect of the basin; it gives us only the topography of its shores.

We must also take into account the hydrography, the disposition of the masses of sea-water it contains. This basin, taken as a whole, forms a vast, deep tank, whose bottom, for the most part, is from nine to twelve thousand feet below the surface. This tank, almost all round, is framed by steep shores which, coming straight up from the bottom to the hills bordering the coast, leave only a very narrow band for the continental shelf. The islands, large and small, Corsica, Sardinia, Sicily, and the Balearic Islands, planted directly upon the deep bottom, are surrounded by tremendous submarine abysses. The lofty summits of their mountains reproduce in relief what the sea surrounding them has in reverse. There are only a few places with broad shallows gently sloping upwards to the coast, for example, in the corridor which gives access to the eastern Mediterranean basin, in the Gulf of Lions, and in a very small number of other places. Everywhere else, the beautiful great blue lake which is so famous, so justly admired, hides, beneath the wonderful surface in which the marvellous bright blue sky is reflected, dark valleys carved out in the depths. As they sail along in the radiant light, the feluccas laden with oranges, the picturesque coasting vessels with their white sails, the liners on their way to the Far East, have dark abysses thousands and thousands of fathoms beneath their keels.

There are several peculiar features about the waters contained in this great reservoir. Apart from those which go down to about three hundred feet below the surface, which undergo variations of temperature according to the season and the weather, they are all uniformly and moderately warm: their temperature remains stationary somewhere between thirteen and fourteen degrees Centigrade. The water of the surface becomes colder in winter and warmer in summer, but in relation to the whole mass, it is like a tiny skin of variable temperature which covers the deep water whose temperature is constant. Consequently it is always subject to the influence of this deeper water. Besides, a part of this deep warm water moves slowly all the time, for there is a regular circulation in the reservoir which affects continually some part of the enormous mass of water which fills it.

The Mediterranean Sea, enclosed between lands which

are temperate and warm, is continually evaporating. It loses more water than its rivers bring down to it, in spite of the considerable volume of some of them. This deficit is made up by the Atlantic Ocean, which sends into it, through the Straits of Gibraltar, a current which moves along the surface, passing along the coast of Algeria and gradually mixing with the rest of the water. But the ocean, when it gives its satellite sea the water it needs to maintain its level, supplies more than is necessary. Consequently, so as to keep the balance, the Mediterranean returns to the ocean the equivalent of this excess. Under the surface current of the Straits of Gibraltar there is a deeper current, going in the reverse direction and carrying off the superfluous water. The former has a temperature varying according to the time of year, and its salinity, that of the Atlantic, is always somewhere between thirty-four and thirty-five grammes of chlorides per litre. The latter is always the same temperature as the depths of the Mediterranean, between thirteen and fourteen degrees, and its salinity goes up to thirty-seven and thirty-eight grammes per litre, the waters of the Mediterranean being more concentrated than those of the ocean.

It is not the tunny, but sea-water which comes through the straits and returns after having made the tour of the Mediterranean. The theory that goes back all the way to Aristotle has credited the tunny with what should be attributed to the currents. The water comes from the Atlantic and finds its way as far as the eastern Mediterranean basin, becoming more and more diluted as it crosses the western basin. It is warmed somewhere between Egypt, Asia Minor, and Greece, then as a warmer, more concentrated current goes back whence it came. Carrying with it a part of the deep waters as it returns to the western basin, this current begins by extending over the shallows between Sicily and Tunisia. From there, dividing up into sheets, it makes its way from south to north between Sardinia and Italy, from the south-west to the north-west near the coasts of Liguria, Provence, and Catalonia, then turns back on itself to go south-west and down to the Straits of Gibraltar. There, striking against the tremendous submarine cliff which, at a great depth, bars the entrance to the Straits, it rises, forms whirlpools which mingle with the new water coming in, and finally empties itself in the Atlantic. So we have an elaborate circulatory system of different waters, subdivided in mass by secondary gyrations, by mixing and remixing with the surface waters which are sometimes warmer, sometimes colder, according to climate and season, by movements towards the coast or away from it towards the open sea according to the direction of the winds. So this great current fills the Mediterranean, stirs its waters, continually renews it, and controlling it, contributes its best known qualities.

The tunnies live in this returning current. Their domain is not topographical but hydrographical. They remain in its waters and follow them, going with them wherever they go. This vast environment is in keeping with their size and profusion. Stenothermic and stenohaline, they only frequent waters which have at least thirteen or fourteen degrees of temperature; they never go into others, whether they are cooled on the surface by the rigour of the seasons, or diluted near the coast by fresh water from the rivers. Living by choice in the open sea, they only approach the coast when the weather is calm and relatively warm. Since they are strong and rapid swimmers, distance matters little to them, and so does depth; they move swiftly about their domain in every direction. Savage and predatory, they give chase ceaselessly to the smaller fishes, mackerel, sardines, anchovies and many others, which live in the same waters as themselves. In this domain which extends in depth as well as in area, they are the wolves, the foxes of the steppes and forests, only more in number and swifter in movement. They display the same supremacy in gluttony, though upon a greater scale, and only yield the palm to the sharks which are even more powerful than themselves.

The tunnies of the western basin of the Mediterranean never leave it; they make their home there and live there all the time. They are caught all the year round. Several fishing ports on the Provençal coast, Carro near Marseilles and Grau-du-Roi south of Nîmes, specialize in them. The sailors must be fearless, not afraid to go out to sea on stormy nights to reach those they seek to catch. They use a strong

net with broad meshes, the " courantille," which they attach
to their boat like a long vertical lattice-work barrier, supple
and floating, and trail it for hours through the night until
day breaks.   The tunnies are so numerous, so frequent in
these waters which they like, that this net, despite its
comparative smallness and weakness, almost always succeeds
in catching, enmeshing, and surrounding them.   The
fishermen, when they haul in their net, often find in its
folds one of those huge creatures, upon whose capture their
livelihood depends.   In an average year, the Gulf of Lions
often furnishes some thousands of fish, weighing all together
about four hundred tons.

II. The " courantille," however, is not used continuously.
It is discontinued every year at definite dates, somewhere
between April and the beginning of August.   This is
because several strange phenomena are to be observed in
the behaviour of the fish.   There are no more signs of a
wandering life, devoted to the satisfaction of a never-sated
appetite.   Another life begins, given up to spawning and the
production of young.   The genetic life begins, then develops,
compelling the individuals, as we have noticed in other
cases, by exaggerating their normal sensitivity, to adopt
habits quite unlike those to which they have become
accustomed.

In April and until the middle of May, a strange sight
may be observed in certain particular places off the coast of
Provence, where the tunny are usually to be found; this is
the gathering of hundreds and thousands of these fishes.
They need shallow water, a calm sea, and a fairly high
temperature.   These qualities they find near the shore, in
certain favourable places to which they return year after
year.   There they gather in considerable numbers, listless;
they have lost their customary ardour and stay without
moving for hours, sometimes for days.   The fishermen are
waiting for them and watch them come.   They have given
up the " courantille " and adopted another device called the
" sinche ", which consists of surrounding these shoals by
walls of nets hastily put out, and pulling them in to the
shore where they can be taken more easily.   Certain
" sinches " in this way capture at a single time as many as
two or three thousand fish.   The way they are unloaded

in a mass and the piles in which they are heaped up on the sands before they are sold and carried away produce an extraordinary impression. Beside the heaps of great inert bodies, spread out and heaped up, the fishermen who have caught them look like busy pygmies, like ants working beside a heap of wheat.

The fish, when they are cut up at this period, show signs of a new status. Often their stomachs are empty, like those of the salmon and the shad, which also lose their appetite during the reproductive period; like them, the tunnies eat either not at all or very little. Again, like the salmon and the shad, their sexual glands are large, voluminous, and richly supplied with blood. All this has a definite significance. These tunnies, preparing to bring forth young, have reached the period of sexual elaboration. All through the winter, for several months, my dissections have shown me the successive stages in the progress of this development. As it approaches its end, in the first half of spring, the genetic life becomes more definite. The tunnies, formerly scattered or grouped in small predatory bands, gather in large numbers, both sexes coming together in these larger bands. When it is getting ready to spawn the species becomes gregarious even to the point of concentration.

About the middle of May, when these preparations are reaching their completion, there is a second strange phenomenon. The tunnies vanish from the coast of Provence and are seen no more there. The bands they formed cease to frequent the regions in which they have hitherto lived; and the fishing season comes to an end, for, from the experience of centuries, the fishermen know that neither their " courantilles " nor their " sinches " would be of any use if they were put out. The disappearance is absolute. These numerous hosts have gone quite suddenly. Yet, at this season of the year, the mackerel, the sardines abound, all the prey of which the tunnies are so fond. They have a happy release from their habitual enemies.

This complete disappearance lasts from two months to two months and a half; then we have the third phenomenon, the reappearance of the tunnies. This occurs during the second half of July or the first few days of August. Then the fishermen bring out their "courantilles" with the certainty that they will use them to advantage. The fish return, not in a body as they went away, but separately. They appear either singly or in little groups and resume their accustomed habits. Keener than ever, they hunt down their prey without mercy. They have ceased to be genetic and have taken up again their wandering life; they no longer concern themselves about reproduction; the only thing that matters to them is the pursuit of food, and to this they devote themselves entirely.

These returning fish, when dissected, display sexual glands that are small and empty in males and females alike. When they went away, their testicles and ovaries were swollen, on the point of maturity; when they return the glands are empty. They must have spawned in the meantime, and the place in which they have spawned is not that in which they customarily live, or in which they have come together. Somewhere there is a spawning place to which they go and from which they have now returned. They disappear only to reappear when the act of spawning is accomplished.

Now, shortly after their flight from the localities in which they usually feed, late in May or early in June, the tunnies suddenly make their appearance in the waters of Sardinia, Sicily, Tunisia, where the tunny nets are waiting ready for them. Until then the species was rare in those parts; now it becomes abundant. The fish who thus appear have large and swollen sexual glands, like those which, a few days before, were gathering together and forming bands. We must conclude that they are the same fish. Still together, they have left their former haunts and gone to others where their reproductive elaboration becomes complete and ends with the fertilization of the spawn in the open sea. The maturation becomes complete during June, and then the spawning takes place. Then the tunnies, having fulfilled their genetic function and become what they were before, separate and disperse, filling anew the whole area of their domain. They have ceased to be the tunnies on the way out; when they again assume their wandering habits they have become tunnies on the way back.

It may be objected that the fish which come to the spawning place are not necessarily or always the same as those which set out from some other place. The facts speak for themselves. When we consider and compare them, the connection is indisputable. After a delay long enough to be accounted for by the journey in question the appearance of one set of fish corresponds to the disappearance of the other and, inversely, when these appear the others disappear, after a similar delay. The tunnies are fish which swim strongly and swiftly. Always active, never still, incessantly on the move, what is the journey from Provence or Liguria to Sicily and Tunisia? Two or three days at the most, at a moderate speed, are enough for such a journey. Since, in their habitual state, they move about all over the western Mediterranean basin, continually in search of food, coming, going, diving, what is such a journey to them? It in no way places a strain upon them, it is but a part of the cycle which they are continually making.

Besides, the tunnies of the northern part of the basin are certainly not the only ones to swim like this to the spawning places. With them come others from other parts, both on the surface and in the depths. Things always take the same course, and the fish always behave in the same way. Arriving from every direction, they all make for the south-eastern angle of the basin and stay in the waters of this spawning area until they have spawned, when they immediately leave it.

Two questions call for an answer with regard to this choice of a spawning place and the rush towards it. Why do the tunnies not spawn where they are, in their customary habitat? And why are they constrained to make this journey which is concerned with spawning and nothing else? We must again let the facts answer for themselves. This region, bordered by Sardinia, Sicily, Tunisia and Tripoli, has under its waters a vast submarine plain from which rise islands and reefs. This submerged plateau dominates the great abysses of the two Mediterranean basins, eastern and western. Over it, hundreds of feet below the surface, sometimes very much less, the sheets of returning water continually pass, leaving the eastern basin and entering the other. These waters retain their qualities both of temperature and salinity. And the tunnies, accustomed to these waters since they are their normal environment, go to those places where they are purest and most perfect, there to accomplish the supreme action of their lives, reproduction. They do precisely what the salmon do, when with the same end in view, they undertake a still more difficult journey and go back to the mountain torrents.

To understand this behaviour we must compare it with that of the other fishes which make these considerable journeys, the salmon, sturgeon, and shad. In each case, there is one indispensable condition which determines whether the

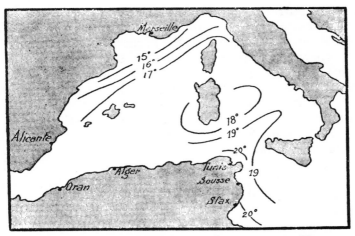

FIG. 31.—ISOTHERMS OF THE WEDDING JOURNEY OF THE TUNNY

Map showing the customary distribution of isotherms (the figures give the degrees Centigrade) in the surface waters of the western basin of the Mediterranean, at the times when the tunnies make their wedding journey.

journey shall be undertaken or not, the preparation and completion of the act of reproduction. The individual fish, when it becomes genetic and elaborates its future germs, becomes different from what it was. Hypersensitive, it reacts to impressions which hardly produced an effect before, if any at all. It is polarized. The tunnies are no exception to the rule. Their sexual elaboration calls for a work of assimilation greater than that necessitated hitherto. This work, in turn, calls for a greater contribution from the environment; it takes more from that environment. Like the shad, the tunny needs heat; it must be provided with a greater number of calories. Drawn to those places where this heat is, polarized thermically like the shad, the fish move automatically, progressively, towards those zones where they find it, and so come to their spawning place, which has a maximum of heat at the time at which they spawn.

In that period of the year in which they travel, late in May or early in June, the surface water, near the coasts of Provence and Liguria, seldom goes above fourteen or fifteen degrees Centigrade. But, going in the direction of the spawning grounds, from which the warm waters of the returning current proceed, the temperature increases, reaching sixteen, seventeen, eighteen, twenty degrees and even more as the season advances, the highest point being reached in the spawning zone itself. The tunnies go to this favourable water as the shad go to the favourable water of their streams. They, too, go against the current, pushing farther and farther in the desired direction and meeting water that is always warmer as they proceed. As their sexual elaboration progresses, they feel a greater sense of well-being which directs them and leads them farther. Their journey is governed and controlled as they go to the spawning place like that of the shad between the banks of their rivers. Less definitely limited, it takes a course of its own, and the fish is obliged to observe this religiously, and so to produce the young that are being made ready within its body.

It is, therefore, a real wedding journey which the tunnies take. Since heat is necessary to their sexual maturity and their spawning, they go where they are best able to secure it. Seasonal fish, they make the most of the season and what it has to offer them. One year is not always like the last. Sometimes climatic conditions are propitious, sometimes the reverse. The journey becomes more difficult, sexual elaboration is not so easily attained, and the fishermen are satisfied or disappointed accordingly. The rhythm of such vicissitudes extends over cycles of years.

The old theory of migration was unable to explain these alternations which result from the very arrangement of this wedding journey. The places where the nets are set, those huge appliances which aim at catching the tunnies when they are making this very journey, are fixed in advance; they cannot be anywhere else. Set up at various, obvious places in favourable waters, arranged according to the prevailing direction of the current, and not far from a coast which can hold them longer, each occupies the position proper to it. And if these waters change in composition, as may happen as the result of alterations in the bottom or to the coast, the tunny nets are affected too, and do not produce their customary harvest.

Speaking generally, the Mediterranean tunnies are self-sufficient; they do not need to borrow from their brothers in the Atlantic. These behave in the same way. Their spawning places are near the coast of Andalusia and Algarve, and there they gather at the favourable time, which is not very different from that of the Mediterranean, although it is not always the same. When they have spawned they return to the ocean without passing through the Straits of Gibraltar. A few stragglers may occasionally cross the barrier. Occasionally too, secondary spawning places may be discovered in certain places. But these are exceptions. In the Western Mediterranean, the realm of the tunnies, they find all they need for their nutritive and reproductive lives alike. Their domain is self-contained.

CHAPTER XIII

A PIECE OF DRIED COD

CERTAIN creatures and objects may be taken as representative of their kind. Not that they are any better or worse than their neighbours in the same category, but they exhibit in an enhanced degree the traits which are characteristic of all. By making them more apparent, they bring them more closely to our notice. And this may be said of the cod, which we may take as representative of the fish which are preserved and used as food.

Everybody knows the smooth, hard, compact flesh, covered with a salty efflorescence, reminding us of the pungent smell of the sea. Triangular in shape, with a shrivelled fin on top, one side is of a yellowish white, the other covered with grey skin. This is the dried cod, salted, sent in bales all over the world, sold everywhere either as a whole or in pieces. No other preserved fish is so well known, so universally sold, so easily served up, or so frequently eaten.

But this dried cod was once fresh cod. Before it was dried and salted it had to be caught, decapitated, opened and cleaned, then spread out and impregnated with salt. It was a fish that went its way as fishes usually do, moving hither and thither in the sea hunting down its prey and satisfying its vital needs. It came into existence as a tiny egg, a minute floating sphere, hardly a millimetre and a half in diameter, lost in the immensity of the sea with millions upon millions like itself. Then it was hatched and became fry swimming about. It grew very rapidly, measuring between ten and twelve inches in length when it was a year old, and between seventeen and twenty inches after two years. It then weighed about two pounds. Its capacity for growth allows it to become still larger, and when circumstances are favourable, it may grow to be a very big fish indeed. Giant cod have been caught more than five feet long, weighing from a hundred and twenty to a hundred and sixty pounds.

The cod (*Gadus callarias* and *Gadus morrhua*, Linnæus) is an oceanic fish that lives in cold waters. It inhabits the

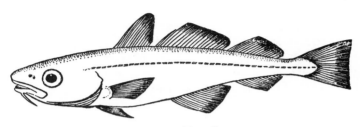

FIG. 32.—THE COD

The Cod (*Gadus morrhua*, Linnæus and *Gadus callarias*, Linnæus).
Family *Gadidæ*, order *Anacanthini*.

northern regions of the Atlantic and swarms there. It seldom goes down so far south as the English Channel. It belongs to the family *Gadidæ*, which is even more important than those of the *Clupeidæ* and *Scombridæ* and quite as varied and rich in abundant and diverse species. This family, with its satellite groups, forms an autonomous section, clearly delimited, among fishes. It may be recognized by the fulness and extension of its fins, which are

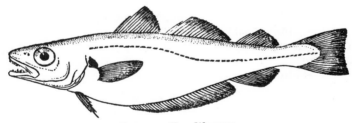

FIG. 33.—THE WHITING

The common Whiting (*Merlangus merlangus*, Linnæus) ; family *Gadidæ*.

supported by flexible, not spiny, rays; by its full caudal fin, which is stretched out fanwise; its relatively large belly, which appears to be somewhat swollen. Unlike the majority of the *Clupeidæ* and *Scombridæ*, the *Gadidæ* are hardly open water or surface water fishes. They prefer the neighbourhood of the bottom, where they stay for considerable periods, and where they seek their prey. They are greedy and voracious, and eat up everything they come across, molluscs, crustaceans, fish smaller than themselves. These habits explain the methods used to catch them, appliances which are able to operate either on the bottom itself or near it, standing lines and drag-nets.

The cod belongs to the genus *Gadus*, which has given its name to the family, and is characterized by the possession of a truly excessive number of unsymmetrical fins. It has three dorsal fins, one behind the other on its back, and two anal fins beneath its belly. Further, and this is its distinguishing feature, the fish of this genus have a fairly full barbel beneath the chin, near its point. The presence of this appendix distinguishes the cod and its neighbouring species from the fish belonging to a very similar genus, the whiting (genus *Merlangus*), which also has three dorsal and two anal fins and in general appearance very much resembles the cod, though it has no barbel under the chin and consequently exhibits a certain difference in structure. The whiting are halfway between the cod and other *Gadidæ* like the hake (genus *Merlucius*), which also have no barbel and are remarkable for their more tapering bodies and less obtrusive bellies, for the fact that they have only two dorsals and one aral, and a general conformation showing a connection with other *Gadidæ* still more remote, which are almost cylindrical in shape, among which are the rocklings of our coasts and the loaches of our rivers. This rapid sketch of the principal representatives of the family gives us an idea of their diversity. Further, we only have to name them to make clear their economic importance. They are in the first rank of the sea fishes which we eat and enjoy. And first and foremost among them is the cod.

It is often assumed to be a migratory fish which appears suddenly and disappears equally suddenly, a fact which, it has been said, can only be explained by migration on a large scale. Actually, however, it is a seasonal fish which reproduces very freely. It has something of the nature of the herring and the tunny. It reminds us of the first by its abundance and its fondness for living in cold waters, but it surpasses it in size and in its predatory capacity for attacking prey of a large size. It resembles the second in its ability to travel long distances in shoals, as the needs of alimentation and of reproduction require.

Dispersed in almost incredibly great numbers throughout the vast extent of their abode, the cod readily assemble in those parts of the sea where conditions are most favourable, either when prey is more easily available, or when they are due to spawn. Appearances and disappearances of this sort, which mean arrivals and departures, have nothing in common with the regular journeys which a genuine migration would entail; they are simply occasional reunions, connected with certain places only and confined to certain fish, moving and changing, with no other purpose than the satisfaction of vital needs. But, none the less, the individuals

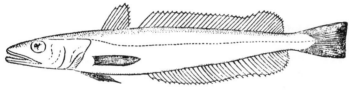

FIG. 34.—THE HAKE
The Hake (*Merlucius merlucius*, Linnæus); Cod family.

which take part in them may be counted sometimes by hundreds of thousands. Composed of powerful, great fishes, most of which weigh many pounds, there is nothing in our life upon land, with its more definite bounds and limitations, capable of giving us any idea of this great assembly hidden beneath the surface of the seas.

Like the tunny and other seasonal fishes, the cod is sometimes nomadic, sometimes generative. When it is generative, which is once every year, it seeks water that is favourable to it, and goes there to spawn. At other times it goes off by itself to the bottom which seems most favourable from the point of view of nourishment, and gathers in greater numbers in those parts which are richest in this respect, ready to move elsewhere as soon as the provender becomes exhausted or is less easily accessible. It frequents especially moderate depths, between a hundred and fifty and three hundred feet, though it is able to exceed this limit when the pursuit of food makes such a course desirable.

It is abundant, therefore, on the submarine shelves where it finds, at one and the same time, the depth it prefers and the wealth of food which its large appetite desires. The shoals of Newfoundland have been famous for many

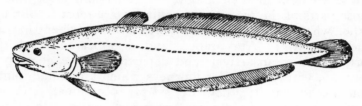

FIG. 35.—THE LOACH
The Loach (*Lota lota,* Linnæus); Cod family.

centuries. A vast population of cod settles there when spawning is over to exploit the ample nutritive resources; and fishermen settle there, in their turn, to exploit this population and turn it to their own advantage. The different changes of fortune to which the fisheries are subject depend upon the changes of fortune which the fish themselves experience in their exploitation of the creatures on which they feed. The fishermen have to take these into account. The cod easily changes its place and its level according to the prey it is after; and that prey seeks the waters whose temperature it finds most pleasant.

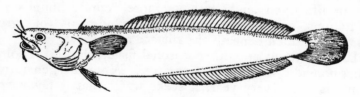

FIG. 36.—THE BURBOT
The Burbot (*Motella mustella,* Linnæus); Cod family.

The cod becomes generative in winter; it usually spawns between January and March. The sexual elaboration and the development of the sexual glands, which assume considerable size, make the fish behave in a manner comparable to that of the tunny. There is a gathering in large bands of both sexes, which proceed together to the maturation which ends in spawning; there is the same search for the favourable water in which are found the calories necessary to that maturation. The generative cod, like the tunny and the shad, needs heat; it becomes thermophile. But, in its case, circumstances are different. The tunny lives in warm and temperate waters, the temperature of which never falls below twelve to thirteen degrees Centigrade. As they spawn in the summer, in order to secure supplementary calories their sexual elaboration polarizes them towards waters that are still warmer, reaching twenty or even more degrees. The cod, on the other hand, is a cold water fish, whose vitality is normally satisfied by a much lower thermality, about zero. The additional calories it needs can

FIG. 37.—THE FEMALE CAPELIN

The Capelin (*Mallotus villosus*, Cuvier, female), family *Salmonidæ*, order *Clupeiformes*. The fish of this species, as large as sardines, abound near Newfoundland, and are hunted by the cod, who eat them. The cod fishermen use them for bait.

be found in fairly low zones of temperature, although above zero. So the cod go and spawn in regions where they find a water at about four to six degrees, water which is favourable from their point of view and sufficiently warm for their purposes, though it feels cold to us.

This favourable water is to be found in midwinter in several parts of the seas in which the cod live. The Arctic Ocean, where it unites with the Atlantic Ocean, has a certain number of islands and shallows which have been raised above the great depths. The Atlantic sends them its relatively warm expanses of water and, from the opposite direction, the Arctic Ocean sends them expanses of almost frozen water. The shallows act as mixing places. Over them, mingling and super-imposing at various levels, pass waters of different temperatures, some at zero, others not quite so cold. The shape of the bottom brings the majority of the latter to a standstill about a few ledges situated not very far below the surface around such convenient regions as the north of Norway and the Lofoten Islands, Iceland and the States of Connecticut and Maine in the United

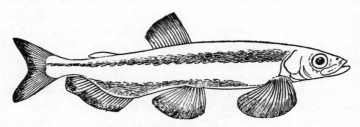

FIG. 38.—THE MALE CAPELIN

The Capelin (*Mallotus villosus*, Cuvier, male). In this species the males differ from the females (see illus. on p. 177) by having larger fins and, along their sides, scales drawn out into hair-like filaments.

States. When autumn comes, the generative cod make for these places in a body. They come there from all directions, complete the process of sexual maturation there, spawn there in the open water; and, when they have finished reproducing themselves, go back to the pursuit of prey, and so to the shoals.

The fishermen take these activities as their guide. In winter they try to catch the cod when it is generative and, in

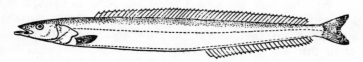

FIG. 39.—THE SAND-EEL

The Sand-eel (*Ammodytes tobianus*, Cuvier-Valenciennes), family *Ammodytedæ*. Fishes of this species abound in the sandy bed of the shoals near Newfoundland where the cod feed upon them.

summer, when it is nomadic. In the first case, they go to the spawning places; in the second, to the shoals where the cod feed so well. The fishing is seasonal, like the fish it endeavours to secure, and has a cycle of its own, with definite features and dangers. It is a deep-sea fishing, and the sea is often rough and difficult. It demands from those who practise it the endurance and experience of perfect sailors. They must be able not only to fish, but to navigate.

When we think of the changes of fortune of cod fisheries, we usually take into account only those incidental features which strike the eye and the imagination; the scenes of embarkation, the losses of boats in the fog, the battling against waves and currents. But these are only momentary episodes, important doubtless, joyful or painful like everything that is human, but only a part of a continuous whole. It is this whole which we must consider if we would know the fishermen's career as it really is, with its uninterrupted labours, its never-ceasing hardships. The fishermen, on board their small vessels, have to handle their tackle with the temperature about freezing, in rain and fog, sometimes a fog which blots out everything for weeks and months at a time. They themselves cut up the fish they catch, and prepare it on boats tossed about by the waves, in narrow, stinking holes and corners. As soon as they have finished one job, they must get ready for another, and the rest they do get is often broken. Yet even this harassing, hard life has its

FIG. 40.—THE WHELK

Shell of the Whelk (genus *Buccinum*). A gastropod common on the sea-shore, used as bait by the cod fishermen.

devotees, so strong is the passion for the sea in those of whom it takes possession that it brushes aside all considerations of hardship. Excluding all else, penetrating, burying its spur in the soul, it implants itself there for ever.

Of all the foodstuffs known to us, fish gives the greatest trouble, the maximum of labour, and the most danger, to secure. Bread reminds us of the delightful vision of fields at harvest time; meat and game, of scenes agreeable enough if we forget the final scene at the slaughter house. We think of meadows, of stables, and dairies. Though game suggests slaughter, massacre, and sometimes battle, all these things happen in the country, on dry land, and the hunter is seldom in any great danger. But fishing is a very different matter. The dangers of navigation cannot always be avoided. A piece of dried cod may have cost a human life,

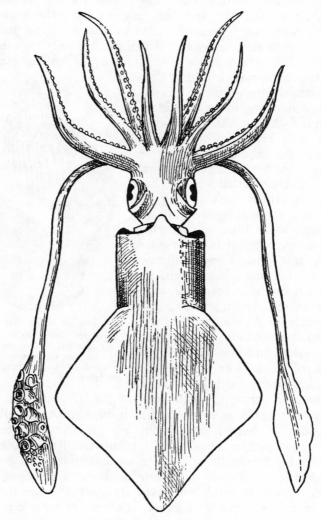

FIG. 41.—THE SQUID

The common Squid (genus *Loligo*). This name is usually given to all the Cephalopod Molluscs, which are open-sea animals, and belong to several genera. Those which the Newfoundland cod feed upon—the fishermen use them for bait—belong to the genus *Onychotenthis*.

and, in any case, has only been secured at the cost of painful and dangerous labour.

This salted and dried cod, although it was caught in the north, is eaten mainly by those who live in warm countries. The principal trade in it is carried on in Southern Europe, Africa, and South America. Its flesh, which is easy to keep and to prepare, is very little affected by these climates. It can be cooked in all sorts of ways, and, like eggs and potatoes, it has the great advantage of being able to be served in more than a hundred different forms. Like wheat and rice, it is an international article of diet; it is found all over the world. In many places the sailor, the farm labourer, make their morning meal of a piece of bread and a little grilled cod, made more tasty by a still more piquant condiment, onion or garlic. Besides, it goes with every kind of sauce, it can be garnished in all kinds of ways and, when fresh meat is scarce, it is an excellent substitute. It is even used for especially delicate dishes, such as the delightfully savoury " brandade ", a succulent emulsion of fine olive oil and mashed cod. It is one of the world's greatest foodstuffs, and is found in more places than almost any other.

So the cod becomes a symbol; a symbol of the utilization by mankind of the nutritive resources of the sea. No other species surpasses it, not even the herring. Vastly abundant and extremely prolific, it maintains its numbers in spite of all the fish that are caught and destroyed. On an average, the total production of the cod fisheries reaches nearly five hundred thousand tons every year, which is equivalent to saying between two and three hundred million fish.

But what are these in comparison with those vast hosts which escape the fishermen and ensure the continuance of their kind, scattering with lavish hand the manna we expect each year? Each female lays several millions of eggs. If we multiply these millions by those of the individuals scattered about in the immensity of the waters, we reach formidable figures—trillions, quadrillions, quintillions—till we lose ourselves in them. It is a manifestation of the boundless power of Nature, which is able to bring such vast numbers into existence and to maintain them.

CHAPTER XIV

THE PASSING OF THE GOLDEN PERCH

I. In late summer and early autumn, usually in September but occasionally in October, the Canal de Sète and all the region round about it becomes at certain moments the scene of a strange, intense animation. Besides all the movement that customarily goes on upon and around it, the boats passing through, the clatter of barrels being rolled over the stone flags of its quays, there are other signs of great activity. The paved jetties, the piles, are dotted with fishermen in considerable numbers, all tremendously eager, throwing their lines into the water, bringing them out again quickly, and throwing them in once more. Other fishermen in little boats are doing the same thing in the middle of the canal. They are all as busy as busy can be. The reason for it is a passing of the golden perch, and these fishermen, hoping to take full advantage of this short-lived opportunity, are trying to get one of these delightful fishes upon their hooks.

When autumn approaches, the golden perch go to the sea to spawn. Until then, they have been living in the pool of Thau, where they spend their life of growth. When they are pubescent, they begin their sexual elaboration in the waters of the pool but, usually, do not complete it there. They need the sea not only to spawn in, but for the final stages of their maturation and, in order to reach it, they take the canal which goes there directly, passing through the town of Sète. Quite frequently they journey in shoals. Their number, which is sometimes considerable, and the relative narrowness of the channel through which they have to pass, make them more accessible, more vulnerable than at any other time. This is a miniature migration of which the fishermen hasten to take advantage.

The pool of Thau is situated at the head of the Gulf of Lions, from which it is separated by a strip of land. It is

182

a part of a system of lagoons along the shore, which goes almost all round the gulf from the pool of Berre, not far from Marseilles, to the pools in the neighbourhood of Narbonne and Perpignan. Like its neighbours, it forms an enclave of the sea with which it communicates only by the Canal de Sète, which is little more than a mile in length and was enlarged and improved by man about the end of the seventeenth century. Its waters are salt. The animals, algæ and marine plants which live in it are like those of the neighbouring coast, but there are a great number of different species which, more sheltered in its restricted area, increase and multiply very freely. It covers about 18,600 acres. Its depth, which is nowhere very great, is seldom more than thirty feet. In summer, the bottom is covered with a luxuriant vegetation of algæ and zosteræ, which is inhabited by a host of varied and abundant little creatures.

This pool and its neighbours are like little inland seas with a miniature hydrography of their own, with little brooks taking the place of rivers. Since it offers to the living creatures of the coast a refuge where they find both shelter and the food they need so much, these creatures flourish there, and they include the fishes usually found in lagoons and estuaries, golden perch, bass, mullet, and eels. The pool of Thau near the Gulf of Lions thus reminds us of what I have said elsewhere of the Bibans Lake, at the end of the Gulf of Gabes. Both are places of asylum for certain fishes, which are safe in them and comfortably settled.

A miniature sea, localized and almost fully enclosed, the pool behaves like the great sea its neighbour, but with certain differences. Since the volume of its waters is much more restricted and its depth less, it is very sensitive to the variations of the seasons; it cools more quickly in winter and gets warmer in summer. Its temperature is often different from that of the Gulf of which it is a dependency. Its content of chloride salts varies considerably, being less at the surface than near the bottom. But these differences are not so great as they might be, thanks to the permanent communication between the sea and the pool through the canal. Not only do the waters of both come into contact and intermingle; but currents form in two opposing directions which sometimes carry the sea water to the pool and sometimes the water of the pool to the sea. These currents go through the whole canal and its dependencies, carrying along with them multitudes of floating animals, especially medusa, and bring an infiltration of sea-water to the pool. Sometimes hardly perceptible, sometimes more vigorous, they succeed each other alternately, one entering the pool, the other leaving it and going to the sea.

All the golden perch have to do is to go along the canal and their journey is over. Isolated specimens are caught in the pool all the year round, but they are caught more easily and in greater numbers when they pass between the banks of the canal. The fishermen who try to catch them are not all amateurs by any means. The professionals are ready enough to take a hand. At different places along the bottom of the canal they set those large winged hoop-nets which they call " ganjoux " with the opening towards the pool end. The fishes, on their way to the sea, strike first against the wings and are then directed towards the opening of the net proper, into which they finally penetrate and so are captured. In some years, in spite of the short time this fishing season lasts, it gives excellent results.

The golden perch enjoys a well merited reputation among connoisseurs, a reputation it had hundreds of years ago with the gourmets of ancient Rome. Its flesh is as exquisite as its appearance is splendid. Its French name, *dorade*, which comes from the Provençal *daurado*, means *golden*, and the Provençal word comes from the Latin *aurata* which has the same meaning. It is a very fair description of the glory of its body when it is just taken from the water. The body has not the elegant proportions which other fish have. It is heavy, bulky, compressed; it has a large head with broad cheeks, with two little round eyes. But it makes up for these defects by a glittering splendour which is seldom found in other fish, from which it gets its scientific name (*Aurata aurata*, Linnæus).

Twenty to forty centimetres long, weighing between one and two pounds, often more, it is a bluish back, shot by shades of all the colours of the rainbow, which gradually merge in the rosy grey of the sides, and the pearly white of the belly.

The sides are traversed in length by narrow bands with

metallic waterings, sometimes golden, sometimes silvery, sometimes bluish, sometimes greenish, but with the gold so predominant that the name given to the fish is justified. Finally, a broad crescent of gold, a real diadem, surrounds the front of the head, crossing the forehead from one eye to the other; and golden plates which are enhanced by a reddish-brown colouring farther back cover the cheeks like the ornaments of a savage chieftainess. The golden perch is really golden. This name, sometimes used in other connections, is better suited to it than to any other fish. The term *Chrysophrys*, meaning " fish with the golden eyebrows ",

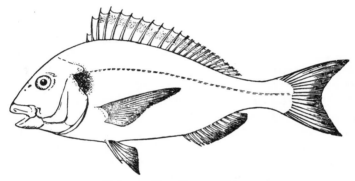

FIG. 42.—THE GOLDEN PERCH
The true golden perch (*Aurata aurata*, Linnæus), family *Sparidæ*, belongs to the order *Perciformes*.

invented for it by Cuvier, and still preferred by many naturalists, also expresses its wealth of adornment and its beauty.

There are, indeed, in the sea and in fresh water, other golden perch and other gold fish. Some of them, like the little red fish which we have in our bowls, and the John Dory with its protractile mouth, are so different from the real golden perch that there is no possibility of confusion. But others, more closely related, bear a closer resemblance. At Paris and in Northern Europe, the name is given to species which, belonging to the same family as the genuine golden perch, and bearing a fairly strong resemblance to it, are distinguished from it, among other ways, by a less striking uniform hue. One of these is the sea-bream

(*Pagellus centrodontus*, Delaroche) which is caught in abundance in the Atlantic Ocean, whose flesh, though it is not so firm, is highly esteemed. The sea-bream is only approximately a golden perch, for there is nothing golden about it and it has neither crescent nor plates on the cheeks, nor glittering sides. Its body is covered nearly all over by a reddish hue, brilliant when it is first taken out of the water, but greyish and leaden later when we see it in the fishmongers' shops. In places where both, the true "dorade" and the false, are exposed for sale, at Sète, Marseilles, and Nice, the sea-bream is called the "Paris dorade," for it is mainly bought by the Paris fishmongers. The real dorade is called the "native dorade."

This "native dorade" is well named. It belongs, in fact, to the Mediterranean and the coasts on both sides of the Straits of Gibraltar. There it frequents the coastal areas, the estuaries, the lagoons, and thus finds its way into many of the salt ponds of the coast, finding there a better subsistence. Its growth in these places is more rapid, for it has a better supply of food. Its thick jaws, with several rows of large triturating teeth, genuine molars, enable it to grind up the hardest of bodies, the calcareous carapaces of crabs and the shells of molluscs. It is especially fond of the cockles which it finds on the bottom, grinding them to pieces between its powerful jaws and enjoying the flesh within them.

One of the pleasant sights to be seen near the pool of Thau is that of the many fishermen of shellfish, in their little flat-bottomed boats, dragging with their hand nets the bottom in which the cockles bury themselves in the sand. The local dialect calls the cockle *Clovisse*. This word, taken directly from the Provençal, means "shut in"; it exactly describes the creature, enclosed in its two-valved shell. The harvest of these shellfish is considerable, and affords the greater part of the livelihood of several hundred homes, through the work of these fishermen. The golden perch are their principal competitors; they are great eaters and also do away with a great many of these famous cockles.

When the golden perch reaches adulthood, it becomes pubescent. This appearance of the power to reproduce is noticeable about the end of the summer season, after the

186

gorging during the hot weather, and is the consequence of an assimilation pushed to the highest degree. As soon as the weather begins to grow cooler, sooner or later according to circumstances, the golden perch, engaged in the process of sexual elaboration, leave the pool to go to the sea. It is now that the fishermen try to catch them on their way. They make the journey in several relays, which means that the fishermen have several opportunities. All the fish caught display voluminous sexual glands in the condition of elaboration. Some, more precocious than the rest and already mature, are already getting rid of their germs.

FIG. 43.—THE SEA-BREAM

The Sea-Bream, or Paris Dorade (*Pagellus centrodontus*, Delaroche), family *Sparidæ*, belongs to the order *Perciformes*.

Their movement from the waters of the pool to those of the sea is, as our observation goes to show, connected with their sexual condition: it is really a wedding journey.

Although the journey is a short one, it is subject to a number of possible vicissitudes. Sometimes earlier, some-times later, sometimes succeeding one another at short intervals, sometimes with a considerable period between them, these journeys offer a considerable diversity. Some are abundant, others scanty. Some are soon accomplished; some seem half-hearted. Certain winds seem to favour them, either when they blow, or in the period of calm which follows them; others appear to be unfavourable. Yet, despite all these various possibilities, one thing is clear; there is always some way of catching them.

II. I have spent some time in studying the habits of these fishes, not only that I might get to know all about the golden perch themselves, but also that I might find out something about the general phenomenon of the migration of those fishes which go to spawn in the sea. If this phenomenon, as in the case of the golden perch, is of slight intensity, on the other hand it may reach an extraordinary fullness, as in the case of the eels. The golden perch, whose behaviour is less complex, more readily ascertainable, less affected by extraneous circumstances, are able to reveal to us what is essential and of primary importance in this migration. Like those seemingly unimportant facts which throw light upon man's character, without his knowing that they do so, by watching the behaviour of the golden perch on their way to the sea we may discover things about them which would otherwise escape our attention.

The first point to note, in this respect, is that these fishes, before they leave for the sea, must come into direct contact with water coming from that sea. They must feel in the pool in which they are still living, the direct action of the sea water which reaches them by the entering current, before they will consent to move, to enter that current and go against it so as, by degrees, to come to the place from which it comes to them, that is, the sea. The golden perch, as they go through the canal from the pool to the sea, go against the current, reach first the canal, and then the sea.

This inverse relation between the current of water entering and the journey of the fish leaving, is constant and complete. The latter is only a function of the former. Nothing happens when the currents carry out the water from the pool. The golden perch would only have to let themselves go with it, to let themselves be carried along, but not a single one of them moves. The excitation brought by the entering current is essential to them, and as soon as they feel it, they begin their journey and carry it through to the end. They hear a summons in this new water, and they obey it. As the salmon and the shad in the sea hear the call of the rivers, so the golden perch in their pools hear that of the sea. The sea must come to them before they decide to go to it. They wait until they feel its immediate action before they conform with the condition it imposes on them. Their migration is strictly determined from without by the action of the external medium.

We can understand the luck of the fishermen when we realize this force. If the currents of the Canal de Sète, both those that enter and those that leave, essentially depend upon variations in the levels of the tides, these being very slight in the Gulf of Lions, several other influences, barometric pressure, the direction and force of the winds, also affect them and often modify them to a considerable extent. Sometimes they are regular in their succession, sometimes irregular; sometimes abundant and rapid, sometimes feeble and slow. These varying circumstances have their effect upon the exodus of the golden perch and change its course. Usually there are more of them when the current against which they travel is stronger and more marked. The current coming before them as though to attract them, the response they make is in proportion to the strength of that current, and is shaped according to the summons it gives.

But this summons, however intense it may sometimes be, does not always meet with the expected response. There are delays, diminutions, sometimes no response at all. So there must be another influence which is able to modify the exodus and introduce variations whilst being dependent upon the qualities of the sea-water, since only the sea-water is able to call forth the journey. We can discover what this influence is by a study of the sea-water compared with that of the pool.

The migration of the golden perch takes place late in summer and early in autumn. At this time the differences of temperature, salinity, and content of oxygen between the sea-water and the pool-water which have come into being during the warm weather, begin to grow less and often end by being reversed. The entering and leaving currents bear along waters which are increasingly alike. Their physical qualities become progressively equalized. During the summer, the water of the pool, usually warmer than that of the sea, becomes more concentrated, the amount of salt in it is increased, and, as a result of its richness of vegetation, contains a greater proportion of dissolved oxygen. This proportion grows less again when the vegetation, algæ and zosteræ of the bottom, begin to break off and corrupt. This is not so noticeable in autumn and there is less difference between the currents in both directions. At the beginning of September, the waters of the pool and those of the sea are often equal in temperature or almost so, usually averaging some twenty degrees, sometimes a little more, rarely less.

Then come the first cold days, the nights grow longer, the hours of sunlight less, and the north winds are keener. The pool and the sea near the shore, suffering the repercussions of these changes, grow colder together, but more quickly and completely in the case of the former, since it

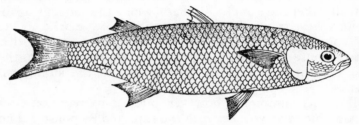

FIG. 44.—THE MULLET

The Mullet (genus *Mugil*), family *Mugilidæ*, belongs to the order *Mugiliformes*. There are a great many species in this genus, and they frequent coastal waters, the pools near the coast, and, for a limited period, fresh waters.

is not so great in mass. The differences are the reverse of those in summer, the pool being colder, and become more noticeable as the season advances and the causes become more effective. Variable according to the weather, sometimes not very great, sometimes very marked, sometimes amounting to three or four degrees or more, it follows that the entering current, coming from the sea, brings to the pool waters that are frequently warmer than those of the pool itself. Now, customarily, the migration of the golden perch takes place when this state of affairs becomes evident. It is the more considerable and important when the difference in temperature in the sea's favour is more marked. When the north wind has blown there are more fish, for the pool is then made much colder; and there are still more if south winds have blown from the sea, driving the warm waters from the open sea towards the coast and forming with them a part of the entering current. The more striking the variation, the more clearly the summons is heard, and the more generally the obedient golden perch set out upon their migration.

Heat, then, is the principal factor, as in the case of most other fishes which make a wedding journey, as the shad and the tunny. Perhaps it is not the only one. It may be that it is accompanied by other sorts of determining activities, which also have a part to play, for the sea-water has many qualities which science is not always able to measure. In any case, the thermic influence, which is of primary importance, appears to be preponderant. Other things being

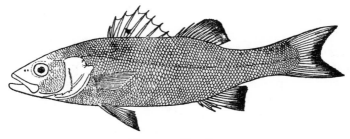

FIG. 45.—THE BASS

The Bass (*Labrax labrax*, Linnæus), family *Serranidæ*,
belonging to the order *Perciformes*.

equal, or at least not particularly unequal, between the waters of the sea and those of the pool, carried along by the entering and leaving currents, it is the thermic influence which is mainly decisive. The rest either counts less or does not count at all.

These journeys of the golden perch have a clear purpose and a very definite cause. The fish becoming pubescent in the pool, there sets about the process of sexual elaboration which demands, for its fulfilment, the taking from the outer medium of a certain number of additional calories. The chill of autumn, diminishing the possibilities of such a borrowing, interferes with the delicate process of the elaboration of the ovaries, and only the entering currents, when the thermic difference is on their side, are capable of improving the situation. The golden perch which they affect in their pool are moved by them. These warm currents, mingling with

the colder waters, create zones of an intermediate temperature, varying progressively. They polarize the fishes,
which make in their direction so as to come into contact
with waters that are progressively warmer, and so approach
the place from which they come. They reach the canal,
enter the water which is favourable to them, work their
way against the current, go all the way through the canal
and finally reach the sea, where their migration is completed.

Led from one end to the other by the direct action of the
environing water upon an organism already prepared to
welcome it, thanks to its sexual elaboration, and consequently
ready to conform automatically to its suggestions, this
migration shows, in its own small way, how great is the
force that instigates it and how definite its direction. This
journey is strictly determined. It begins only when it is
solicited, summoned by the coming of favourable water.
It takes place in this same water, in the direction imposed
upon it by the water. So, harmony being realized between
the conditions present in the interior environment and those
of the exterior environment, the golden perch go to the sea.

They do not leave the neighbourhood of the shore, for
they find there what they were seeking, what their organism
desired. They complete their elaboration, mature their
reproductive elements, then proceed to spawn, the individuals among them showing important differences, as
is the case with most fishes. The fertilized eggs are
hatched in the sea, where the fry begin their growth during
the winter. The parents continue to frequent the sea
waters and go on growing there, later reproducing themselves
in the sea, still keeping to the neighbourhood of the coast.
They do not trouble to return to the pools from which they
came.

But the fry do not behave in this way. Because of their
more active respiratory system, they feel a greater need for
dissolved oxygen, which the adults feel less. As, in the
spring, the currents leaving the pool for the sea bring with
them a water that is already warmed, which the rains of
the season make relatively rich in oxygen and poor in
chloride salts, the fry, sensitive to these influences, polarized
by them, move in their direction. They go against them,
pass through the canal, and take in the opposite direction

the journey which their parents made before them. They go from the sea to the pool, enter it, settle there, take advantage of its wealth of nourishment; their growth is speedy there, and then they return to their sea as their parents did before them. So, in spite of the autumnal exodus, the population is maintained, thanks to these continual renewals, to these journeys which succeed each other every year according to the season; natural circumstances, in their alternation, laying down the law and imposing the obligation.

The golden perch has a biological cycle entailing a change of environment, like the other species of migratory fishes which alternately frequent the sea and the fresh water, but the direction it takes is contrary to theirs. It is born in the sea, but leaves the sea to grow in the salt or brackish water of an estuary or a pool; then, when it is pubescent, it goes back to the sea to spawn. The main feature of this cycle is the spawning in sea-water; the migrations in both directions lead either to this spawning or away from it. The shad is anadromous; its spawning takes place in fresh water; the golden perch, on the other hand, is thalassotocic (from *thalasse*, sea and *tokos*, childbirth), since its reproduction takes place in the sea. This spawning in the sea, though the reverse of what happens in other cases, follows the same sort of law. If the direction is different, the cause and the compulsion are the same. Its object is spawning and its guiding principle, likewise, is the determining harmony with the environment.

III. The pool of Thau is only a tiny realm compared with the sea. The golden perch seem only a small group when we think of all the hosts of creatures that live in the sea. We might be inclined to consider that their case is interesting, remarkable even, but only of limited importance, without any special significance. But this would be a mistake. The contrast of direction with that taken by the anadromous fishes, based upon an essential identity of determinism, shows that this condition, far from being isolated, is related to a general reason, upon which, at different stages, all the migrations of fishes depend. Then too, in this particular case of spawning in the sea and the journey undertaken to the sea to accomplish it, the golden perch are not alone. Several other species which, like them, live in these pools along the coast, have similar habits, especially the mullet (genus *Mugil*), and the bass (genus *Labrax*), which are also fish that spawn in the sea.

The golden perch are usually the first to try to make this journey to the sea. More precocious than the other species in their sexual development, they more quickly display the consequences of the thermic hypersensitiveness which results from it; they get away more quickly. Sometimes certain mullet, especially the large-headed species (*Mugil cephalus*, Linnæus), have already gone before them, perhaps influenced by some other factor; but, usually, their imitators follow them, and the journeyings of these fishes, going on throughout autumn, continue to midwinter. The eels go with them about the same business. So there is work for the fishermen to do for several months on end. Their tackle, set out at the regular places which the fish pass, and always prepared in the same way, does not always reap the same harvest, for the circumstances which affect the golden perch affect the other migrants in the same way.

The pool of Thau has a position peculiar to itself, and for this reason is able to afford us remarkable evidence. One of its creeks, that of l'Angle, situated between Bouziques and Balaruc-les-Bains, has an abundant spring of warm water, a real submarine geyser, which comes up straight from the bottom. Its temperature is practically constant, usually about twenty-one degrees. This spring has made for itself a vast reservoir, a hundred feet deep, and from it the water comes up with such force that, when it reaches the surface, it makes an expanse of ripples thirty-five feet or so in diameter.

This spring, which is called *Vise* or *Bise*, from which the name *Abyss* has been coined to denote the depression from which it comes, is part of the system of the thermal waters of Balaruc. Like them it is slightly impregnated with a sodium salt. Its emergence in the pool, with the water of which it is being continually incorporated, results in a diminution of the degree of salinity about it, and creates there a zone in which the temperature is constant in the neighbourhood of twenty degrees. During the greater part of the year this particular feature is not noticeable, for the heat of the pool itself is equal to, or even higher than, that of the spring. But not in winter, especially the coldest part of winter. The neighbourhood of the *Vise* then forms a relatively warm zone, a place specially sought out by those fishes which are sensitive to heat. They often come there. In the middle of winter, the fishermen in this part of the pool catch many mullet and bass, often hundredweights at a time.

The story of the golden perch, and that of its rivals, has something to teach us. As the life-history of the trout teaches us what to expect of the salmon, so the golden perch prepares us for the study of the eel.

CHAPTER XV

First Part: The People of the Eels

I. THERE are extraordinary features about the lives of many migratory fishes, but none, perhaps, more extraordinary, more startling, than those we meet with in the eel. In unexpectedness, in diversity, the eel is the rival of the salmon; in many respects it outshines it. These two species, so different one from the other, one starting out from the very bottom of the sea to spawn in fresh water streams, the other, moving in the opposite direction, going down the rivers, leaving the ponds and lakes, to bring forth its young far away in the depths of the ocean, have much in common. They are both impelled by the same impulse and, in a way, they balance one another. Their realm covers almost the whole field of the world of waters. Their journey takes them across that world, overcoming one difficulty after another, from one end to the other.

We all know the crawling, snake-like fishes which live everywhere, swarm in almost all waters, bury themselves in the mud of rivers and lakes like giant vermin. They are as much at home in the salt pools of the shore as in the pure mountain lakes. They are found in stagnant ponds and in running water, in clean water and in foul. In this the eel is unlike all other fishes; nothing seems to frighten it away, no circumstances are beyond its powers of endurance. It seems to be as comfortable in good conditions as in bad. This extraordinary power of adaptation, this prodigious vitality, give it a quality of originality that is all its own, the more accentuated because of the incredible way in which the eel increases and multiplies. Wherever eels are found they are found in swarms. We do not often see them, and not for long at a time, because they hide whenever they can; but occasionally, when something fetches them up to the light of day, we are astounded at the number of them even in places where their presence was hardly suspected. Their life is a tissue of riddles, and this capacity for survival, this readiness to be content with what Fate brings them, is one of the first of those riddles to claim our attention.

Eels and the other fishes of their group take the place in the world of waters of the snakes we know on land. They have the same shape, the same humble, crawling mode of life. Both snake and eel have a long body devoid of functional members. They are similar in still another important respect, the readiness with which they adapt themselves to circumstances, the ease with which they are able to comply with the exigences of their environment. These feeble creatures make up for their feebleness by a capacity for resistance which animals from whom more might reasonably be expected either do not possess at all or in a much smaller degree.

This group of fishes, because of its principal characteristics, is given the name of *Apodes*, from the Greek word meaning " limbless." I have had occasion to refer to it elsewhere, particularly when dealing with the poison of the muræna. Here I am concerned only with the eels. The genus *Anguilla* of the order of Apodes is a family in itself. It is recognizable by the small pectoral fins—these do exist though they are very small—by the blunt, truncated snout, by the dorsal fin which begins far back behind the head, and by the thick skin, in the substance of which are contained the tiny scales. The head, in spite of its smallness, has a well-cleft mouth, with fine teeth in jaws which are not the same size, the lower one coming out and round the upper one, like a spoon.

The eel is often mistaken for a fish of another genus, the conger, which belongs to another family. So great is the resemblance between them that the conger has often been called the " sea eel." The similarity does not go beyond appearance. The conger always lives in the sea and never ventures into fresh or brackish water: its jaws are the same size; the dorsal fin comes up close to the head, the skin has no scales either inside or out. The two fish are as different from one another as a dog from a wolf, or a donkey from a horse.

The eel's skin is particularly interesting. It is thick and flexible, and renowned for the slipperiness which makes it so easy for the creature to escape, to slip through the fingers of anyone who tries to grasp it. It is polished and smooth, with a surface that is devoid of roughness since the scales are enclosed and not external. It is covered all over with a thick layer of sticky mucus, secreted by a host of tiny glands in the skin itself. This mucus adds to the slipperiness of the body, the more effectively on account of the shape of that body, which is long and cylindrical, without any

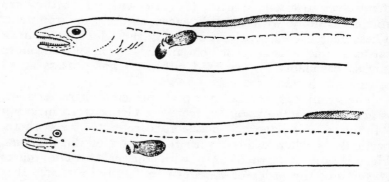

FIG. 46.—THE EEL AND THE CONGER

Heads and foreparts of the Eel (genus *Anguilla*) and the Conger (genus *Conger*), showing the differences between them. The Eel (below) has a more powerful lower jaw and its dorsal fin is set lower down than that of the Conger (above).

projections. The undulating suppleness of the creature is another factor which tends to the same end. The eel squirms in order to escape more easily.

This characteristic is so obvious that it has become proverbial. The possession of enclosed scales, which is confined to the eel alone among the *Apodes*, is still more remarkable. Fishes usually have a garment of scales which covers their whole body in such a way as to form a resisting envelope which serves as a protection to the delicate skin beneath. Here the scales are lodged actually in the skin, so that the creature is bare instead of being clothed, and looks as if it had nothing on at all. If we take a piece of the skin, scrape it and examine the scrapings, or let it dry and then examine it, we can see the scales like little oval plates. The largest are seldom more than two or three millimetres in length. They are made up of a host of little grains in concentric rows, distinct, not touching one another. They do not seem to serve any useful purpose. Whether these organs are regressive or progressive, or whether they are merely representative, their small size and the position they occupy makes them seem very different from those which, in other fishes, are placed on the body itself and do afford effective protection. Here is another puzzle which makes the eel seem stranger still.

The European eels belong to a single species, *Anguilla anguilla*, Linnæus. Careful study forces us to this conclusion. But it is not what the fishermen think, or even some naturalists who, observing certain differences, have made those differences the basis of distinct and formal categories. They distinguish between eels with a snub snout, a pointed snout, and a snout that is neither snub nor pointed; between yellow-bellied eels and eels with white and pearly bellies; between lazy eels which love to hide in the hollows between the rocks or to bury themselves in the mud and active eels which crawl along or make progress with a characteristic undulating movement. But though there may be some reason for these groupings, and observation makes it clear to us that there is, the distinctions are not definite enough or sufficiently important to justify us in forming definite species to allow for them. They are purely individual, due to such factors as age, sex, time of year, or the degree of sexual elaboration that has been reached. The whole group, despite its polymorphism, is a unity and must be so regarded. Whatever their size, colour, behaviour, or shape of head, all the European eels belong to one species, and this, in vast multitudes, inhabits the greater part of our land waters.

The species is to be found practically all over Europe. It occurs as far north as the 70th degree of latitude. It goes south to the Mediterranean and even beyond the continent of Europe to Northern Africa, Egypt, Tripoli, Tunisia, Algeria, Morocco, in fact, almost to the tropics. It appears also in the Mediterranean islands, Corsica, Sardinia, the Balearic Islands and off the coast of Northern

Africa in the Atlantic, the Azores, Madeira, and the Canaries. The area it covers, the realm which it has made its own, is greater in extent than that of any other fresh water fish. And not only does the eel surpass these other fishes in this respect, but also in the ease with which it seems able to exist anywhere and everywhere. The trout has a field of activity of almost equal extent, but it is compelled to live in water that is flowing and pure. It settles in a few chosen places and is not found elsewhere. The eel is everywhere. It thrives as comfortably in the warm waters of Northern Africa as in the colder waters of Northern Europe, in the lakes of the plains as in the pools among the mountains, in marshes as in brooks and rivers. It is found in great numbers over a larger and more varied area than any other fresh-water fish.

The fact that the eel is so extraordinarily universal makes its absence, when it is absent, the more remarkable. Now, though it is so abundant in the countries whose shores lie along the northern half of the Atlantic Ocean, including the Mediterranean, it is never seen in the countries of the Southern Hemisphere which are washed by the southern half of the ocean. It is not known in West Africa below the Equator. The extraordinary thing is that we find exactly the same state of affairs in the New World. On the Atlantic shores of North America we find a species of eel, *Anguilla rostrata*, Lesueur, which is closely related to the European eel, from which it differs only in the possession of a smaller number of vertebræ. (The American species has 103 to 110 while the European eel has between 111 and 119.) There is hardly any difference in appearance and behaviour. This American species is found as far south as the Caribbean Sea, but no farther. It never reaches South America. No eels are ever seen in South Africa or South America on opposite sides of the Atlantic Ocean, whereas the northern regions of the northern hemisphere abound in them. The complex of riddles which centres around the eel is rendered even more striking by this strange problem of geographical distribution.

But this is not all. The two Atlantic species, the European and the American, compose a relatively definite group within the genus *Anguilla*. In this respect they differ from another group, that of the Indo-Pacific eels, which is much more varied. We know of at least a dozen different species in that group. Yet the odd features of the one group are found in the other, and we find them manifested in identical oppositions. The whole of America, south as well as north, has no eels on its Pacific shores, whereas the coasts of Japan, China, part of Australia, and South-east Africa have eels in most of their lagoons and rivers. In the fresh waters which flow into that sort of inland sea bounded on the north by Cochin-China, on the west by the Malay Peninsula and the island of Sumatra, on the south by Borneo and Java, no sign of an eel is ever seen. On the other hand, there are swarms of eels in the rivers of Java and Borneo which empty themselves into the Indian Ocean.

But there is a solution to the mystery. If we look at a map which gives the physical features, noting both the contours of the land areas, the depths of the oceans, and the directions of the currents in those oceans, we find that the regions which have eels in their fresh waters are always bordered by seas of exceptional depth, or are visited by currents which pass over those depths. The situation becomes clearer when we remember that when the eels are very young, while they are still fry, they come from the sea; that they begin life far out at sea and live there for a time before they begin to penetrate the rivers. They are originally deep-sea creatures. Rising from the depths to approach the shore and enter the rivers, the particular part of the land to which they will go is determined by the part of the sea from which they come. They can only approach the land when their home in the sea is within immediate reach.

II. The eel is a deep-sea fish. It is brought out of its native waters, drawn up from the abyss to live in fresh water. Beginning as a child of Thetis, it has the singular, the unique power of being able to leave its native cradle and to go for its growth in the realm of Cybele. The Oceanid becomes a Naiad, the familiar of streams and lakes.

Although the order *Apodes* to which the genus of eels belongs is made up of species whose original home is in the depths of the sea, some of them, the congers and murænæ, for example, are able to exist on the continental shelf near the coasts, though they show a preference for the deeper waters near by. The eels go even farther, they pass to the land itself, and make their home for a considerable period in fresh water. An extraordinary—one might almost use the word startling—thing about them is that such an astonishing adaptation is possible. An eel buried in the mud of a pool affords a spectacle which, in the other fish of its group, could only be found in the darkness and slime of the depths of the sea. This fact explains some of the peculiarities of its behaviour and appearance. The eel, in fresh water, behaves as a deep-sea fish behaves.

It is extraordinarily greedy and gluttonous. Nothing comes amiss to it. Carnivorous, it will eat any kind of food, will pursue any kind of prey, will feed upon any fleshy substance. In a fishpond, the presence of eels in any number may easily become a plague. The eel destroys and consumes everything capable of being eaten, exploits to the fullest extent the places in which it takes up its abode and, when it finally takes its departure, leaves nothing behind it. When it has exhausted the possibilities of any one place, it leaves that place, goes elsewhere, and begins all over again. If this is impossible, if circumstances compel it to remain where it is, it stays motionless, rolled up in a hole or in the mud, and waits till times improve. It is capable of living for weeks or even months without food but, when some happy chance gives it the opportunity, it stuffs itself to a state of repletion. Though most other fish do this to some extent, no other fresh-water fish can rival the eel in this respect.

The eel has a similarly extreme capacity as regards breathing. The different fishes which live with it in the pools and brooks cannot leave the water to which they are accustomed, from which they must draw unceasingly the dissolved oxygen they need. The eel is different. It is able occasionally to go on land, to travel between one pond and another, or from a stream to a well some distance away. It can do this because it has gills which can store away a certain amount of water, leaving it free to absorb the oxygen of the air for a time. The same peculiar characteristic enables it to live in polluted water where insufficiency of oxygen would be the death of most other creatures. The eel, however, making use of its emergency capacity for breathing directly from the air, is able to exist in such places.

Its methods of locomotion are equally capable of adaptation to circumstances. The fact that it has no limbs hardly seems to be any drawback at all. The flexibility of its body, the power of its muscles, enable it to move from one place to another with a rippling motion. The eel moves like a snake. Possessing only one means of locomotion, that of the play of its undulations, it makes use of that means on all occasions and always succeeds in doing what it sets out to do. When it wishes to move over the surface of the ground, it crawls with a sinuous motion; when it wishes to bury itself in the ground, it bores its way with the same undulating motion. When it wishes to swim in the water, it acts in exactly the same way, undulating its way forward. This single method, as in the snake, is all sufficient. In spite of the infirmity which gives it nothing but a limbless trunk, it can go wherever it wishes to go.

In spite of these peculiar qualities, the eel sometimes comes into conflict with natural factors which put a limit to the action of those qualities and even make them ineffective. It is sensitive to cold and light; it endeavours to escape from them and to find warm shady places. It is most active during the warm weather when it pursues its prey more insistently and gorges itself with food. The water in which it lives is, at this time, always warm, and provides it with all the heat its organism needs. When autumn comes and the water becomes colder, there is a definite slackening down of activity. When winter sets in, the eels become quiescent. They cease to move about, dig themselves in, bury themselves in the mud, roll up and go to sleep, and remain so as long as the weather is cold. In this state of dormant existence they hibernate, not moving, not eating, breathing only enough to keep them alive. When spring returns and the water becomes warmer again, they come out of their torpor and resume their active life. Their hibernation has come to an end. For them there are two successive, alternating seasons in the year; the summer season, which is that of their active life, and the winter season, when their life is at its lowest ebb. Their whole existence is governed by this double cadence, and, sometimes more sometimes less, according to the climate, always conforms to it.

But the eels are not the only fresh-water fish to behave in this way or to hibernate. In streams and ponds they are often accompanied by others which, when the cold weather arrives, go to sleep in the same way. The carp, the tench, most *Cyprinidæ*, pass the winter in a state of lethargy, hardly moving and hardly eating. But the eels, who always stand out from the rest, go, as usual, to extremes. Generally speaking, they are the first to enter this hibernating stage and the last to emerge from it. They are not content simply to remain motionless upon the bottom; they look for a suitable place beforehand, delve into it, bury themselves, so making preparation for the state of lethargy and taking the precautions which seem necessary for their protection. This ability to slow up their vital processes is extended to other actions. Should their pond dry up, they dig deeper into those parts of it which still remain moist. There they can wait quite a long time until the supply of water becomes more adequate. Where other fish, their neighbours, would perish, they are able to survive. Consequently, it is very difficult to get rid of them from the fishponds when it is necessary to do so. In this respect the eel has only one rival. The catfish (*Ameiurus nebulosus*, Lesueur) is as capable of resisting drought as the eel itself. This fish is indigenous to North America and was introduced to Europe nearly half a century ago. It frequents the muddy waters in which the eel takes such delight.

The eel seeks darkness with as much eagerness as it seeks warmth. It is to be numbered with the nocturnal creatures of the waters which become active only when it is dark. It retains the impression acquired in the depths of the sea where it was born; it moves, gives chase, eats, only during the night. It spends the daylight hours sleeping in a hole, buried in the mud, rolled up, doing its utmost to escape the faintest ray of light. If eels are kept in an aquarium and a beam of light is suddenly brought to bear upon them, they get into a panic immediately, dash off in all directions, finally piling one on top of another in the darkest corner, pressing as close to one another as they can in their eagerness to get away from the light they hate. And in their natural haunts, the fishermen who wish to catch them must set their tackle by night and take it up again in the morning, when the darkness is past. This persistent, unescapable dread of the light is a controlling factor in the life of the eel and makes it obvious to us that the eel is indeed a creature of the depths.

These restrictions upon the activity of the eel are not very far-reaching. They do not affect adversely the other characteristic features of the fish. Especially they have no ill effects upon that extraordinary capacity for resistance and adaptation which the eel displays at every provocation. It may be that certain characteristics of their internal organization have something to do with this.

People who have to handle eels, who cut them into little pieces, are well aware that their blood is poisonous. If these people have hands in perfect condition, without a scratch, contact with this blood will not do them any harm. The skin itself is protection enough. But the slightest cut may be serious, for the poison can take effect through it and there may be inflammation, mortification, suppuration, sometimes oedema complicated by lymphangitis and infiltration. The toxic principle, called *ichthyotoxin* (or fish toxin) is found dissolved in the blood serum; it is part of the humours which are developed by certain parts of the organism and carried by the blood through the circulatory system. It is found in many fishes, but in the eel it has a greater potency than in any other. A tenth of a cubic centimetre of serum taken from an eel, if injected into a rabbit weighing a couple of pounds, will undoubtedly kill it, so strong is this venom. There is certainly some relation between this toxic quality of the eel's blood, itself produced by the presence in the serum of an infinitesimal quantity of a peculiar substance, and the extraordinary capacity for survival in almost any circumstances which the eel displays. Researches into these poisons tend to show that their use either for attack or defence by the creatures in which they are present is only supplemental, collateral as it were. Their main purpose seems to be concerned with rendering the processes of assimilation easier. Their business is primarily to facilitate the personal, internal processes of nutrition. The eels, which are very well circumstanced in this respect, possibly find in these poisonous products the strength which gives them such astonishing powers of resistance. Their humoral secretions are of such a nature, of such importance, that the eel perhaps draws from them the energy which enables it to adapt itself to circumstances and places of every kind. Its will to live, which is so strong, so complete, may be based mainly upon these peculiar secretions.

It is this untiring energy which is the most striking characteristic of the eel. The elusiveness with which it slips from between our closed fingers, the strength of its narrow body, are only the outward signs of a still greater elasticity, an enhanced strength which is inherent within the organism. This humble, crawling animal has powers of endurance possessed to the same extent by no other creature of its kind. In it they exist to an imposing degree. And when we realize the intensity of this individual life we are better able to appreciate the vigour which the creature displays in its reproductive life, especially in the journey which that life necessitates. The former is the measure of the latter. The eel indeed possesses all the necessary equipment which it will need when it comes to undertake its long and difficult wedding journey.

CHAPTER XVI

THE ASTOUNDING JOURNEY OF THE EUROPEAN EELS

Second Part: The Wedding Journey across the Ocean

I. EACH year, some time during the autumn, the eels set off upon this journey and continue to do so until the middle of winter. If about this time some feel the temptation to indulge in the winter slumber, and try to bury themselves in the mud and to roll up motionless, others keep on the move, crawling, swimming, even more agitated than they seemed to be before. These are the strongest, the oldest. In them, this increase in vitality is simultaneous with the coming of puberty and the beginning of sexual elaboration. The others, younger, still unaffected in this respect, go on leading their accustomed lives, while the latter, starting a new life, that of reproduction, take up a new line of behaviour. Occasionally some give signs of such a new life at other times, but the great mass do so only during the autumn. For the European eels this is the prelude to the great exodus across the Ocean. They set out upon their great enterprise and prepare themselves for its accomplishment.

The initial episodes remind us of the golden perch and the mullet when they migrate before spawning; they choose the same times of the year, they show the same signs of pubescence, they make the same drive towards the open sea. In this they are exactly alike and the eels do no more than other migrants which go to spawn in the sea. But their migration is on a much larger scale than that of the other fishes. Not only are they very much more numerous and consequently much more impressive in this respect than other migrants we have considered, but they start at a greater distance from their goal, have a longer journey before them. They are found practically everywhere, in running fresh water as well as in stagnant, and they set out from all directions to the sea. When they reach the coast, they do not delay in coastal waters, as the mullet and golden perch do, but go right out to sea, and make for the depths. Theirs is a terrific journey rivalled only by that of the salmon.

When their time has come, the fresh-water eels go to the rivers and go down with the current to the sea. They leave ponds, pools, and lakes, and seek the outlets. They go from the brooks to the streams, from the streams to the rivers, and so to the sea. They have only to let themselves be carried along. Semi-active, semi-passive, they prefer to travel by night. During the day they stop, bury themselves in hollows, and go on again when evening comes. Often, several of them curling up together form a confused heap, which the current rolls round and round as it carries it along. Fishermen, who wait for their coming at this time of the year, capture enormous quantities of them. Those which escape finally reach the estuary and so come to the sea.

The eels of the lagoons, the estuaries, and salt ponds near the coast behave in the same way as the golden perch and the mullet, their companions, and, like them, make their way to the sea through the communicating channels. But they do so in a way peculiar to themselves. They seldom move except by night, and they need a cloudy sky, or the absence of the moon, a darkness that is practically complete. If, at the same time, the wind blows from the sea, stirring up the waters of the pond, disturbing the mud in which the eels are awaiting the moment for departure, and bringing through the canal warm currents from the open sea, all is for the best; the summons is heard, and the exodus is accomplished in a few hours. In Corsica, one night of wind and terrible storm with thunder and lightning, such as one sometimes gets in autumn, I saw a pond empty itself of almost all its inhabitants. When morning came, the fishermen had a splendid time, and the pond itself was left with hardly a fish in it.

Despite the darkness which covers them, the darkness they like so much, the eels do not mistake their road; they never go astray, but find their way straight to the sea. They go back, in the opposite direction, along the road they took several years before when they came from the sea to enter the waters of the land. Then they were tiny elvers. Now that they have grown, they are going back to the sea to spawn, to lay eggs from which new elvers will come, which, in their turn, will make again for the waters of the land. So we have a perfect cycle, with a going and a coming, whereby the numbers of these creatures are kept up wherever they are found despite these annual departures.

These travellers who set out and complete the first stage of their journey on the threshold of the sea-water are extremely numerous. It would be difficult to gain a real idea of this journey without first taking into consideration their prodigious quantity, which may be calculated approximately, but sufficiently, by taking the total number of fish caught by the fisheries permanently established to capture them in the lower reaches of the rivers, and in the channels which bring them from the pools. For many, doubtless, these fisheries mean the sudden end of the journey, but others, still more in numbers, escape and find their way to the sea. But the numbers of those caught will serve to give us an idea of those which are not caught and so we may get a rough notion of the total.

When I consider the production of a typical pool near the coast, that of Thau, for example, of which I spoke in the previous chapter, I find, in an average year, that its quota of eels amounts to about sixteen to twenty pounds per acre. As the total surface covers twenty-nine square miles, the average yield for a year amounts to between a hundred and thirty-four and a hundred and seventy-eight tons. Admitting that the eels which escape are hardly as many as those which are caught, we must allow an equal number for them. Consequently, the pool of Thau alone sends to the sea, each year, at least three hundred and fifty tons of eels representing, in round figures, between five hundred thousand and six hundred thousand fish.

The pool of Thau is surrounded by other pools, like itself peopled by eels, sometimes more richly. We must increase the figure I have given if we wish to give the total of them all. Now we are only taking into account the eels which leave the Mediterranean coast of France, and their number already runs into millions. If we add to it those of the still larger pools, just as richly populated, in the Adriatic, in Corsica, Sardinia, Tunisia, and Algeria, and of the estuaries, lagoons and all the rivers on the coast; if we add all these up, we arrive at enormous figures, tens of millions, hundreds of millions, which alone can give an idea of the swarming hosts of these travellers on their way to the sea in this migration. And that is only for the western basin of the Mediterranean.

Then, turning to other districts, if we take into account the corresponding Atlantic coast, which stretches from Morocco to the Baltic, a much greater distance, our imagination fails us. By hundreds, perhaps thousands, of millions, the pubescent eels set out each year upon their journey to spawn; go down to the sea and lose themselves in its depths. We have to think of this swarming mass of squirming, crawling creatures on their way across the ocean, to understand fully what this migration means. It is a sight which no eye can see, which our imagination alone can picture to us, though its magnitude bewilders us.

II. These travellers, launched in an almost boundless immensity, leave behind them the confined places in which, until now, they had spent their days. They are predestined. Their new behaviour is in keeping with their budding puberty. Hitherto, there has been no sign of anything unusual about them. But when their time comes and their sexual elaboration begins, the force which compels them to start their journey takes possession of them and holds them in its grip. They set out, pushing straight forward and never thinking of turning back, as if they had given up all idea of returning. So their migration is begun.

Both sexes are equally affected. In spite of differences of form and size, all, at the same time, display an equal animation. The males are the smaller, seldom more than sixteen inches in length; their other measurements, especially their circumference and their diameter, retain their due proportion and so preserve the grace of the body. They seem almost dwarfs beside the females, which, longer and more powerful, sometimes reach a length of a yard or more, with the rest of their bodies in due proportion. The small head of the males has a pointed snout, while that of the females is more rounded. Such differences have often led to the sexes being considered different species. But the points of divergence are only variations arising from a sexual dimorphism, in which the principal difference is in regard to shape and age, the males becoming pubescent earlier than the females. So, dwarf males and giant females, all carried along by the same impulse, they set out together to play their appointed part in the spawning that is to come.

In them all, the sexual glands duly begin to develop. Tiny, until now, and difficult to see when the creature is dissected because they are so delicate and transparent, they increase and become opaque, so rendering themselves easier to see. The ovaries of the females, especially, gradually allow the young ovules to be discerned. These are minute, and their number exceeds hundreds of thousands, approaching even a million. Under this influence, the individuals change their mode of life. The genetic excitement takes possession of them. Instead of becoming sleepy they continue to move about, to undulate in the water, in spite of the approach of hard weather. They cease hunting their prey and no longer eat. In the grip of the reproductive anexoria, their stomachs and intestines generally empty, they live upon the reserves which, accumulated in their flesh, make them firmer, stronger, fatter.

As in the case of the salmon and the shad and many other fish, the succulent qualities of this flesh, filled as it is with juices, are at their finest. These eels are at the most tasty and delicate stage. " Fine eels " the fishermen and shopkeepers call them to distinguish them from those which are not pubescent, whose flesh is softer and much coarser in flavour. These winter travellers, caught in a body at the moment of departure, are at their very best from the gourmet's point of view. Now that they have given up their search for nourishment and have lost the muddy flavour they used to have, their white, firm flesh gives every satisfaction to the epicure.

The changes due to the development of the reproductive powers are not only internal. A corresponding transformation is manifested externally. The colour changes. Before the beginning of puberty, the eels, males and females alike, had a green and yellow coloration, dark brownish green on the back and bright yellow under the belly. These colours now partially disappear. The green back takes on a shade of purple. The yellow of the belly gradually fades away and is replaced by a pearly white. The creature preparing for the production of young and beginning its wedding journey arrays itself in a new coat. " Silver eels," " White eels " they are called, and the name fits them well, so great is the difference in the tints of their bellies from what it used to be and from that of their younger brothers and sisters still. Further, their eyes bulge out more, seem larger, more in the males than in the females.

Dressed in their wedding dress, the eels set out upon their wedding journey. Gripped by the excitement of that sexual desire which is gradually developing within them, they move and twist about incessantly as they crawl or swim. There is a degree of agitation about them which indicates their anxiety to reach the coast, the first stage in their journey. And when they reach it, they go straight on, as if the enormous distance to be covered compelled them to avoid all possible delay.

III. The disappearance of the eels as soon as they arrive at the sea is really very remarkable. They literally lose themselves, leaving no trace behind them, as though annihilation in this immensity were their fate. In spite of their huge numbers, none are ever caught, no matter what tackle is tried. Their flight is complete; they make a clean escape. Like the young salmon, when they enter the salt waters, they go straight out to sea and to the depths.

Where do they go when they disappear like this? In certain countries, Denmark, for example, where fishermen catch the eels as they go through the straits, some have been marked in the hope of finding out where they have been if they should be caught again later. Some, indeed, have been recaptured in the North Sea, more rarely in the English Channel, thus making it clear that their direction was that of the Atlantic Ocean. But then all trace of them is lost, and the ocean itself has revealed nothing of their secret. The whole people of the eels buries itself in the waters of the ocean and loses itself there. We can trace their course so far and no farther, and now we are confronted by a riddle which offers us no clue to its solution.

It is a very old riddle. It is connected with that of the reproduction of the eels, a problem which has been discussed for centuries without any acceptable answer being forthcoming, in spite of the eagerness with which investigations have been conducted. This species of fish being more abundant than others, and found wherever there is fresh water, its eggs have never been found, nor its fry when they have just been hatched. With any other species at the same reproductive stage, you will find its spawn, its spawning places, and can follow the first stages of its growth. There is nothing of the sort to be discovered about the eels in fresh water: all we know is that at the beginning of puberty they hasten to the sea.

Imagination has supplied the deficiencies of experience. All sorts of legends have been coined about the reproduction of eels. The slightest little fact, the twistings and turnings of the descent, the struggles in the pursuit of prey, in self-defence, the presence in the body of tiny parasitic worms, have served as pretexts for many hypotheses. When we have disposed of all of them, two facts emerge: on the one hand, the descent to the sea of the large pubescent eels; on the other, the return from the sea of the elvers, the fry of the eel, whose growth has already been considerable. Consequently, it is clear that the spawning and the earliest stages of development take place in sea-water only. The eel goes to the sea to spawn; its eggs hatch there; its fry go through the first stages of growth there and, when they have become what we call elvers, they leave the sea and go to the rivers. The spawning takes place in the sea. But where, and how?

Here we come upon an additional complication. The phases of the descent, of the flight to the sea beyond the neighbourhood of the shore, prove that the spawning is carried out in the great depths of the sea. The eel which comes from the abyss returns to the abyss to bring forth young. Now, among the fish which inhabit those depths or which live near them, there is a group of creatures whose curious appearance has long attracted the attention of naturalists. These are the *Leptocephali*. This name is given because of their tiny heads (*leptos*, puny; *kephale*, head) to a small fish with a body as clear as crystal, oblong, and flattened

out towards the top. Like oval-shaped leaves, suspended
in the water by their edges, and not able to swim very well
because they have only tiny fins, they let themselves be
carried along by the currents, their flatness facilitating this
process. Several species of them are known, nearly a
hundred in fact. They are found in every sea, and it is
known that they are not perfect beings but larvæ which
will ultimately change their form and become young

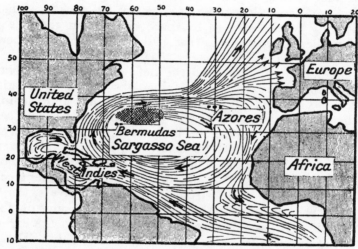

Fig. 47.—Map of the wedding journey (migration and spawning) of the European
eels. The currents and their direction are shown by continuous lines and by
arrows. The spawning place is shaded. North and east of it is the Gulf
Stream moving towards Europe and North-West Africa.

individuals complete in structure. These larvæ are peculiar
to the order *Apodes* to which the eel belongs, and all
the species of this order undergo such changes. Their
eggs, when they hatch, produce Leptocephali which must
themselves change and assume their final structure. The
larval type of the European eels is the *Leptocephalus
brevirostris*, Kaup, and the successive stages of the metamorphosis of this creature have been observed and described
minutely, in the fullest detail.

But the riddle is not yet solved. It has shifted, has
become more complicated, but it still remains. The only
new fact is that the fry of the eels is originally a lepto-

cephalus, and that it must undergo a metamorphosis before it turns into an elver. We are all the more convinced that the first stages of the development take place in the depths of the sea. But the main question remains unanswered. Where does this spawning take place? How, in what circumstances, does the eel reproduce? On the one hand, the pubescent eels disappear: on the other hand, all we find in the sea are the leptocephali which will ultimately become elvers. The problem remains. We are unable to trace out in the ocean the route taken by the eels before they reproduce and, consequently, no solution is forthcoming. Our direct inquiry leads to a dead end.

In the last few years, a brilliant piece of work has enabled us to get round the difficulty, and secure the answer for which naturalists have been searching so long. It is due to a Danish ichthyologist, the late Professor J. Schmidt. As eel fisheries have considerable economic importance in Denmark, it was considered desirable both in the interests of protection and, if possible, of repopulation, to find out exactly all that goes on in the life of the species. Professor Schmidt devoted many years to the study of these questions. In the course of the researches necessary, he made several successive cruises on board ships specially fitted out for the purpose, the *Thor* and the *Dana*. He undertook his investigations methodically, with the utmost determination, and without slackening. Proving, by his own example, that Buffon was profoundly right when he said that " genius is unflagging patience," it was the combination of tenacious patience with scientific knowledge that enabled him to succeed in his task.

Finding it impossible, with all the appliances at his disposal, to locate the migrating eels in the sea, because they were too elusive and too mobile, he concentrated upon the leptocephali which are more numerous and less active; they can be taken from the currents in which they are suspended. Occasionally, a single cast of the net will bring in hundreds of them. He then discovered a remarkable fact about the distribution of these larvæ. They appear in the Atlantic Ocean in order of size; the largest close to the shores of the old world, and the smallest to those of the new. Difference in size being evidence of difference in age, for the smallest are bound to be the youngest, this was as much as to say that the leptocephali of the eel are distributed in the Atlantic in order of age, the oldest on the European side and the youngest on the American side. There are no exceptions to this order of things. It is categorical, progressive, and regular.

Here was a ray of light. Since the larvæ of the European eels scattered about the ocean are younger and younger as one approaches the American continent, it is obvious that their earliest youth, their first days, must be spent on that side. All that was necessary after this discovery was to cruise about those regions, taking bearings in one place after another, and to steer a course in the direction indicated by the harvest of leptocephali as they became progressively smaller. So the place was reached where the tiniest larvæ were found, just hatched from the eggs. This was obviously the place where the eels spawned. It was reached, not by following the parents on their way to spawn, but by collecting the results of that spawning in the very place where those parents actually put forth the eggs. The final cruise which took the naturalist to the spawning place of which he had been in search was taken in 1921 and 1922, dates of very great importance in the study of the subject, for they provided a formal solution to a problem which has been puzzling people since the days of antiquity.

This spawning place, where the European eels meet for their wedding, is in the open Atlantic Ocean, between 48 and 65 degrees of west longitude near the Bermudas and the northern shores of the Sargasso sea. Here, at a depth between 110 and 160 fathoms, the spawning takes place at the beginning of spring, between three and five months after the eels leave Europe, months devoted to the journey across the ocean. The spawning takes place in midwater, at a temperature of about twenty degrees Centigrade. Each female expels millions of tiny eggs, which float freely in the water. At this temperature, only a short period of incubation is necessary, and the eggs soon hatch. At the beginning of April, the fry, small and tenuous, like threads, measure only twelve or thirteen millimetres in length. The myriads of them fill the waters in which they have just been born. At the very beginning they have the flat shape of the leptocephalus, and they keep it for a fairly long time, growing all the while.

This wedding rendezvous, this place where the wedding journey ends, is close to that of the American eels, to which they go after an exactly similar journey. But they have not so far to go, only a quarter or a fifth of the distance, and their spawning place, relatively speaking, is almost near at hand to them. The archipelago of the Bermudas, so named after the Spanish navigator Bermudez who discovered it in 1522, is about six hundred miles from the

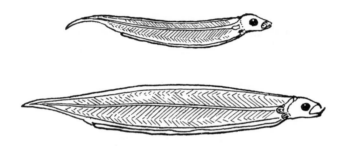

FIG. 48.—FIRST STAGES IN THE LARVAL DEVELOPMENT OF THE EEL

First stages in the development of the eel after its hatching (from Professor J. Schmidt's sketches). Above: a very young larva measuring actually eight millimetres. The older larva (below) measures twelve. These stages mark the beginning of the various stages shown in Fig. 49.

southern coast of the United States, in the latitude of Cape Hatteras and Chesapeake Bay. Close to it is the northern boundary of the immense floating prairie of sargasso (gulf-weed) where brown algæ (*Sargatium bacciferum*), dragged by the waves from the subtropical coasts, then taken by the currents and caught in the whirlpool of the mid-Atlantic waters, continue to live in scattered tufts of dark golden colour, floating on the surface, kept there by their spreading branches swollen with gas.

Not far from this marine prairie, the coral reefs of the Bermudas rise above the waves, surrounded almost perpendicularly by vast abysses which go down three or four miles in depth. The nuptial rendezvous is deep down immediately below them. Towards it crowd the multitudes of eels in their millions. Many hundreds of feet below the surface their sinuous masses twist and turn at a level to which the light of day never penetrates. Then, suspended in the water, the two sexes come together, intertwine, and the monstrous marriage, for which such a long preparation has been necessary and for which the participants have come so far, is consummated beyond the reach of

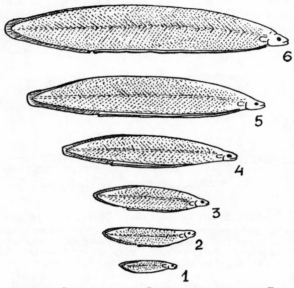

FIG. 49.—GROWTH OF THE LEPTOCEPHALUS OF THE EEL

Stages in the growth of the Leptocephalus of the European Eel during its return journey across the Atlantic Ocean (from Professor J. Schmidt's sketch). Nos. 1, 2 and 3 show the first year's growth; 4 and 5, the second year; and 6, the third year. Then come the phases of metamorphosis shown in Fig. 50.

human eye, and the only signs of it, the only proof that it has ever taken place, are the eggs and the fry that have just hatched from them.

IV. Our imagination may, perhaps, reconstruct for us the likely stages of this great journey which takes the eels for two thousand and more miles across the Atlantic. First, we may call to mind the vigour and endurance which the creature customarily displays all through its life, and so, we may realize that no effort, however great it may appear,

is beyond its powers. Then we may try to get an idea of
things as they are, or rather, as they must be. When I
look at the tank in my aquarium which contains the eels,
I see how they swim. They advance with an undulatory
motion; they beat the water with their whole body, especially
with the rear portion of it, for this is thinner but more
supple and mobile than the other. In spite of this serpentine
appearance, they move in a straight line, and keep up their
swimming for a long time. They do not swim very quickly,
covering, on an average, eight to twelve inches a second.
But that is thirty-nine to fifty-nine feet a minute, more than
half a mile every hour, twelve and a half to fifteen and a
half miles a day, if we are justified in supposing that they
keep up the same rate of progress for so long a time.

Now, upon their wedding journey, the generative eels,
driven onwards by the excitation of the spawning for which
they are getting ready, move without stopping, without
resting a moment, especially during the night when the
daylight does not immobilize them. In the sea, when they
have gone down almost to the depths where the rays of
light do not penetrate, there is nothing at all to interfere
with their progress. They can then put forth all their
strength and go at full speed, eight to twelve miles every
twenty-four hours. Observations which have been carried
out under natural conditions confirm the conclusions to
which our study of the behaviour of eels in the aquarium
leads us. The eels passing through the narrows from the
Baltic on their way to the North Sea, actually do swim at
this pace, if we may judge by the evidence provided by
those which have been marked, put back in the water, and
caught again later. On the other hand, a pace of from
eight to twelve miles a day means that over six hundred
miles can be covered in between a month and six weeks.
The distance from the Old World to the spawning place
taking from four to five months, at this rate of progress, it
is that actually taken by the eels in the journey which they
begin in autumn and complete about the end of winter or
the beginning of spring.

Working upon these premises, we may imagine what
an extraordinary spectacle these myriads of generative eels
must present as they journey from the rivers and lakes in

which they have been living until now. The creatures which used to crawl and bury themselves have now taken to swimming. Their sexual development, as it follows its regular course, drives them along in a continually increasing state of excitement, and they become more and more active. Love drives them along. Their sinuous hordes, after leaving the coast, cross the whole breadth of the continental shelf, and reach the slopes that rise perpendicularly from the great depths, over which they pass across the ocean. It is a long way and their journey a painful one, but their vigour is immense and eventually triumphs. Nothing of this journey is to be seen above the waves, for it is all going on in deep water, many hundreds of feet below the surface. But it does go on; it reaches its goal. And as it goes on, the sexual elaboration increases accordingly; the milt of the males matures; the ovules of the females complete their development. When the goal is near, when the eels reach it, now ready to bring forth young, they proceed to spawn. The journey is ended.

This gigantic migration, this swarming of creatures swimming, winding their way through the darkness of the waters, startles the imagination. Doubtless the mighty gluttons of the deep take their toll of the multitude, they become the prey of sharks and cetaceans which find in them a manna which is theirs for the taking. The eels were many when they set out upon this journey, and doubt-less, the majority never arrive. But enough remain, in spite of all the losses sustained on the way, to bring together at the meeting-place a goodly host.

Not all the eels set out upon this hazardous journey. Some, at the period of puberty, cannot, for reasons con-nected with the locality, leave the pool or lake in which they are too closely imprisoned. Like the sterile trout of the deep lakes, and for the same reason, their ovaries, for these eels are usually females, then change and atrophy. Rendered sterile, naturally castrated, like pullets, they grow fat in the same way, but go on living and growing larger. Eunuch eels of this sort have been kept in captivity for twenty or thirty years. Huge specimens weighing many pounds have been caught. But these eunuchs are in the minority. The greatest number find their way to the sea when the proper time comes, then set off across the ocean, like a vast people migrating to the west, setting off each year on the same journey, inspired and guided by the urge to produce young.

V. What is the force which drives all these creatures to undertake such a journey? Who supports them in its accomplishment, despite so many difficulties, those due to weakness of body, and to obstacles in the environment? What is the call they hear which causes them to undertake such a vast migration? And why are things not so arranged that they can produce young in the coastal waters where they are, instead of being compelled to this perilous, wearisome crossing of the ocean, which takes so long?

To me, it seems that the answer to these questions is to be found in things themselves, which must be considered as a whole as well as in their relationship to one another. There is no difference in this respect between the eels and the golden perch, the mullet and the bass, their companions in the pools along the shore. In spite of some small differences in detail, the essential circumstances are the same. Sensitive to warmth and absence of light, the species exalts this sensitivity at the time when the elaboration of germs brings in its train an increase in vitality. The creature, rendered hypersensitive to the physical conditions of its surroundings, is polarized towards them and allows itself to be guided by them. Fleeing from the light, it lets itself go towards zones which are progressively deeper, from the ponds to the streams, then to the rivers, finally to the sea, in this respect doing what the young salmon do when they go down. Seeking for warmth, they answer the call of the warm waters of the open sea and make for them, leaving the coast behind. The golden perch and the mullet, coastal species which, like the eels, are guided by a similar impulse and set out as they do, do not go beyond the waters which border the shore; but the eels which flee the light and love the abysses, push their journey farther and continue it to the depths.

The shores of Europe are bathed by expanses of warm water that come from the open sea, and these are particularly noticeable in the autumn, when the shore waters begin to get colder. These expanses provide the eel with a favourable environment of which he does not hesitate to take advantage. The eels plunge into them, go through them in the direction from which they come, for they find a temperature more and more to their liking all the time. Getting farther and farther from the shores they have left and reaching the open sea, they soon come upon the current of the Gulf Stream from which these warm expanses originate. There they settle, finding the temperature always more and more favourable, and strive to go against the current. The migration is continued in the Gulf Stream till it reaches its end.

The Gulf Stream, formed in the Gulf of Mexico, starts out towards the north as it enters the Atlantic Ocean, then turns   stwards by degrees, till it finally strikes the coasts of Europe and Northern Africa. At its origin, the dark blue water, contrasting in colour with that which surrounds it, advances at a speed of between four and four and a half miles an hour, at a depth of between two thousand five hundred and three thousand two hundred and fifty feet. Its temperature, which is very high, is as much as twenty-seven or twenty-eight degrees. As it moves onward, turning eastwards, it slows up and spreads out to a breadth of a hundred miles and more. Its speed decreases proportionately. So it passes the archipelago of the Bermudas, then Newfoundland, and beyond, now flowing eastwards, it spreads out in a vast fan, whose branches, crossing the ocean in its whole breadth, finally reach the Old World. On the way, its temperature drops continuously, but it is always higher than that of the surrounding water.

Urged forward by their thermic polarization, the eels proceed against this current and go up it so as always to be reaching a higher temperature. Like the salmon and the shad in their streams, they go against the current, using the only method of progress which their limbless bodies will allow, swimming by undulation. Their generative excitement increases all the time. Their sense of well-being increases continuously; the preparation for reproduction is nearing its desired end. Then, in waters becoming warmer and warmer, still advancing in the direction which allows them to receive more and more calories, the eels reach the zones where they find the water that is favourable to them, whose qualities harmonize completely with the demands of their reproductive system. They have matured their germs on the way, and now proceed to spawn. Their eggs, ejected by the mothers in mid-ocean, like those of the tunny, the cod, and the sardine, are fertilized where they are and hatch a few days later.

We can only presume that this is what happens, for we cannot actually observe or investigate the course of events. But other migratory fishes, which we can get at more readily, make us believe that this is what probably takes place. From first to last, the behaviour of the eels seems as if ordained, directed, rigorously determined by a continual concordance between the physical condition of the sur-rounding waters and the organic condition of the interior environment as its sexual functions are being developed. When sexuality makes itself apparent, organic conditions effect a realization of their compelling force. The eel is bound, inevitably, to do what they would have it do. And, in return, it is able, despite the feebleness of a body almost deprived of fins, to accomplish the extraordinary feat of crossing the Atlantic.

It is in the same case as the salmon; both are controlled by the same law. In spite of the differences in the direction which is taken and the impulse which causes it to be taken, the course is the same. The salmon, impelled by the needs of its respiratory system, leaves the marine abysses to go and spawn in the mountain torrents. The eel, drawn on-wards by its desire for warmth, leaves the land waters to spawn in the depths of the ocean. In both cases the goal is at the utmost limit of the waters, and the manner of the journey is determined by an ineluctable law. For weeks and months, the salmon forces its way obstinately up the stream to find in it places that are more and more favourable. In the same way, the eel, for month after month, strives persistently to find around it the water which most befits it. In both cases, the journey which has to be made, the distance which has to be covered, are of secondary im-portance; the creature is concerned simply with keeping itself in its water, with making progress towards a greater degree of well-being. It would turn round and round in a circle if circumstances decreed that it should obtain the desired result by so doing. But Nature has disposed things in such a way that progress happens to be made in a straight line. It is only to us, who consider the journey in terms of our own experience, that it is astounding. It is not at all so to the eel, which measures things by an entirely different standard.

Besides, this remarkable journey is remarkable only in the case of the European eels. Those of other parts of the world have not so far to go. The eels of the United States, when they get down to the sea, find themselves quite near their spawning place. The Indo-Pacific species, which are still better situated, reach their favourable water almost immediately. They are able to spawn near the abysses at hand, and have no need to set out on a long migration. In Nature, things are accommodated to the different conditions of existence. And the journey is made, if it is necessary, in accordance with the order established by the common action of all the forces of Nature.

VI. We have solved the problem of the reproduction of eels, but not completely. The main riddle which the species propounds to us brings in its train a number of secondary riddles to which we do not yet know the answer. How is the journey really accomplished? How, and by what means, is such a migration carried to a conclusion, a migration no one has ever seen, which can be reconstructed only by the imagination working upon what is known of the manners and customs of the creatures concerned in it? Doubtless by swimming, by going against the threads of the warm currents, and keeping deep enough to avoid the action of the light rays which come down from the surface. But is the journey made in compact, closely knit bands, like those of the elvers which go back up the rivers, or in little isolated groups, or by individuals? Do the sexes make the journey in common, or do they form distinct groups, which come together only when they have reached their goal? In the Atlantic abysses, where there are only occasional shallows, do the eels move onward continually, or do they rest for short periods of time? None of these questions has been answered.

Another problem is that of the Mediterranean eels. Each year, they pile by millions into the deep reservoir of that inland sea, and then disappear without leaving a trace. Do they stay there? Or do they find their way to the ocean and join the army of their Atlantic fellows, and go with them to share whatever fate may await them? The evidence is contradictory. So far, no very young leptocephali have ever been found in the Mediterranean; and this fact, which tends to show that the eels do not spawn in this sea, makes us presume that they go to the ocean to spawn there with the others. In that case, they must cross the Straits of Gibraltar, the only way open to them. Yet, at the time when one would expect to find them going out, not a trace of them is to be seen in the Straits. The tremendous eddies which stir to the bottom the currents which abound everywhere in it ought to bring back a few of these travellers which are in such numbers, but they never bring back any. Is there really any movement through the Straits, and do the Mediterranean eels go to spawn in the Bermudas? Do they pass along the bottom in a gigantic caravan winding its way to the ocean favoured by the current leaving the straits? Or is there somewhere in the Eastern Mediterranean a spawning place hitherto unknown, where the fry, after they are hatched, stay deep down in the water before dispersing? This is still a puzzle which we may discuss, but cannot really solve.

The most fascinating of all these supplementary riddles is that of the ultimate fate of the parents when once they have spawned. Each year, at a fixed date, these myriads of eels assemble in the same place to bring forth their young. We might presume that, when they had done so, we should find some trace of them besides the fry which were hatched on the spot. But, contrary to our expectations, there is not a sign of them. They have disappeared completely, and their disappearance remains complete. Neither the ocean in the neighbourhood of the spawning place, nor the land nearest to it, ever show traces of these parents who have just brought forth their young? Do they die when they have spawned, exhausted by the trials of their long journey, worn out by the organic losses of reproduction, as is often the case in similar circumstances with other migratory fishes, such as the salmon and the shad? Or do they go on living, changing both their abode and their customs; do they return to the depths of the sea, go down into the abysses over which they have just put forth their eggs? Like the most closely related genera, the muræna and the conger, whose life goes on, whose growth continues until their bodies assume enormous proportions, do they too become giants, able to come up again from the abysses and, each year, participate in the processes of reproduction? A new riddle, but one which we cannot solve. Nature has not yet revealed her secret.

Is the eel, which dwells for a time in the waters of the land, a species that belongs there, or is it rather a denizen of the abysses, which simply comes to spend its youth in the ponds and rivers, and then goes back to the abyss, to go on growing and live the rest of its life there? Is it, as we know it in its final form, to disappear as soon as it has spawned for the first time, its growth and its life then coming to an end? Or is it the young edition of an unknown creature, which begins its growth on land but ends its days in the waters of the abyss, extending its prodigious empire, vaster than that of any other creature that lives on most of our continents and in the depth of the oceans? All this is still unknown to us.

What a fascinating journey of exploration it would be, if we were only able to make it, that would take us into these dark abysses where the waters of the vast ocean are at rest, abysses of greater extent than the continents, deeper, broader than the highest mountains that earth can show. The eel and the salmon travel through them. It may be that they are deserts with but a scanty population, peopled, here and there, by animals of which oceanographic cruises have brought us back a few examples. It may be that they teem with animal life, a life which finds no counterpart elsewhere, giants, unknown monsters. It may be that, down there, some parts are poor and some rich. This is the great mystery of the depths of the sea, a domain which we cannot reach, whose perpetual darkness extends even to our knowledge of it, which is but in tiny fragments which we have to collect piece by piece.

CHAPTER XVII

THE ASTOUNDING JOURNEY OF THE EUROPEAN EELS

Third Part: The Journey of the Elvers up the Rivers

I. THE estuaries of the rivers, the lagoons along the coast, the entrances to the pools along the shore, in all the districts which the eel frequents, are invaded, every year, in a very strange and unusual manner. This invasion begins in November or December, reaches its height in January, February and March, when the cold waters are richest in dissolved oxygen, begins to drop off in April and finally comes to an end, though it will begin again the following autumn. It is the extraordinary phenomenon of the ascent, the invasion of the brackish and fresh waters, by tiny eels which have come from the waters of the open sea, arriving in vast hosts, penetrating all the openings, then making continual, gradual progress, until they spread themselves all over the districts to which they have come. It is a genuine, a complete invasion, beginning with the frontier of the coast, gradually reaching the interior, extending in all directions, and ending in a tenacious occupation.

The eels which arrive in this way are tiny fry, measuring, on an average, two to three inches in length and less than a tenth of an inch in diameter. Like little supple sticks, they have already, despite their small size, the external shape of their species, the cylindrical body, the small head, the well cleft mouth with the lower jaw protruding slightly, the undulating method of swimming in the water, and the serpentine method of crawling along the bottom. The only difference between them and the adult eels is in their size and their extreme transparency. Often one can only see them and make them out against the light, or when the light falls in a certain way. The little black stains which are their eyes make us aware of their existence. These miniature eels, like worms, apparently made of the purest crystal, swimming along in the water and easily taken for that water, may readily pass unperceived.

They make up for their small size by their astounding numbers. They are given various names in different places, called *elvers* in England, *civelles* and *piballes* on the Atlantic coast of France and *bouirons* in the Mediterranean, *angulas* in Spain, and *cieche* in Italy. They are caught and used as food. The fishermen catch them in nets with a very fine mesh. All that is necessary is to dip these nets in the water when the elvers are passing, lift them out again, and they will be full of crystalline, squirming creatures. Sometimes a bucket will bring them up by the hundred. If we try to calculate the total number of these tiny invaders, the figures run into thousands of millions. We have only to multiply the millions of mother-eels which cross the ocean to spawn by the millions of eggs they produce within their bodies, to understand the meaning of these vast numbers. There is nothing on earth, not even in the world of insects, neither the dense swarms of locusts nor the bands of ants which set out on a marauding expedition, to approach this startling profusion hidden away in the mass of the waters.

In one of my attempts to calculate their numbers, I found that the railway stations of the Department of the Landes, in 1906, despatched, for the making of preserves or for ordinary consumption, seventy-three tons of elvers that had been caught there. As a pound in weight corresponds to something between seven hundred and fifty and a thousand of these fry, the total quantity thus despatched represents an average of a hundred to a hundred and fifty million individuals. But this enormous figure only represents those sent by train. It takes no account of those dealt with by other means of transport, nor of those consumed locally, and still less, of those which escape the fishermen. To get a true idea, the number should be greatly increased, multiplied by ten or a hundred, perhaps by more. And this is the coast of a single French Department. But extended to the whole of Western Europe, it may give us an idea of the prodigious quantities of young eels which, each year, make up the invading army. Such a number is beyond our powers of calculation, and it is equally impossible to destroy. The invading hosts, which no human agency has brought together, which have come into existence simply by the harmony of natural conditions, escape, thanks to continual renewings and their magnitude, the decimation which destroys more active fishes. They may sometimes be reduced, in one place or another and from one year to another, but they never disappear.

This invasion has its hours, its moments. It is particularly strong at night, for the future eel already tries to avoid the light. When the sea is rough, when a strong tide drives the waters of the open sea to the shore, more fry come to the estuaries, especially when there have been a number of invigorating floods. Then the bands which go up the rivers are even more tightly packed. Sometimes, in certain circumstances, there are so many that they become more than usually visible. After the dawn, during the dull grey mornings, the elvers keep up their progress towards the higher reaches. They seek those places where the force of the water is not so great as to interfere too greatly with their efforts; they keep as near as possible to the banks, and under cover of them. There they gather in great numbers, waving about, swimming against the stream. Often, piling themselves one upon another, they form a dense heap, a quivering moving cordon which moves as it goes up the watercourse. This is a strange company in which myriads of active individuals make up a sort of total unity, like a troop of unmeasured proportions which, because it is so dense, can be seen in the water through which it is passing.

Sometimes, in the lower reaches of the Loire, this cordon extends unbroken for several miles, a yard across and half a yard thick. Millions of elvers form it, quick moving and sinuous. When it is broad daylight they break up, stop, spread out over the bed of the river and bury themselves in the mud, or hide among the pebbles. When night falls, they come to life again and go on their way, reassemble as though in response to a bugle call, and reform the cordon, within which each, striving to make progress itself, takes what advantage it may from the efforts of its neighbours and the community as a whole.

It may be that this cordon, made up of these puny elvers, represents on a smaller scale and in the river waters, other cordons, formed in the same way but by the great adult eels which cross the ocean to go and spawn far away. If that is so, their long journey is made in common. And the giant cordon, living, moving, made up of these large eels, crosses the Atlantic like an enormous cable which lays itself in the bosom of the waters.

If I go back to the little elvers in my aquarium, I see that they already show the characteristics of their species. They move hastily about the tank. Some swim, others crawl along the bottom; some stay still for a moment, their heads uplifted. Those that move are the most numerous; at this age the creature is more eager to keep on the move than anything else. They undulate in the water, making the greatest effort with the hind part of their bodies; the fore part oscillating from right to left and back again, as though to tear asunder the liquid masses of the water and so make progress easier. Those on the bottom stretch themselves, spread themselves, raise their delicate heads with the black eyes. They are eager to bury themselves in the sand, to curl up in the holes. They hunt all night and often stay motionless all day. The light frightens them; makes them disperse and scatter.

I take one of them and, to examine it more closely, put it on a glass slide and look at it under a lens. I can see clearly the way in which the little animal is made, drawn out like a stick of crystal, cylindrical in front and slightly compressed at the back. Its length, hardly more than two and a half inches, is practically twenty-five times its diameter. It is so transparent that, within it, I can make out most of its organs. A thin brownish line that goes from end to end shows the position of the spinal marrow above the slender vertebral column. With the two black spots which are the eyes this is the only touch of colour which the body shows. In the front part of the trunk, below the belly, a few yellowish, pinkish, whitish masses, very light in hue, represent the viscera which end in the narrow intestinal cord. Thin transversal zigzag lines show the segments of the musculature. The principal fins, the dorsal and the anal, frame the trunk like thin transparent edges, one running along the back, the other along the belly, joining at the back. There they form, as they spread, a full terminal palette, which contains within itself, in its axis, a narrow terminal brush, a sort of miniature caudal fin.

This slight, delicate organism, whose tiny skeleton is still cartilage, yet has behind it a long career both as regards age and complexity. It came out of its egg, still more tiny than it is to-day, nearly three years before. It began as a leptocephalus, a flat, oblong larva, and, in that form, began to grow. After undergoing a metamorphosis, it became the elver that it is now. It has lived long and hard. It has covered vast distances in the sea. Yet, when one looks at it, it seems rudimentary; it shows no sign of all that it has gone through. At the same age, a carp or a trout is a quite powerful fish, weighing a pound or two and measuring many inches in length, capable of reproduction. Yet this elver is still a puny little fry, whose organism is still incomplete, a long way removed from the time when it will be able to fashion within itself the germs that will develop into young.

II. The cruises and investigations of Professor J. Schmidt have thrown light upon this history from its beginning. When the young eel is hatched in the deep waters of the spawning ground, near the Bermudas and the floating fields of the Sargasso sea, it measures hardly more than a few millimetres in length and a fraction of a millimetre in breadth. Fine, transparent, the remarkable feature about it in these minute proportions is the relative size of its globular head, which has long projecting crooks. As it grows and its proportions become more generalized, the young fry gradually assumes the characteristic features of the leptocephalus, with head now proportionately small, teeth which no longer project, a compressed body, oblong, shaped like a leaf with a lance-head. In June, three months after it has hatched, it is twenty-five millimetres long. Three months later, it is between thirty and forty millimetres. It grows regularly, still remaining flat, lanceolated, and the only important change in it is that of growth.

This growth takes a long time. It goes on through the rest of the year in which it was spawned and the year afterwards; it occupies three years, or rather three summers; at least the European eel does, for the United States eel takes only two years to grow. In any case, the extraordinary point is the excessive slowness with which it grows. When this growth approaches its end, the leptocephali are no more than sixty to eighty-eight millimetres long; compared with most other species of fish, and when their almost advanced age is taken into consideration, they seem like dwarfs. But this characteristic is common to them all. The vital energy of the creature, which is either too weak or too much employed for other purposes, does not seem to concern itself with growth. The small intestine, beneath the belly, where it occupies only a small space, does not seem to fulfil the function which usually devolves upon it. Doubtless these eel fry, floating larvæ, nourish themselves directly on the substances dissolved in the sea-water after the manner of other floating animals, and the scantiness of such a system of nutrition may explain the slowness of growth.

Besides, these leptocephalic larvæ are practically inert and passive. All they attempt to do is to keep themselves suspended; their little fins have very little power to move them. On the other hand, their shape allows the water to carry them along without any difficulty. Hatched in the neighbourhood of the place where the Gulf Stream begins, caught in its current, they are carried along by it, floating in the water, almost a part of it, thanks to the transparency of their bodies. Their hosts, borne by the current as leaves are borne by the wind, go wherever it goes. So they cross the Atlantic Ocean and come to Europe. The journey takes three years. Born of mothers who had made the same journey in the opposite direction, they are brought back to the place from which their mothers came by the very current against which those mothers had to swim, as the salmon fry come down the streams and rivers which their parents went up to give them birth. Certainly these vast hordes in their long journey are, like their parents, a prey to the rapacious fishes which find in them a very ample and satisfactory source of nourishment. During the three years of their crossing they doubtless lose the greater part of their effectives. But in spite of these disappearances, enough of them remain, when the journey comes to an end, to make up the vast number of the elvers who go up to the land waters.

At last, its long period of growth at an end, the larva is ready to undergo its metamorphosis. The leptocephalus becomes an elver while it remains suspended in the water of the sea. Today we know the successive phases of this change. The principal natural history museums of the world possess specimens representative of these stages, mostly thanks to the Danish naturalist Professor Schmidt, who has done more than anyone else to describe them. I have before me, as I write, some which have been sent me,

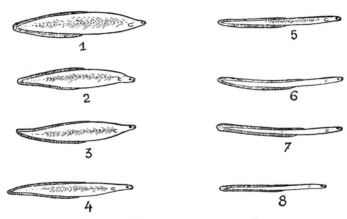

FIG. 50.—METAMORPHOSIS OF THE EEL

Stages in the metamorphosis of the Leptocephalus into a young eel or elver. Half natural size. Nos. 1 to 5 show the change of the Leptocephalus into a transparent elver (this takes place in the sea). Nos. 6, 7 and 8 the change into a pigmented elver (this takes place in brackish and fresh waters). After this the creature has only to grow to become the eel we know.

and they form a very striking series. The change begins with the head, or, more exactly, behind it; its attachment to the trunk grows shorter, and turns into a sort of neck. Then an identical change takes place at the other end of the body, near the tail, the attachment of which to the trunk also becomes shorter. After this, the two extremities now being freed, the restriction begins to affect the middle. When we examine the series of these larvæ in process of transmutation, we see that the body gradually loses height and spreads out in length. By degrees the oblong shape, like that of a flattened shuttle, which is that of a leptocephalus, disappears and is replaced by another, that of a cylindrical rod. The larva becomes an elver. Henceforth it ceases to be the almost passive organism, borne along by the water, which the currents have transported across the Atlantic. Henceforth it behaves as an active, mobile organism, which its new shape allows to swim by its own power.

But while it changes in form and behaviour the larva remains transparent. Before, it might easily have been mistaken for the water which surrounded it. It remains transparent during its metamorphosis, and will remain so until after it has entered the rivers and canals. But if the organic apparatus of which it is composed remains hyaline,

FIG. 51.—THE ELVER

Transparent elver, almost twice natural size, showing the connected fins outside the body, and, inside, the digestive tube, the notochord, and musculation.

it none the less undergoes considerable alterations which prepare it to assume its final structure. One of the most remarkable of these changes is that in the intestine, which grows shorter; the anal orifice which was at the end of it is brought up to the front part of the body. The anal fin goes with it; it extends gradually towards the front and becomes longer. Further, the organism contracts upon itself, as if it were tightening up its different parts. When the metamorphosis is complete, the elver is smaller than the leptocephalus from which it sprang. Not only has it lost height by becoming rod-shaped, it has also lost length, in a proportion varying from an eighth to a tenth of its original size. This is a phenomenon which may be observed elsewhere, in similar cases of metamorphosis from the larva stage: the butterfly often has a body smaller than that of its caterpillar and, among the batrachians, some of the toads, like the Pelobates and the Alytes, have, when they produce young, offspring larger than the parents.

This metamorphosis goes on in the sea, but not far from the coastal waters. We may conclude that the physical conditions of this new abode have some effect in producing it, perhaps a determining effect. These waters, in certain places and at certain times, are richer in dissolved oxygen, and less laden with chlorides than those of the open sea. They attract, they summon to the coast, the fry of those species which, beside the eels, grow in the estuaries and coastal ponds. We may presume, therefore, that they also attract the fry of the eels, and that the greater facilities they provide for respiratory oxydation activate the changes and let loose the metamorphosis. However that may be, the leptocephali, when they come in contact with these waters, change into elvers, and the latter, instead of staying any longer in the sea, hear still more loudly the call of the fresh waters, swim towards them and go up the estuaries. Now the ascent begins. Now the land waters are to experience the invasion of these tiny eels which have arrived from the open sea, the prelude to the gradual invasion that goes farther and farther inland.

When the elvers enter fresh or brackish water, they are still almost perfectly transparent, as if they kept within themselves the clear limpidity of the current which has slowly brought them there. But now there is a change. The first stage of the metamorphosis manifested itself by the transformation of the leptocephalus into an elver; the second will appear as the change of the transparent elver into a fry that is both opaque and pigmented.

As it continues to ascend, getting farther and farther away from the sea from which it came, going always more and more into land waters, the elver continues to undergo organic changes. Pigments deposit themselves in its skin, which becomes, consequently, a yellowish green colour. Now it loses its transparency; it has adopted the colours it will henceforth wear. By April and May, most of the elvers have already their final coloration, and this is the more complete and the more early as the season is precocious, for heat favours the formation of the pigment. Inside the body, the skeleton consolidates itself; it loses its cartilaginous structure and becomes bony. The different parts of it, though they are still small by reason of the small dimensions of the organism, in spite of this smallness and especially as regards the head, acquire a hardness which is not found in the transparent elver.

These new transformations are accompanied, like those which went before them, by a reduction in the size of the body. The leptocephalus grows smaller when it becomes an elver; the elver, in its turn, grows smaller when it becomes a pigmented fry. In length it loses about a tenth and in thickness from a third to a quarter. These pigmented fry, at this period of their life, are tiny, threadlike creatures, measuring hardly two and a half inches in length and two to two and a half millimetres in diameter, their little heads being a little broader than the trunk. Now they have all the characteristic features of the eel, appearance, colour, behaviour, attitude; all they have to do now is to grow.

FIG. 52.—SCALE OF THE MALE EEL

Diagram showing the construction of the scale of a male eel of the mountain torrent. The zones of growth show that the creature has lived five years since its scales began to form, and that its total age is about ten or eleven. Enlarged about thirty times.

Myriads of them often fill the sandy, muddy regions which they are so fond of in the ponds and the lower reaches of the rivers. If we suddenly pull up a handful of this mud, we see them squirming, crawling.

Looking at them so, numerous, delicate, and frail, one would imagine that they had only just been hatched, and it is not difficult to understand the ancient legends which made them be born from the mud, or brought into existence by a sudden viviparous act of reproduction. It was impossible to imagine, such as they really are, the real facts, the natural facts, so different from what usually happens. No presumption, no imagination, however daring, could have got anywhere near the full reality—the distant spawning, the crossing of the ocean, the metamorphosis. These tiny creatures, far from setting out in life, are already aged. Hatched more than three years before, they have gone through a complex metamorphosis and their small size by no means signifies youth.

Before them, these fry have the vast domain of the land waters. They get ready to occupy that domain, to go everywhere it is possible for them to go. Setting out from their bases, the mouths of rivers, they invade the interior without ceasing, they deploy their forces as they proceed, and neglect no place which they are capable of reaching. Their extraordinary numbers enable them to try everything.

This tenacious penetration, crawling, obstinate, goes on under the water, silently, far from our eyes; its principal movements take place at night. Each year the ocean brings new armies, all fresh, which carry on the invasion, doubling and reinforcing the hosts of their predecessors. Each year

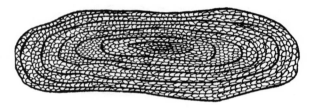

FIG. 53.—SCALE OF THE FEMALE EEL

Diagram showing the construction of the scale of a female eel of the mountain torrent. The zones of growth, separated by concentric lines, number eight. Hence we may presume that the creature has lived eight years since its scales began to form. This date being five or six years after its hatching into a Leptocephalus in the ocean, its age must be about thirteen or fourteen. Enlarged about thirty times.

the land waters are invaded by these hordes which, come from the sea. It is a continuous invasion, an invasion that never ends, having no counterpart in nature except the returning exodus to the ocean, there to produce future invaders, the exodus of the eels who have grown fat and prospered in the conquered realm. Its numbers are its strength. A living wave of assault thrown forward by the waves of the sea, the sea brings it in the surf which strikes against the shore, carrying it beyond the limits which enclose itself, and extending its powers even beyond its own domain.

III. After this, the eel shares the fate common to all living creatures; it grows, it develops. Now that it has assumed its final form, the eel goes on developing that form until pubescence interrupts it and substitutes that of pre-paration for reproduction. This growth is slow, slower than that of the other fishes near which, in the fresh water, the species now lives. Two years after its meta-morphosis, five years after it was hatched, the creature whose scales are now first beginning to form in the skin itself, seldom measures more than eight inches in length. The rhythm of physical development proceeds at the same slow pace.

Puberty makes its appearance at times varying according

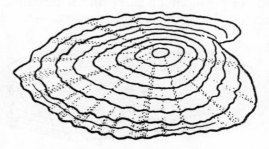

FIG. 54.—OTOLITH OF THE FEMALE EEL

Diagram showing the construction of an otolith of a female eel of the mountain torrent. The number of concentric zones of growth, eight in number, corresponds with that of the scale represented in the preceding illustration. Enlarged about thirty times.

to sex. The male eels are precocious like the males of several other fishes. Usually, they become pubescent four, five, or six years after their arrival in fresh waters. Their length at this time is about sixteen inches at the most. The females, who are slower, go on growing for several more years. Their length and breadth often become double those of the males, sometimes even more. The dispro-portion of size between the sexes is more marked in the eels than in most other fishes. Thus accentuated it is the cause of the remarkable contrast which we notice when the eels set out on their wedding journey, the males younger and smaller, the females older and larger, crossing the Atlantic together.

Such a diversity of age and sex gives a peculiar interest to the studies which have been made upon the growth of eels. We try to calculate this growth by reading the scales, although in the eel these are small and enclosed in the skin. I scrape a fresh skin, and dig out of it the tiny scales. I macerate the product of this scraping in a little water for a day or two; then the organic matter of the skin decomposes and the scales, now free, collect at the bottom of the vessel. I have only to pick them up and put them on a glass slide, then I can examine them through a microscope.

Then I see that each scale is shaped like an oval plate, its substance made up of tiny grains, arranged in concentric layers. When I compare a number of them, taken from individuals of different sizes, I find that they are larger in proportion to the size of the individual, and that, on the other hand, the number of their concentric layers is greater as they themselves are larger. There is, therefore, a definite relation between these factors, from which we are justified in concluding that it is possible to decide the age of the eels from the number of the layers of their scales. It seems, as in the other species of fishes which have been investigated in the same way, that each of these layers takes about a year in the making. So we may find out the age of the creature, at least from the date at which the scales began to form. As the result of this examination, we discover that the male eels, when they set out on their wedding journey, are usually between eight and ten years old, that is, from the time when they were hatched, and their female companions are between twelve and fifteen. The cycle of generations in the eel, therefore, is renewed at a much greater interval than is the case with other fishes.

There is a real value in such rough approximations, but we must not lose sight of the exceptions. They must be regarded as a fair means of arriving at an average, not as justifying a categorical statement in each individual case. They are only approximations and not capable of precise affirmation because the layers which indicate growth may be confused and multiplied in individual cases. Our investigations may be corroborated by further observations of the otoliths. This is the name given to the calcareous concretions in the cavities of the inner ear which are found in fishes, including the eel, though less in number than we find in other vertebrates. Relatively large, they grow, as the scales do, by the successive apposition of concentric layers, and so follow the gradual growth of the head in which the inner ears are situated.

To observe these otoliths, we must treat the eel in a special manner; cut off the head, separate it from the trunk so that it may be more easily handled, detach the lower jaw with a pair of scissors, cut an incision longways in the middle of the skull, then separate the two halves and look at them through the cut. So I see the place the inner ear occupies in the skeleton of the skull, and in that inner ear I see a little whitish, transparent nodule, which I take out with fine pincers and put on a glass slide for examination. This is the principal otolith, a lentil-shaped concretion, between one and two millimetres wide; its circumference is roughened in a few places. When we look at it through the light, we find that it is made up of concentric layers enclosing one another, some of which are clearer and others darker, the number differing, as a rule, very little from that of the scales. So the two figures provide us with data which, considered in relation to the observations carried out directly on the fish itself, enable us to assert, if not to define, the extraordinary slowness of these creatures in attaining their full development.

Yet the eels are flesh-eating animals, even rapacious eaters. They are certainly not less so than most of the other species which live beside them. Most often the contrary is the case. If, in the case of these other fishes, the food they eat tends to make flesh, it does not seem to do so in the eel. Everything about their organism seems to move slowly, to prolong youth far beyond the usual time. Here I am forcibly reminded of the idea I have already put forward, that there may be a possible relation between the extreme powers of endurance possessed by the creature and its slowness of development. It seems that the strength used up in the process of living manifests itself rather by activity than by the creation of flesh, or by the development of organs. The assimilation manifests itself more in the direction of energy than that of matter. Like those thin, dried-up humans whom we colloquially describe as "all nerves," who spend themselves in activity, the eels, having the same sort of nature, become what they do become in this strange manner.

Finally, during this stay which they make with us in the land waters, they offer two more riddles for our solution, one concerned with the place in which they choose to live, the other with procreation, which are intimately related to one another, and appear to be connected. Though the eels seem to live everywhere, those we find in one place are quite different from those we find in another. Here, we find the small eels, the future males, in the majority: in most of the pools along the coast, in the great rivers, and their principal tributaries. There, the large eels, the future females, seem to predominate. One pond regularly presents us with large-sized specimens; another usually has nothing but the smaller ones. These eel populations go by localities, each having a character of its own, its percentage of small and large eels, which will later develop into males and females. What is the cause of this distribution and what is its result? How comes it that certain regions are different from their neighbours and show no resemblance to them at all, although the invasion which came from the sea was the same in every case? It is to some extent a question of ease of access, possibly of the availability of food, but mainly of sex, since these localizations result in the segregation of the sexes, at least partially.

When the elvers come from the sea, is their sex already determined, virtually present in their organic humours before being localized and developed in the reproductive glands? Or is sex simply generally latent in them, leaving to the future and to circumstances the decision about the direction it shall ultimately take? Is the eel unisexual in its early stages? Or is it sexually indifferent during the long period of its youth, like a hermaphrodite, which can, later and as circumstances determine, turn into a male or a female?

Early observers were inclined to decide in favour of the former. It is a fact that the smallest elvers, those which come at the beginning of the annual invasion, seem for the most part to become males. But, though this is true, later investigations have shown that the problem is more complicated. We have come to assume that the eels, still neuter when they arrive from the sea, assume one or other of the two sexualities according to locality and abode.

Several facts seem to show that an eel, already provided with the attributes of future maleness, may, if the localization changes, alter its sex, and become capable of acquiring the characteristics of femaleness. In this case the sexes must be naturally reversible, at least from maleness to femaleness, if not in the opposite direction. This phenomenon has been produced artificially on some of the batrachians, and Nature, in the eel, would seem to effect it more regularly and more definitely.

Whichever way we turn when we are considering this strange creature, we find surprises and exceptions. This slippery, crawling animal goes through the world enveloped in mystery. In itself, like the serpent, it seems to enshrine, in one feeble body, all the riddles of creation. Instead of dispersing, they concentrate here, and show that the essential vital principle, although it creates forms and figures of flesh that it may manifest itself in them, does not imprison itself within the limits of these forms. Going beyond the apparent limits set by material structure, form and organization are not always the most important, or the fundamental, factors.

CHAPTER XVIII

I WAS walking slowly with a friend along the river bank. It was a delightful spring morning in Brittany. The sun was high in the sky, and it lighted up the flowing water, making each ripple of the surface glitter like a diamond. Everywhere the water flashed and sparkled, save for a few dark patches where the bank itself cast a shadow, or trees overhung the stream, and in these places the transparent water seemed to open and reveal itself so that the pebbles on the bottom were clearly visible. The broad stream, flowing steadily, peacefully, moved onwards swiftly, continually, smoothly, as though for ever. Framing it, as it were, the hills were adorned by fresh spring foliage and early blossoms. The pollarded oak trees, short and stumpy, were covered with leaves, the gorse was punctuated by specks of gold. And overhead, the dome of the sky was free from clouds, and its blue, as reflected by the water, broke up into tiny pieces and shared in the glory of the flashing light. Everything, the air itself, scented with the perfume of the meadows, breathed calm and serenity.

" It is really a lovely day, the sort of day we seldom have at this time of the year," my friend said. " The rainy season will not be long now. At least, I hope not, for we need it in the fields. But the rain will swell the stream, and this water, which is so pure now, will be a yellow, muddy torrent. Let us go as far as the old dam. At the foot of it we shall certainly see the salmon that have just arrived from the sea, which have not yet been able to get past it. Only a day or two, and they will be gone. As soon as the rain comes and the waters are in spate, there will be more water over the dam and the salmon will be able to get over it. Now they can't. There is not enough water, and they cannot get a sufficient start."

The friend with whom I was walking was also my host,

who had invited me to spend a few days with him. I had known and valued him for many years. Formerly a sailor, a great hunter, a great fisherman, a great reader, he had retired for family reasons before he was officially due for retirement, and had settled down on his estate, not far from a river in Brittany famous for the good fishing that is to be had in it. There he lived the life almost of a recluse, seldom travelled, and then only on business, governed the parish of which he was the mayor (re-elected always without opposition), and was delighted when, at any time of the year, his old comrades, his friends of all sorts, came to visit him. A very open and plain-spoken man, disguising perfect good humour beneath a somewhat brusque and distant exterior, he invariably displayed the greatest common sense and the keenest possible desire to oblige his friends.

We walked without hurrying, allowing ourselves to take in all the charm of the delightful day and came at last to the dam, stretched across the stream like a low wall, hardly more than three feet high, over which passed, from one bank to the other, the broad sheet of water which broke in foam before continuing its way towards the sea. At both ends of it, near the banks but more particularly on our side, the current was swifter, the foam more abundant, the eddies more violent. We saw what we expected to see. A number of salmon, several of which were quite large, were trying to make their way past the obstacles. Leaping up, one after another, they came out of the foam, sometimes completely, sometimes only half uncovered. It was only the fact that there was little water, that the fall was too small, which prevented them from getting right over it. They all fell back and disappeared, only to try again. They kept at it, let themselves be carried back, came up and leapt again only to fall back once more, but their efforts never slackened.

We had seated ourselves side by side on a fallen tree. We watched them. After some minutes of silence, my friend said:

" This regular yearly journey of the salmon is a strange business. The peasants, when they see all this activity at the foot of the dam, say the salmon are playing. But this incessant coming and going seems a funny sort of game;

it looks more like hard labour than amusement or recreation. As far as one can tell, the fish is not out for amusement. It may get some satisfaction from what it does, but there seems to be very little pleasure or relaxation about its actions. It perseveres, it keeps at it, it wears itself out. It is tired, but not satisfied; it comes back as soon as it is able. It is content only when it has got over the dam and then it finishes this play, as soon as circumstances make it possible to do so. Then there is an end to its excitement; it will go and find a hiding place in some hole in the bottom, or under the shelter of the bank, and there it will stay for week after week without moving, letting the water flow round it, and not making a single movement.

"But just think how things take their course; how they follow one another absolutely methodically. It is the middle of spring. These salmon, which arrived only a little while ago, were living far away in the sea only a few weeks before. They were quite comfortable there; they were growing fat there. Yet they never hesitated to give up that comfort and start out on the journey that has brought them here, and fetched them up against this dam. You and I know where they are going and what they are after. But do *they* know, do *they* understand? They will stay in this stream, hiding away, eating nothing, moving very little, all through the summer and all through the autumn. When the flood waters allow, they will go higher and higher, until they come to their spawning places. In midwinter, they will produce their young. Their little ones, in those places where the water is always cold and swift, will have about them conditions favourable to their growth, which they could never have had in the lower reaches or in the sea.

"Beyond a doubt, intelligence endowed with foresight could not do better, or act more wisely. If I were in their place, and, like them, were obliged, for my children's sake, to put up with conditions other than those which satisfy me, I should do as they do. I should behave as they behave. Under the guidance of paternal love, I should leave the places which suited me and go to those which would suit my offspring. I should leave the sea and its depths, I should seek out the mouths of rivers, I should go up their flowing waters and, finally, I should come to the places most suitable for spawning and the growth of the little ones. But I should act in this way deliberately, understanding what I was about, remembering what I was leaving, mentally foreseeing and hoping to attain what I desired and what awaited me. Have the salmon any such knowledge? Have they the understanding which my powers of thought and my memory give me? Have they an understanding of things, either like our own, although unable to show it in our way, or different from ours, based upon some unknown process of reasoning? These are questions which always come into my mind when I look at these leapings and activities from this particular place."

Beneath the blazing sun the water streamed over the dam evenly and without stopping. The great fish continued jumping, leaping, raising themselves as though they tried to see beyond the dam what there was behind the barrier that made them weary. The scene did not change.

"The very obstinacy of these salmon gives you the answer," I said. "There is a significance about their movements. If they had the slightest intelligence, that is to say, any faculty at all of bringing their actions into harmony not only with what they feel now, but with past sensations and future sensations, they would not behave as we see them behaving. They would not wear themselves out like this. They would realize that the efforts they are now making are quite useless, and they would wait until circumstances were more favourable. They would be gifted with powers of reflection which would guide their conduct. It is only necessary to look at them to realize that they have no such powers, that they do not, in fact, reflect. They hurl themselves against this barrier, and keep on coming back to do the same thing, driven on by an irresistible force which brings them back incessantly. They obey their orders, which are to go up the stream, and they obey without attempting to change anything. A sailor like you ought to understand why they do so, unconsciously, and without the exercise of any reasoning powers."

"Yes," he said, "I can understand that they do exactly what is demanded of them, contenting themselves with doing it well. But, when I was given orders, even if I did not argue, even if I did exactly what I was told, I realized that my superior officer had thought out the order he gave. My behaviour, even if, so far as I was concerned, it was a matter of strict and unquestioning obedience, had been thought out and calculated by the one who imposed it upon me. But, where is the superior officer whom these salmon obey? What duty of obedience have they? I only see the fishes themselves and the water which contains them. Where is the one who gives orders to them and directs their conduct?"

"Now we're getting at it," I said, in my turn. "We will admit, if you like, for the sake of argument, that there is in them, as people often say, a migratory instinct, to which they conform and which takes the place of a command. Now we must see of what this instinct consists, what this hackneyed expression actually means. It is sometimes considered that instinct is a form of intelligence that has become mechanical, that an instinctive action performed today was, once upon a time, an intelligent, voluntary action, the primitive nature of which repetition for generation after generation has transformed so as to render it automatic, unreasoned, and to cause it to be performed without any need for the use of will. It is also considered that instinct has developed little by little, progressively, like a sort of natural training brought about by circumstances in which the incapable are weeded out, the others being retained as they make themselves fitter. These ideas are presumptions, hypotheses, which, for my own part, I refuse to accept. I cannot follow an argument unless it is based upon reality and conforms to reality. If it does not do this, I stop and begin again. I have only to take your remark and reality is there at the outset. We can only see the fishes and the running water. There is nothing else. Nevertheless, we can see that there is this obligation, this order, which constrains each salmon, compels it to obey, induces it to pass over the dam. That obligation is the only real factor; it is in the salmon, or in the water, or in some relation between the two. That is where we have to look.

"It cannot reside in the salmon alone. We are not

dealing here with land animals, in which the action of gravity accentuates the individuality of each creature and confers upon it a more definite apparent independence. In the salmon, which floats suspended in the water and loses the greater part of its weight in that water, the physical part played by gravity is of much less importance. The water contains it and supports it; the fish is dependent upon it. The problem is correspondingly simplified; we have not to take an outside term into account. There is only the creature itself and its environment and their relation one to the other. It is sufficient to observe the behaviour of the creature, its mode of life, its determination, to be convinced that the environment activates and directs it, and that the essential influence comes from that environment.

" What in fact is life? A succession of mutual giving and taking between the animal and its environment, interchanges of matter, interchanges of energy. The being takes from its environment what it needs for its life, and gives back what it has produced within itself. Life is the sum of intimate reactions in response to certain actions of the environment. In order that it may be maintained there must be harmony between both. The satisfaction of living comes from the reasonable equilibrium of the reactions of the creature to the actions of the environment. This produces an entente which is maintained so long as the equilibrium is preserved, but alters and changes if there is any alteration in the equilibrium.

" What is any single individual living salmon? A creature simple in appearance and in the way it is made, but double as regards the use it makes of itself. In one body it contains its own person and its posterity. Beneath its scale-clothed skin it has an individuality of its own, but also the possibilities of series of successive generations in which it is itself incorporated. Its single body works towards two ends; first towards its own self-preservation, then towards reproduction. These two directions often come together and become one. But in the salmon, they remain separate, they become clear through isolation. The fish which we see trying to leap over the dam have no other purpose in life than reproduction. They have ceased to try to keep themselves alive for their own sakes, to digest the food on which they normally live, to assimilate its substance. Now they are devoting themselves entirely to the preparation of their germs, they are getting rid of the matters they formerly possessed so that the germs they are about to elaborate may make use of them. The previous equilibrium, that of the person, has vanished. Another equilibrium is coming into existence and becoming established, hence these new forms of behaviour and an alteration in the harmony which has hitherto existed.

" Once, in the depths of the sea in which they used to live, the vital actions of these salmon were concerned only with growth. This growth monopolized their efforts. They took from the surrounding water the oxygen they breathed and the prey upon which they lived. The equilibrium was established in such a way as to permit the maintenance of their persons and its development. Then things took a different turn; the needs of posterity declared themselves, and the organism gave itself up to its new task, that of reproduction. There was a change of equilibrium, for this organism demanded less on the one hand and more on the other. Its demands for nourishment grew less, and its demands for more oxygen took on a new urgency. As a consequence of this disharmony, the satisfaction it formerly experienced disappeared; its sense of well-being vanished. The individual was compelled to find a new satisfaction, and this necessity was the origin of what has been called its migratory instinct.

" This instinct is certainly nothing more than an organic intuition, limited to the search for a specialized satisfaction and a progressively increasing sense of well-being. The salmon, no longer finding about it the proportion of oxygen necessary to the satisfaction of its new needs, leaves its old home and goes in the direction where it will find an increasing proportion of oxygen and consequently what it has hitherto lacked. From the strictly mechanistic point of view we may say that it polarizes itself; but, taking a wider view, since it behaves as a sensitive organism, we may add, with greater accuracy, that it acts in response to an intuition unceasingly brought into play by an external action which is increasingly accentuated. The organism feels what it lacks and what it must do. That is all it feels;

249

that is all it experiences at the moment; but the impression is sufficient to guide its conduct from moment to moment, from place to place. It is an immediate intuition, continually renewed, which progressively increases the sense of well-being by allowing the function which now becomes the controlling one, that of reproduction, to fulfil itself more easily at less expense of labour and effort.

" It is this continually alert intuition, the result of the creature's vital sensitivity, which makes up what we call instinct. By itself it cannot achieve its end, it is only able to perform the necessary act with the aid of exciting circumstances present in the environment. It must have a harmony, a coming together with these external conditions: otherwise it remains shut in and leads nowhere. And this harmony belongs to the moment, for it is born of the adjustment of these conditions to the immediate needs of the living body.

" Instinct actually consists of a series of adaptations or accommodations, leading from one to the other with inflexible determination. Here we have the authority from which emanates the command resulting in the execution of the order. It does not exist in the individual alone, for the individual is possessed of the means to obey, but nothing more. It resides in the association and direction of natural things, which allow the surroundings, the environment, to act upon these means and to set in motion their functional mechanism. Their determinism is a harmony, or rather a succession of mutually related harmonies; in it the physical conditions of the environment regulate and direct the organic conditions within the creature itself.

" The salmon which are detained here, at the foot of this dam, have come there because external circumstances, as they work out at the moment, have brought them there. If those circumstances had been different; if they had not been able to satisfy the increased respiratory demands, the salmon would not be here. The migration is automatic. The fishes set out upon it because the natural course of events does not permit them to act in any other way. They go on and on like slaves, like a flock of sheep led by an invisible shepherd, a shepherd who is always there. And the object of this direction is the production of young, the conservation and perpetuation of the species. So we see where Nature's true power really is. It has its harmony, its combinations of harmonies, which, at one and the same time, govern the activity of all and the actions of the individual. The movement as a whole, embracing what is living and what is not living, consists in a sovereign cohesion."

The sun was nearly at its zenith. The glorious spring day was becoming more glorious still. Space, filled with light, seemed to increase in extent, to grow deeper before our eyes, as though its immensity, becoming greater still, would lose itself in the infinite. The blue sky seemed vaster, the transparent air lighter. Distant points in the landscape stood out, one behind the other, making us aware of the existence of other distances, invisible to our eyes, present but inaccessible. The world about us was filled with life. Insects fluttered past humming; birds flew from branch to branch, then settled and began their song. All Nature gave evidence of the animation within it, constant, co-ordinated. And as we looked upon it all, intuition appeared as the very expression of its soul, with which the sentiments which rose in us beneath this influence were in perfect harmony. The ambiance, so exquisite, so generous, acted upon our minds, activated our thoughts, brought them to birth, developed them, at first indistinct and confused, then gradually more precise. Such moments as these one has only at the beginning of summer, moments only too rare, only too fleeting, when we realize things better, as they appear rejuvenated and glorious after the rest and darkness of winter.

" You spoke," I said, " of a foreseeing intelligence, and you said that the salmon, in their blind dash forward, behave as well and in the same way as an intelligent being would do who was possessed by desires similar to theirs. Irrational instinct and intelligence possessed of will would follow the same line of conduct to attain the same end. The two would thus be equivalent. But is there so great a difference as there seems to be between instinct and intelligence? Is not everything, in the last resort, instinctive? Intelligence seems to be rather a choice of instincts than an entirely new quality. The salmon, in its water, has a limited intuition, for its being is not capable of more. But the intelligent being, possessing intuitions of greater extent and scope than those of the salmon, would, none the less, follow the line of conduct which the salmon's intuition fixes upon, as being the most suitable for the occasion. Instead of acting blindly, it would act like a reasonable being, taking account of causes, but, none the less, under the impulsion of external forces.

" That is the point I was anxious to make. In the instinct of the salmon there is an intelligent part which really governs and directs, and this intelligence resides in the supreme co-ordination of things around us. If I were a poet, I should talk about the inarticulate music of the spheres, and, before the wonderful scene which we now behold, before this symphony of sound, of vision, of odour, all of which at this moment strike upon our senses and produce a repercussion in our minds, the expression would be a just one. We attune ourselves to the harmony of that music. Our own individual intelligence consists in opening ourselves to its influence, in welcoming it, receiving it, listening to it so far as the means at our disposal permit. So, on a larger scale, we do what the salmon in its water, the insect on its plant, do on a small scale; the origin is the same. Nature has a soul, compact of all the energies which traverse it, made up of all the movements which give life to it, even in the depths of the sea. Life is spirit, and all creatures, in varying degrees, are inspired by the breadth of that spirit. There are differences in quantity, but the essential quality is the same. Each individual life, intelligence, or instinct, is a reflection of that general life, continuous in space, continuous in time, which penetrates all things. If, in instinct, there is but a tiny spark of it, if intelligence is able to choose its own ray from a more brilliant torch, both are lighted together and take their flame from the same fire.

" The study of Nature, beginning on earth with the contemplation of realities, mounts higher and higher until it attains the highest degree of spirituality. It leads the way stage by stage, halting occasionally and making sure of the facts which, considered from another angle, might seem to be fictions. If the physical governs the organic, the psychic, even the moral, this physical in turn is governed by the supreme law which it has received from the creative omnipotence which brought it into being. Nature has a higher intelligence and a morality of its own, whose presence we feel not only around us but within us. Instinct has but a tiny morsel of this higher element; intelligence is enabled to possess more. If the intuition of the one is limited and concerned with a single end, that of the other is much more varied and extensive.

" The ideas of beauty, of goodness, of justice, when we come to contemplate living Nature and to examine the life that is in Nature, assume a precision and a truth hitherto unsuspected. Innate in us, or seeming to be so, they take form in it. Everyone who looks upon a scene so beautiful as that which lies before us must feel this. In the sense of well-being which takes possession of us, we feel arising within us aspirations to something better, an attraction towards the infinite. We actually become better.

" And when I say this, I am not forgetting all about the salmon and the dam which is proving such an obstacle to them. I am still the naturalist concerned solely with realities, who will only agree to think on lines supported by realities. I come back to them at intervals to give me a fresh start. What are these fishes doing here? What brought them here, summoning them with a call they could not fail to hear? In more scientific language, what is the final purpose of this phenomenon? You know as well as I do: it is reproduction, the foundation of a family, the maintaining and safeguarding of the species by the establishment of successive generations. Their instinct carries them in that direction, though it is itself ignorant of what it does, for it is incapable of such foreknowledge. Our intelligence, on the other hand, reflecting the light of Nature on a grander scale, is clearly able to discern that purpose.

" This work of reproduction, which is the ultimate purpose of the journey, being done and finished, what will become of these parents who have been carried far from the retreats in the sea in which they have hitherto lived? Most of them will perish: very few will return to the hiding places from which only the need of love has brought them forth. These vigorous salmon who go to their loves, go also to their death. They are destined to be sacrificed to the fate which awaits them. You said just now that the salmon were playing. The word is truer and deeper than it seems. Moved by a force superior to their strength both in power and in diversity, they are playthings indeed, and not only they, but all living creatures.

" They show us on a small scale, but none the less truly, one of the parts of the general movement of life which is governed by the superior harmony and the supreme intelligence of all things.. These fishes give us a lesson in philosophy. That intelligence, dominating time and space, considers the whole of creation at once. Its purpose is to preserve life as a whole, all life, in what essentially constitutes life, that is to say, the succession of one generation after another. To it, individuals are only the means it employs to arrive at its ends. The collective life of families and generations goes beyond individual life; the parents are of account only in so far as they have children. The salmon are altruists in their own way, altruists who sacrifice their personal existence in order to save the existence of the whole. They are so involuntarily, by compulsion, without reason or reflection; but because of this obligation which Nature forces upon them, they show more clearly how strong is the impulse which animates them. If we do not feel this impulse in ourselves, it is because it exists elsewhere.

" Certainly, the great metaphysicians, the greatest idealists, the most fervent mystics, have drawn from themselves, in spiritual contemplation pushed to the degree of paroxysm, the thoughts which they have expressed. Spirit is best made known by spirit. But we are justified in presuming that the creations of their minds are largely recollections. Their more perfect intellect has been able to give a body to that which others do not see at all, although it exists outside us, and is reflected in each one of us. Our spirit is like a secret mirror in which are reflected the lights of the general spirit. Clearer in some people, tarnished in others, it none the less represents the vast stage on which Life plays the drama of its magnificent and eternal prodigies. We take back into ourselves, for ourselves, that which is going on outside us.

" The physicists, the chemists, the naturalists, try to get at this external world impersonally, and to see things as they are, as they present themselves to the senses. In spite of the difficulties of so doing, often in spite of the impossibility of so doing, they do find something. If what they find is limited, their results, none the less, have a definite value. They serve, in a small degree, as terms of measurement. They enable us to corroborate and to define. The scientific study of Nature may in this way rise to the highest degree of which the mind is capable; where reality comes into direct contact with spirit, where both agree and confirm each other.

" But then they meet with the same obstacles. These salmon, held back by the dam, leap out of the water as though they would see what is beyond the barrier; then they fall back. We too have a dam before us, and matter detains us, keeps us at its feet. We start out, full of the noblest desires, to try to learn more; but our fleshly senses restrict our efforts and we fall again, after having contemplated for too short a time a small part of what we wished to see. Life has a secret, and it keeps that secret jealously. Whence comes it? How does it maintain itself, and how far does its power extend? Towards what ultimate goal is it striving? And especially, since we are ourselves directly interested, what miracle gives our own life, which is incorporated in the general system which governs other existences, the power to judge, to know, to exploit as it does, all that goes to make up life as a whole? These are riddles before which knowledge, limited to what it learns from the observation of material facts, is powerless. ' What do I know?' Montaigne asked. We might say ' What do I know of what I know?' "

" The things of this world, like those of the world above, proclaim the glory of God," my friend said aphoristically, as he got up. I have always noticed that the finest dissertations upon such subjects end with a quotation, or an invocation. So each of us satisfies himself in the manner determined by his beliefs and his temperament. For me, who am a believer, the answer to these questions is not to seek. But that does not prevent the existence of problems which demand solution, and our intelligence, trying to find even a partial solution, is not ill employed if it strives to set itself more in harmony with that supreme intelligence which inspires the whole world. . . .

" But it will soon be twelve o'clock. In spite of the loftiness of our conversation we are not pure spirits. It is time to think about lunch, the more so because I have invited two of our friends, and they have probably arrived already. Let us go back and find them."

CHAPTER XIX

THERE were four of us to lunch round the table in the dining-room, four old friends: the master of the house who had invited us to stay with him in Brittany; one of his old friends in the navy who had now become an admiral and was commander-in-chief of the neighbouring port; a business man, the proprietor of a number of factories for the preserving of fish in various places along the coast of Brittany; and myself.

" I'll tell you what we're going to have," our host said, looking round to see if everything was ready, " Grilled salmon, and roast leg of mutton with new potatoes. The salmon was caught this very morning, not far from the dam where we were sitting," he added, turning to me. " The mutton comes from the salt marshes. It was a little black-haired Ushant sheep, which no more than three days ago was still feeding on the spray-covered grass. The potatoes are out of my own garden, and they are prize-winners of which my gardener is extremely proud. You see this is a real Breton lunch.

" I should have liked to offer you oysters to start with, and I asked the people at the beds in the Belon river for some. But they told me that the close season had begun earlier this year and that the oysters wouldn't taste so good or so delicate as they should. We shall have to go without the oysters. But to make up for it, our friend the manufacturer, for that's the name we are supposed to give the members of that important corporation whose members devote themselves to the preserving of fish, has brought with him a choice selection of his most tasty products. There they are in front of you, looking as good as they undoubtedly are. They fill up the table. While the salmon is grilling over the wood fire, and the mutton is being cooked to a turn, we may busy ourselves with them. But,

257

whilst eating them—and I see you haven't wasted any time in making a start—our friend will tell us what they are, for so much art has been brought to bear on their preparation that it is not always easy to recognize them."

"That's easy," said the manufacturer, helping himself liberally. "You recognize the sardines in oil. They have for long been the main source of my firm's reputation. My predecessors prepared nothing else except the tunny you have there, the pieces of which are also preserved in the best olive oil. In their time that was enough to build up a considerable business, but today things have changed. Consumers demand more nowadays; they must have a greater variety, and competition is becoming keener and keener. Not only have I been driven to produce things like those which can be had abroad, as good if not better, but I have had to invent new products. I make experiments, and put the result on the market.

"I have completely transformed my old factories. I pulled down one after another and reconstructed them on a larger and more regular plan. Instead of the little separate departments you used to know, I have built large, well-lighted, well-ventilated sheds, where the work is carried out from beginning to end in one room. The fresh fish comes in at one side and goes out at the other, finished, packed, either in boxes or crates. I am able to follow and control at a glance the different stages of preparation from first to last. I do everything myself without any outside help. I make my own boxes in all sizes and shapes, my tubs, my crates. Among my workmen, besides those who are experts in the actual work of preserving fish, I have tinsmiths, tinkers, and carpenters. I even have mechanics and fitters to make any repairs that may be necessary to the machines. With all these improvements, I am now free to devote myself to research and to produce on a large scale, ready to set to work in any direction that the results of my research appear to indicate.

"You have there slices of sturgeon, prepared like tunny, but perhaps finer in flavour. Unfortunately, the raw material—the sturgeon, that is—is becoming rarer and rarer in this country. Those whitish filaments are cooked elvers caught on their way up from the sea. Them I put in boxes for my Spanish customers. Then there are pickled anchovies, like those you get in Provence and Roussillon, filletted herrings which are cleverly smoked before being macerated in oil, other herrings that are rolled and cooked in a sauce strongly spiced with pepper and juniper mixed with cumin, mackerel in white wine, cods' tongues salted and dressed, sardines in tomato and pimento, and shrimps' tails with the shell taken off, which are used as dressing. But these are only a few of my experiments, those with which I am satisfied both as regards appearance and flavour, and also from the point of view of sales, for they are very successful. But I am still experimenting. Preserving has become a complicated science. All sorts of industries and businesses have become associated with it, from metallurgy for the making of boxes to international law for protecting the sale of products, passing through all the stages of preparation and presentation. I have quite enough to do."

"The results are really exquisite," our host said. "But you can see for yourself how greatly we appreciate them. We are listening to you, but we do not lose a mouthful. The senses have all the play they can hope for here. The eye delights in the different shades of all the dishes set before us: there are pink, scarlet, pure white, pale yellow, dark brown with dashes of blue, silver, and gold. The rainbow has contributed all its colours. Then the sense of smell has every reason to be content. These exciting aromatic odours serve as an envelope to still another, more delicate odour, which they enhance while, to some extent, they disguise it; I mean the odour of the sea, of rocks beaten by the waves. Finally, after sight and smell, taste comes into play. Still more delicate and discerning, it perceives the most diverse and delicate flavours, and gathers up into itself the final sensations, those to which the others lead. So we have a most remarkable harmony, a sort of symphony of hors-d'œuvres, which unites in itself the harmony of three sensitivities and brings to this table, by these material perceptions, an echo of the original symphony, that of the ocean with its eternal dialogue between the waters and the winds."

"Yes," I said, "the word is well chosen. It is a real symphony. But, as in all symphonies, the impression we obtain is not only due to the notes played by the instruments, as it is here by these delightful dishes; it is produced further by their combination in an orchestra, and by their preparation. Not only their preparation in the factory, where the manufacturer displays his knowledge and skill, but by their previous preparation in nature itself, where these creatures are fashioned. This delightful flesh which we consume with so much pleasure has been made of other flesh which, in nature, was consumed and absorbed as prey. Without it, we should not have the other and, though it might exist, it would be no use to us. We should gain no advantage from it. I will take what we have before us and, while we are still enjoying it, go through the various fish and you will see the extraordinary diversity which is hidden beneath the apparent simplicity of this food.

" These sardines, anchovies, mackerel and herrings which the fishermen catch so regularly in abundance, feed and maintain themselves at the expense of creatures smaller than themselves. They consume them, nourish themselves upon them, make use of their flesh to build up their own. Most of these fishes have fed upon tiny floating crustaceans, whose bands, whose hosts, contain millions upon millions of individuals. The fragile, delicate flesh of these hosts of creatures is a prey which has only to be swallowed and digested by the fish who feed upon them. We ourselves, when we eat these sardines and herrings, are through them consuming and using for our own nourishment the swarming multitudes of those tiny creatures suspended in the immensity of the ocean which we could never know, still less reach, in any other way.

" Then take these elvers. Their tiny mouths can only allow prey still more tiny to pass, microscopic creatures which would be invisible to our eyes, if we could look into the water which contains them. This prey, upon which they feed, is also devoured by the tiny crustaceans upon which the herring feeds. The nourishment we take begins upon an even lower scale, beyond these crustaceans, since beneath them, forming their flesh, are representatives of the most elementary forms of life. They are, doubtless, not alone, and the organic substances dissolved in the water add their share to this primitive source of nourishment. If the oysters which we might have had to begin our meal had been served to us, we should, in their flesh, have tasted, as in all the shellfish, the product of a similar system of nutrition. The simplest, the smallest creatures, scattered and suspended in the water, are at the very basis of this chain of eaters and eaten; they are the first term of an alimentary cycle which, beginning with them, ends in ourselves. Thanks to the intermediaries, the floating crustaceans and nomadic fishes, we are able to have our part from their prodigious swarming.

"Looking again, I see there pieces of tunny fish. We have now gone beyond the fish of middle size, like the sardines and herrings, and come to a fish which reminds us, though it exists in greater numbers, of the larger animals we hunt on land. The tunny is a heavy, corpulent creature. It is also a beast of prey, keen on pursuing its victims, hunting down animals smaller than itself, deep down in the open sea. Our friend the manufacturer, when he set his produce before us, gave us sardines and mackerel caught by fishermen near the coast. But, when he offered us the tunny, his offering came from much farther afield. These fine fish were caught out at sea, where they live, where they feed, where they are a menace to their prey. Thanks to them, we consume the flesh of sardines, mackerel, and various other species which, if they could live away from the coast, would have escaped the activities of the fishermen. So we make use of, in another form and in another way, flesh which, without them, we should be unable to use at all.

"These are fish of the open sea, but the same is true of deep-sea fishes. We have just enjoyed these slices of sturgeon. And, when we have the chance, we enjoy the delicate flavour of the caviare made out of its eggs just before they are spawned. Of what is food of this sort composed; how does it come into existence? Of the flesh of shell-fish which would be no use to us, but upon which the sturgeon feed at the very bottom of the sea. The realm from which we draw our own nourishment grows larger. It fills the whole sea, the coasts, and extends from the surface to the abyss. The intermediaries of the cycle of nutrition are like what the law calls 'persons interposed';

they bring us, preserve for us, what, without their agency, we should never be able to obtain.

" Then again, there is the debris, even the dead bodies, from which we ourselves could hardly profit. These shrimps and larger creatures like them, lobsters and all the astonishing legion of the different sorts of crab, eat refuse. They are the scavengers of the sea bottom. Their appetite and their activity let nothing escape them. Far away in the water they scent out the emanations which come from dead flesh. Eagerly hastening to the spot, they are anxious to get what they can from it, and they make the best use of their time before decomposition is complete.

" So nothing is lost. This precious living matter, this flesh which forms the body of every being, taken and retaken in the alimentary cycle, passes from mouth to mouth, from stomach to stomach, from individual to individual. Each time it is broken up and unmade, that it may be digested; then it is made again under another form; its materials are recomposed; and it is re-lived until there is another change. Finally, it reaches ourselves; we reap the harvest. What we receive in this way is indeed the fruit of the sea, engendered and borne by the sea, just as the land offers us its fruits."

" You might add the salmon to your list," our host said, " It deserves not to be forgotten. See, it is just ready for us. The grilled slices are cooked to a turn, covered with a napkin so that they shall not get cold. With them, as an accompaniment, are two sauces, one sweet, *à la hollandaise*, the other piquant, aromatic, and highly seasoned. Personally, I prefer not to have any. I would rather have a few drops of lemon juice. I enjoy the flesh itself better that way, and appreciate its exquisite flavour without any extraneous element. All its delicious savour is preserved, exhaled by this flesh, which is firm without being hard, and of that delicate rose colour which adds to its attractiveness. This fish has every quality, from elegance of form when it is alive to the delightfulness of its taste when it is suitably cooked and eaten. In its own field, in relation to ourselves and our fondness for good cheer, it is indeed king.

" But of what is this delectable flesh? If I may continue along the lines you set out, of what flesh has it been built up? This salmon has consumed nothing in the stream in which it was caught; it has lived upon the reserves of food stored up in it, reserves which are now transferred to our use, for our nutrition. It took no more from the coastal waters through which it hastened so as to arrive more speedily at the river which was more favourable to the demands of its life processes. Its flesh was fashioned far out at sea, in the depths. The elements were taken from the strange creatures which then lived beside it, the large red shrimps, the black fishes with phosphorescent flashes. Out of their flesh the salmon has made its own, hunting them down relentlessly in the neighbourhood of its lair in the darkness. It brings us tribute from the depths of the sea. When we eat it, we enjoy a distant product with a special savour like those exotic fruits which deliver to our sense of smell, to our palate, the scents and savours of the country in which they ripened. This fruit of the sea comes to us from distant, inaccessible places, and when we gather it we share in a series of strange circumstances peculiar to the salmon alone.

" Old legends tell us of the people of the gnomes who live in dark forests into which no human being ever goes, and of places underground in which they devote themselves to the strangest labours. Only at night do they go forth and haunt the places wherein human beings dwell. Some of them must pay tribute to the powers of light and open day. At times agreed upon, their messengers bring that tribute, made up of magnificent, glittering things, made and fashioned beneath the earth in the darkness of unknown caverns. The salmon are such messengers from the depths of the sea. In the same way, they give us with their flesh the tribute paid to human power by the labour of lives lived beneath the dark mass of waters. But this time we are dealing with reality, and not with fairy tales."

" I like the word ' harvest,' " said the admiral. " It brings back to me memories and impressions of many years ago. More than once I was detailed for duty on the guard-ship which is sent out during the fishing season to the coasts of Newfoundland, Saint-Pierre, and Iceland, to watch over the interests of our fishermen. When I was beginning my life in the navy, thirty years ago, I was a midshipman on one of those ships; afterwards I was lieutenant and later commander, though, in between, I sailed in many other ships to many other places. I have seen the changes that have been brought about and the gradual extension of the cod fisheries. Nowadays, there are more and more large boats, some of them steamers, some sailing ships with auxiliary motors. They are nothing less than floating factories, manned by a considerable crew, with all they need on board, and able to prepare and salt their cod on deck before they send it down to the holds. When the ship is full, they return, to come back again later if the season is suitable, and the owner desires.

" In the old days, the system was more interesting, and there seemed to be more activity. Most of the boats were simple two-masted boats, with just enough room for the crew and the fish. The men were often obliged to go on shore to get the supplies they needed, even to salt their cod. They worked on land almost as much as on their boats, got their catch ready there, put it out to dry. They spread out their fish on the shore, gathered it up into piles if it should happen to rain, and spread it out again when the storm was over. The shore where they were working, covered with disembowelled codfish, looked like a field bearing a strange harvest, which was waiting to be gathered and cleared away. The heaps of piled-up cod were like so many sheaves, like those in a wheat-field. It was really like a harvest, brought forth by the waters of the sea each year, and carried at a fixed date to the shores where it was gathered. No other term so well expresses what I used to feel when I saw it. Our fishermen were like a peculiar order of farmers gathering this harvest and getting it ready to put into barns.

" My impression was strengthened recently when I was inspecting some of the southern fisheries. I visited some of the places where the cod are dried. Some of them might almost have been called scaffolds, for the fish are hung side by side in them by hundreds and thousands, so that they can be dried more readily by a current of air. They might be taken for fruits hung up to be preserved, fruits of a special category, produced by the sea."

" Your remarks," I said, " confirm what I was saying.

This nourishment which the fishermen bring us from the sea, a form of nourishment mainly composed of fishes, is indeed a harvest which nature provides for our use. Thanks to it, we are able to take advantage of conditions and things which themselves are beyond our reach, and which consequently we are unable to use. As I have said already, it brings us the tribute of a host of creatures, of which we should have been deprived without its aid.

" See what there is on the table now. The leg of mutton is served surrounded by *pommes fondantes*. This meat is that of a sheep which has grown up in the scanty pastures of the Island of Ushant. This sheep has built up its meat by making use of the nutritive material it found in the grass, a material which we ourselves could not use directly as it does. So far as we and our requirements are concerned it plays the part of an alimentary transformer. Those pastures, and the pastures of the whole world, would be no use at all to us if the cattle did not make themselves our intermediaries. Thanks to them, mankind is able to take advantage of a foodstuff that would otherwise be completely lacking. Then again, these potatoes grew in the garden we can see through the window. They were born there. They drew from the earth, from its mould, the principles which allowed them to develop, which, if the potatoes had not been there, we should never have had. They too, in their own way, are food transformers, and, with them, all the useful vegetables, leaves, seeds and fruits. An immense cycle of giving and taking of food which embraces the whole of Nature finally ends in us and at our table. Every living being finds in that cycle the satisfaction he needs. It is not devised for our use alone; but we benefit from it more than the others, for the last word rests with us. This sort of metampsychosis of the flesh, the passage of flesh from one to the other, finds in humanity, among all its avatars, its principal goal. It is the conquest by man of the products of Nature.

" Refer all this to the living world of the waters, and you will gain a better idea of it. Think for a moment of the tackle which the fishermen use. In spite of the ingenuity of its construction, in spite of the cleverness of those who use it, it cannot capture everything. The creatures they have to leave are many and diverse. Some of them, too small, tiny, microscopic in fact, could be of no immediate use. Others, too large and too strong, are only caught by accident. Others again, like those on which the salmon feeds, live at great depths which the fishermen's accustomed tackle cannot reach. Still others keep far out at sea, where fishing vessels never go. For all these various reasons, the fishermen are helpless; they can concern themselves only with certain species, always the same, which are more easily accessible. Now these species, amongst which the migratory fishes occupy the principal place, live upon prey which always escapes us. They fashion their flesh with the help of this prey and, having thus produced it, bring it themselves to the fishermen's nets. These creatures are food transformers, as the cattle are in relation to the meadows and these potatoes in relation to the garden, and this piece of bread in relation to the field in which the harvest ripened. They give us, in the form of food, the product and result of their own feeding. They are actually the fruits of the sea.

" The fishing of the migratory fishes penetrates, fortunately for us, to the most intimate and extensive of the living resources which the water contains. Without it we should know practically nothing of these resources. Huge quantities of possible sources of food, a vast host of different creatures, would spend their lives without humanity's benefiting in the least from them. That is why it is of such importance from the economic point of view. Nature being organized in such a way that, thanks to the fish we catch, we may profit by what our eyes can never see and our hands never touch, we are able to use for our own advantage the nutritive resources of this world to which our own physical conformation will never allow us to attain. We use it even in its most secret and remote regions.

" The comparison with the cattle of the meadows, in respect of this alimentary transformation, is all the more remarkable when we are dealing with the migratory fishes. The cattle live in herds which we watch over and control, which, at the proper time, give us the products we expect from them, a harvest of milk, a harvest of meat. Except for the supervision of breeding, the migratory fishes are the same in the life of the waters. Many of them arrive in troops, in shoals, at regular times, in places at which we know we shall find them and catch them, and they furnish us with the products we desire. Although we have no sort of supervision over them and have no way of giving them help, nature does for them what we are not able to do. It gathers them like a vast, immeasurable herd which it brings up, keeps alive and guides, and, in a word, places at our disposal. These are Neptune's flocks, manifold and changing, entrusted to the care of Proteus, who also changes."

" Quite so," said the manufacturer. " But our satisfaction would be very incomplete without the intervention of another factor, my own industry, in fact. The products of the land look after themselves, preserve themselves, with a little care on our part. Here is our dessert. In front of me are apples, pears, walnuts, all last season's fruits, since those of this year are not yet ripe. They were gathered months ago, and all that has been necessary has been to put them in a dry cupboard to keep them intact and even to improve them. If necessary, in the cold part of the year, butcher's meat can be kept, but only for a few days, unless we treat it in some way with cold, salting, or smoking. But it is quite different with fish; their flesh is too delicate, decomposes too easily; the goods are too perishable—to use the regular expression. If its principal qualities of flavour and digestibility are to be retained, it must be dried, kept in refrigeration, or sterilized in boxes hermetically sealed.

" What use would this profusion, this abundance, which you have just remarked upon, be to us if we could not take advantage of it ? This harvest of the fruits of the sea would be hardly any use, when we consider our needs. We must therefore profit by its abundance, and not allow any of it to be wasted. It is my own industry of preserving which does this for us. I remember the story which tells of the days when the salmon, more plentiful than they are now, frequented the streams of Brittany. It seems that the peasants, labourers fed by their masters, asked that they should not be given salmon more than three times a week, because the flesh, in spite of its delicacy and flavour, became objectionable in the long run because it was too fat. They used to eat fresh salmon, for nobody in those days knew how to preserve it. Certainly, when the season for salmon was at its height, a great number must have died, for the consumption was not enough to account for all. It is different today. The countries which are still well provided with salmon smoke them, salt them, put them in boxes, lose, in fact, nothing of the harvest which enters their rivers from the sea.

" When you come and see me, I will show you, beside my desk, a showcase in which I have put samples of the various preserves which have been sent to me from all over the world. You will see boxes of all sizes and shapes, of every colour, coming from very different parts of the world, and differing in contents. Some have designs upon them that are veritable masterpieces. Then you will realize the importance of the factory, and realize that the part it plays is of the utmost significance."

" I shall be glad to see your exhibition," our host said. " I have no doubt it is extremely interesting and instructive, and I shall remind you about it the next time I come and see you. But before we leave the table, I should like to go back to the idea of fish, especially migratory fish, as a natural food from which we profit without having to bother about breeding it. I have become a landsman, but I still have the mind of a sailor, and questions about fishing always interest me. Now fishing, if this idea is the correct one, acquires a supreme, though often unrealized, importance among the diversity of human occupations. Since we are obliged to keep ourselves alive, to take our food, from the products which nature gives us, the fruits of the land may be easily accessible, but those of the sea escape us in the water. And those are the fruits which the fisherman must go and gather, outside the reach of our hands, beyond our sight.

" Here is an interesting contrast between land and sea. Both have their own game, their own stock of beasts, but they are constructed and situated very differently. On land, in civilized countries, the cattle have the advantage as regards quantity. It is to the cattle we turn for our usual food. Game is a food *de luxe*, which we often do without. On the other hand, in the world of the waters, the herds we ourselves maintain, which we breed, are limited to a few fresh water species. The wild game, produced naturally and independently of us, is greater as regards diversity and quantity. It is at once both game and cattle, since, although it remains wild, Nature breeds it as if it were domesticated, directs it and places it at our disposal, and our fishermen catch it and bring it to our tables. Thanks to the fisheries, we get all the benefit. In the utilization by man of the resources of Nature, the work of the fisherman supplements that of the farmer."

We had left the table and, seated comfortably in arm-chairs on a terrace on to which the dining-room opened, we enjoyed our coffee and smoked our pipes and cigars. It was that moment of relaxation after a meal which is so restful. The body being satisfied, the mind seems clearer, more open, light and immaterial. When matter becomes drowsy, the mind begins to stray. Anecdote, confidence, and easy chat take on a new vivacity. We looked toward the distance full of lightness and calm, and I remembered my morning walk with our host, and our conversation beside the dam.

"Do you remember," I said, turning to him, "the conversation we had a few hours ago? We were discussing the essence of things and we soon found ourselves face to face with difficulties which brought us to a standstill. Our conversation at table was more profitable. Our considerations upon the migratory fishes took us much further. What is it, in fact, that we are really trying to find in Nature? A meaning that we can accept, that is beyond possible objection. The fishes give it to us. What do they represent, if not a form of use so perfect, so complete, that it is a sort of revelation? Scattered everywhere, spread over the immensity of waters, they come and let themselves be caught in certain definite places. We profit by them. We use nets, and with such tackle we capture them. But they themselves are like a prodigious moving net, a living net, into which all the resources of the world of waters are brought for our use, that we may benefit by them. The harvest is sown and cared for by Nature; we gather it and make use of it.

"For, in Nature, everything comes back to questions of use. Its total movement is made up of the sum of the efforts which creatures spend themselves upon so as to get the best out of themselves and their surroundings. If the profound essence of this movement is in the realm of the inaccessible, we may, at least, trace its direction.

"Living Nature, in order that it may exist, takes its materials from the brute world; it takes them incessantly, and always in greater numbers. Never tiring, it takes what it wants, and shares among its parts, all of which are bound up with one another, the resources which it so acquires. It takes possession of the inanimate which contains it and activates it, and so builds itself up and maintains itself. Its tremendous energy is always striving to create, making use of the environment upon which it depends. This gives it a purpose which consists in so using the means at its disposal, and a morality which we ought to take into account, for it has a reality, a duty, a sanction of its own.

"We turn a part of this power to our own advantage. We utilize for our own purposes the resources which Nature has so lavishly distributed and, by our industry and our science, we often put our own power in its place. We shelter our human achievements behind the achievement which it called into being. We must, therefore, follow its rules and try to understand them. We must strive to know Nature, to know how to use Nature, and, bringing ourselves into harmony with Nature, to profit by the understanding which it has brought into being."